# TWENTIETH CENTURY VIEWS

The aim of this series is to present the best
in contemporary critical opinion on major
authors, providing a twentieth century perspective on their changing status in an era
of profound revaluation

Maynard Mack, *Series Editor*
Yale University

# SPENSER

## A COLLECTION OF CRITICAL ESSAYS

Edited by

*Harry Berger, Jr.*

Prentice-Hall, Inc.    A SPECTRUM BOOK    *Englewood Cliffs, N. J.*

Current printing (last number):
10  9  8  7  6  5  4  3  2  1

# Acknowledgments

The editor would like to express gratitude and appreciation to the following for services of all kinds, from intellectual through scholarly and high-stenographic to string-tying and word-counting: Professor Richard B. Young, Mrs. Charlotte Cassidy, Miss Sharon Overgaard, Mrs. Phyllis Halpin, Mrs. Judith W. Ball, Miss Carol Wilson, and last but most, Mrs. Harry Berger, Jr.

# Contents

# SPENSER

# Introduction

*by Harry Berger, Jr.*

The primary aim of this anthology is neither to sample the most influential critics, nor to present the varieties of "critical approaches" to Spenser, nor to trace the shifts of sensibility and response occurring over the centuries during which his poetry has been read, discussed, interpreted, and evaluated. The aim is rather to make available essays which, in the editor's opinion, illuminate in a substantive and perceptive manner as much of Spenser's *oeuvre* as a volume of this size and scope permits. Thus all the essays included here are interpretive studies centering on individual passages, poems, and sections of that *oeuvre*.

In introducing an anthology of this sort, it is tempting to try to classify and relate the different kinds of critical method that recent interpreters of Spenser have put into play—the rhetorical, the allegorical, the numerological, the iconographic, and the archetypal (or mythological), for example. But most commentators worth their salt do not actually take rigorous stands within classifiable "positions" except when they are functioning poorly; they work more or less *ad hoc* with whatever equipment they bring to the poem and whatever "method" they feel any particular poem calls for. A more useful set of distinctions derives from the problems of scale and distance Spenser's poetry has always posed for critics as well as for anthologists: It is too extensive a body of work to be viewed comfortably in a single sweep of the eye. Its extensiveness seems also to keep it from easy access by the opposite approach, that is, line-by-line analysis. Recent full-length studies have consequently depicted Spenser in the middle distance, reading the work book by book or poem by poem, but not reading too closely. This approach has been more rewarding than the extremes apparently fixed by the limited space and aims of periodicals: the panoramic essay that tries to wrap up a whole book or even the whole *Faerie Queene* by restricting attention to Spenser's imagery, myths, allegory, or themes; and the spot-picking, usually scholarly, essay that glosses a particular passage without trying to relate it to the larger units or larger movements in Spenser's thought and work.

There is another, more familiar problem associated with Spenser's work, and it is to this that I shall address my remaining remarks. For a long time he was more the poet's, gentleman's, or scholar's poet than the poet of students or of casual readers. His poetry was praised (or condemned) for such qualities as its literariness, its unworldliness, and its quaintness; its unhurried spaciousness and expansiveness; its pictorial, rhetorical, and musical refinements, not to mention its refinements of noble sentiment or alluring sense; and its syncretic assimilation of the most diverse gobbets of classical, medieval, and renaissance culture. When the first waves of the "new criticism" washed across the decks of academe, he was quickly swept overboard because of his inability to write like Donne, Eliot, and Allen Tate—though to be fair to his detractors, the Spenser they disliked was the Spenser presented to them through the somewhat fusty gentility of the Variorum Edition and not the Spenser we have more recently been enabled to recover through the agency of that very new criticism, in its aspect of close interpretation. Spenserians of the fifties and sixties have clearly benefited from this aspect, and have combined it with other benefits received from such sources as the long line of studies of Renaissance culture from Burckhardt through Cassirer to Wind, the iconographic and iconological approach practiced by many art historians and especially associated with the work of the Warburg Institute, the investigations of such European philologists as Auerbach and Curtius, and the related achievements of intellectual historians in this country.

In this editor's opinion, much recent Spenser commentary has suffered from the conservative influence of literary iconography and intellectual history, solid and important though these forms of inquiry be. This conservatism perhaps develops in reaction to the tendencies of some "new-critically" trained readers to see "modern" complexities in a Renaissance poet. Literary interpretation seems indeed of late to have drifted farther away from the arms of the more hardheaded historical disciplines; it has opened itself to breezes from psychology, epistemology, anthropology, existentialism, and phenomenology, also to impulses from the approaches to cultural history deriving from Hegel, Dilthey, Cassirer, and others. Though the skepticism of the intellectual and literary historians is useful as a needle with which to puncture the metaphysical balloons often floated on such winds, I believe it is less valuable as a positive approach to Spenser—and not only because these historians frequently have been reluctant to acknowledge forms of evidence different from theirs as equally real or "hard," but also because they seem often to presuppose a notion of historical relativism that is misguided.

It used to be fashionable to justify Spenser's poetry by frankly admitting its datedness; he was considered a period piece, a poet of his age but not for all time. His life spanned the crucial decades from 1552 to 1599, during which the process of assimilating the achievements of the continental Renaissance rapidly intensified, and radically altered English culture. Spenser has long been treated as a paradigm and showcase of this process, the embodiment of the Elizabethan literary Renaissance. As some of the following essays may suggest, this in itself is a judgment that needs considerable qualification. Spenser did not simply swallow his sources and influences; like Chaucer and Wyatt before him, though in a different manner, he took a critical stance toward the more idealistic and Neoplatonic manifestations of the Renaissance in France and Italy. But the significant flaw lies in the assertion that since the Renaissance was a very different culture from ours, we cannot appreciate Spenser unless we change thinking caps so as to put away modern preferences and assumptions. So simple a formulation can no longer be taken seriously, not because we now believe that all ages, like all mortal men, are fundamentally the same, but because we know that a so-called Renaissance thinking cap cannot get us any further toward, or into, the so-called Renaissance mind than a Darwinian, Freudian, or new-critical thinking cap. All are equally perspectives on, not avenues into, that mind; all are equally interpretations made "from here" which may enrich, but cannot exhaust, the ever-changing, ever-growing career of a poem—a career whose course through later minds and times is as much an essential part of the poem's being, or becoming, as the words of which it is constituted. Any age or period may be characterized in its differentness by terms, descriptions, concepts, and approaches that arise from and reflect our contemporary situations, our own problems and concerns. It is possible, for example, to apply to earlier cultures terms drawn from Freudian, anthropological, or biological contexts of theory and practice, so long as those terms signify perennial insights and persistent facts of human nature and so long as we do not ascribe to earlier cultures the particular functions or distortions imposed on the terms by their modern contexts. With this caveat in mind, I should like to sketch out a framework for both Spenser's poetry and the essays that follow, by enumerating four familiar aspects of what may be called the Renaissance imagination.

First is the new dignity of fiction and make-believe, the new interest in the ability of poet or artist to create a relatively autonomous, yet explicitly artificial and imaginary world, the second world, or second nature, described by Leonardo da Vinci and Sir Philip Sidney among others—"second" because it was set over against the first world of actuality in which men found themselves, the world created by God, and including angels, stars, planets, men, kingdoms, trees, and elements. The notion of an ideal place or "space" artificially prepared and rigorously bounded off from actuality, a place where the mind may project its revised and corrected images of experience and where the soul may test and enlarge itself—such a notion lies at the roots of a variety of phenomena identified with the renaissance enterprise. Among them are the theory of perspective in art, the gradual return to an Aristotelian emphasis on the plot as the center of fiction and to the Neoplatonic enhancement of this idea in various descriptions of the diversified unity of the godlike poet's creation, the development of pastoral as a simplified and experimental play world, and the corresponding development in scientific thought of the idea of experimental method in connection with the idea of a closed world, that is, a specially controlled environment into which the experimenter temporarily has withdrawn.

The second world, with its emphasis upon serious make-believe and meaningful play, provided many artists with a means of counteracting, and often of ironically portraying, impulses to despair, escape, or wish-fulfillment that they may have perceived in themselves, in their fellow men, and in more systematic form in such cultural tendencies as alchemy, hermeticism, utopianism, astrological determinism, "philosophical" thaumaturgy, and some influential strains of Neoplatonism. For the poet can claim that only in a patently second world is it possible to indulge fully and legitimately the mind's absolute impulses toward total pleasure, total knowledge and power, utopian visions, and universal harmony. The controlling awareness that we are only making believe provides a limiting frame within which we can abandon ourselves to pleasure or seriousness with all the more intensity. Closely connected with this exaltation of the imaginary world is a dialectical awareness of the tensions and interrelations between fiction and actuality. The more you stress the reality of illusion, the self-sufficiency of artifice, the more conscious you can make the reader of his shifting relations—involvement and detachment—to the esthetic experience. When the rhetorical, painterly, and theatrical conditions of the respective media become part of the artist's subject, visibly displayed elements of his fictional world, the reader or spectator is forced to become conscious of the boundaries between art and life, and indeed of his character as reader or spectator. Once these boundaries are stamped on awareness, the artist may freely manipulate his perspective, allowing himself and his audience to cross and recross the boundaries, to destroy them or re-establish them.

A second aspect of the Renaissance imagination, connected with the first, is an interest in experimenting with the stylistics and semantics of visual and verbal presentation, communication, and symbolism. This topic has received much and varied attention in the last four or five decades, perhaps most notably in the work of Ernst Cassirer, Erwin Panofsky, George Kernodle, Rosemond Tuve, Rudolf Wittkower, Frances Yates, Edgar Wind, Ernst Gombrich, Marshall Mc-Luhan, and Father Walter Ong. Their studies of various kinds of images—logical, rhetorical, pictorial, theatrical, allegorical, emblematical, symbolical, typographical, and so on—have taught us to expect the most dynamic interplay between presented forms and their referents, the most fluid and delicate shifts of shape and emphasis attending that interplay. They have helped us loosen up our too fixed and categorical notions of the ways in which Renaissance thinkers, writers, and artists conceived of such image-genres as similitude, metaphor, symbol, allegory, emblem, and personification. They have also shown us that the intelligible center of a work like *The Faerie Queene* is to be sought less among its discrete allegorical moments and pictures, its isolated emblems, personifications, and tableaus, than in the process whereby its narrative surface changes in continual flux from one to another semantic relation, at times sheer immediacy, at times almost wholly mediate, at times opaque, at times transparent.

The third and fourth aspects of Renaissance thought are even more closely interrelated than the first two. The third is a concern for precise definition of the spirit of the age, its differences from previous ages, its debts to and antecedents in former cultures—in short, a concern for what might be called the culture's self-image. If the second world is characterized by self-sufficiency and frequently by romantic unreality—by differences from the first world—it may just as frequently be used as a reflecting or refracting surface to beam back the image of the first world. Thus many Renaissance thinkers who affirmed the richness and significance of the second world, and who identified the quality of their age with their image of its quality, felt that they possessed the means of creating its ideal image, of preserving it from the depredations of chance, change, and ignorance, and of presenting this self-interpretation to the future.

The fourth aspect is perhaps the most familiar element of this concern—the development of historical consciousness, the self-generated
idea of cultural renaissance as a blueprint for action. The revival of
learning was but one feature of a more pervasive set of attitudes and
activities that seem in retrospect to have been dialectical in an Hegelian
sense, that is, founded on consciousness of medieval darkness as an
historical gap separating Renaissance "self" from Classical "other," the
other being the self-there-and-then that the self-here-and-now creates
and with which it interacts, first setting it up as an exemplary ideal,
then showing it to be superseded by the Renaissance present. What
history denied the ancients, so far as we know, and made available
to the moderns was this sense of different periods as different fields,
bounded universes of culture whose very distinctness one from another
allowed them, like the first and second worlds, to encounter each
other in dialectical play.

The relevance of these four aspects of Renaissance thought to
Spenser will be manifest in various ways in the essays that follow, if
the reader has not already felt them at work in his own experience of
the poetry. I shall therefore restrict myself here to suggesting two
points of connection: The first concerns the organizational value of
the distinction between first and second worlds to the major classifi-
catory division of the *oeuvre;* the second touches briefly on certain
features, both representative and unique, of Spenser's historical sense.

1) Critics and philosophers have always found appealing the use
of the term *world* to describe the form and content of a particular
fictional experience—hence the temptation to equate "fiction" with
"fictional world" and, in my own earlier remarks, with "second
world." But if we have in mind a short work, a lyric or first-person
poem like *Prothalamion,* the term *world* seems somehow excessive or
hyperbolic. Yet it would be a mistake to assume from this that such
a poem is less fictional and imaginary, more autobiographical and
historical, than *The Faerie Queene.* Rather we are confronted with
different modes of relation between the speaker and his subject. In
the first-person lyric, the speaker is normally his own main character,
though he may share the spotlight with a friend, lover, or reader
whom he engages in implied dialogue. In the epic and narrative modes,
he tells us about other people, places, and events. Thus narrative experience happens mainly to others, lyric mainly to the self, and in
this sense the plot of narrative may be thought of as external to the
speaker, the plot of lyric as internal. Hence narrative plot is con-
ventionally distanced by location in the past tense relative to the

teller, whereas lyric plot unfolds now, in a period of time congruent with the utterance of the poem.

It will be useful at this point to distinguish between the person who makes the lyric poem and the experiencing self whose voice we hear as the poem. Most poems are thought out in advance, adjusted to metrical and other patterns, put down on paper, revised, and filed away or sent off as finished products. But the poet may want this product to be read as if it were an image of the mind in process. He may want you to observe not merely his vision or revision but his effort to see. His subject may be his own activity, the difficult and peculiarly human activity of trying to master experience from within. It is in this sense that the event he creates is both subjective and imaginary, and it is imaginary, as I am using the term, whether or not it happened to him in real life. From this standpoint the problems to which the Intentional Fallacy addresses itself cease to exist. Whether, in any poem, the speaker is or is not identical with the real poet does not make much difference, and if our knowledge of the real poet's life and background helps us to understand the speaker, so much the better. So long as we recognize that genetic criteria are more appropriate to biographical and historical study, while "cognitive" criteria are more appropriate to interpretation, we may apply both kinds whenever we find them helpful. In this general context, *fictional* should not be understood to mean "unreal" or "illusory"; rather it should suggest to us that, for the duration of the work, we are to give ourselves wholly to the presented experience, and to respond as if the work before us is all there is. And since the word *fiction* connotes something made as well as something made up, we may expect fictional experience to be more completely articulated, more vivid and coherent, than any counterpart in actual life.

The division of Spenser's *oeuvre* into minor poems and epic poem reflects by and large the distinction just made between lyric and narrative modes. The minor poems may be called subjective in either a personal and quasi-autobiographical sense or an impersonal and theatrical sense. The first sense is best exemplified by *Prothalamion, Amoretti,* and *Epithalamion,* and the second by poems in which Spenser impersonates or tries out various kinds of conventional attitudes in order to present through first-person enactment their strengths and (more often) their limitations—*The Shepheardes Calender, The Teares of the Muses,* and *Mother Hubberds Tale,* for example. Still other minor poems embody various combinations of these two forms of subjectivity, some closer to the personal, others to the impersonal:

*Virgils Gnat, Muiopotmos, Colin Clouts Come Home Againe,* and the *Fowre Hymnes.* In different ways, these poems deal with the relation between poetry and life or portray the dilemma of a man torn between the urge to write poems and the demands imposed by love, mutability, vicissitude, society, and sheer survival in a world dominated by knaves, fools, and fickle patrons. By their very nature, then, the minor poems are precariously poised between the first and second, or actual and fictional, worlds—between the brazen world surrounding the poet and the green or golden universe of Faerie which he has imagined. Many of them reflexively explore the various functions of poetry—recreative, plaintive, and moral—from the lyric standpoint of the poet facing the first world. In contrast with this, the poet adopting the epic mode withdraws into the second world, breaks free of the limits of actuality, and translates his concerns into the narrative that unfolds his model universe. It is precisely the distinction between lyric and epic/narrative modes that allows us to note the unique and original development occurring in the later books of *The Faerie Queene:* The voice and problems of the lyric speaker—as Spenser (personal) and Colin (impersonal)—penetrate the second world of Faerie and make increasing demands upon our attention.

2) My own view of Spenser's historical sense is set forth at some length in my contribution to this anthology. Therefore I shall confine myself here to some generalizations and examples. Among the variety of Renaissance stances taken toward antiquity, Spenser's readers should be aware of the following: the cyclical view, which sees the Classical spirit reborn and revived in Renaissance times; the linear view held by Christian humanists who, since they believed in the novelty of history and the uniqueness of events, felt that the past could only offer, as Jonson was to put it, "guides not commanders" and that the approximations and models drawn from Classical or Christian antiquity would have to be adapted to the quite different needs of the present; and finally, and perhaps more important than the others, the familiar paired contraries rooted in pessimism and optimism—the thesis that history is a long decline from a golden age at the beginning of time *versus* the belief in patterns of evolution (from simpler to more complex states) and progress (from worse to better states). Pessimism may give rise to elegiac, nostalgic, idyllic, heroic, or antiquarian retrospects, to chiliastic or apocalyptic prospects, to movements of escape from bitter world and self toward other places, other times, and other selves, the more remote and unreal the better. Pro-

gressive optimism appeared in a number of forms: in various Neo-platonist and hermetic figures (Gemistus Pletho, Ficino, Pico della Mirandola, Bruno, Paracelsus and Paracelsians, and many others); in those whose preference for the vernaculars over Latin and Greek was based upon nationalist as well as modernist arguments; in those who, while respecting the ancients, discarded many of their customs and beliefs (especially religious) as outmoded superstitions (Tasso, for example, who would admit antique gods in his poem only as fictional conveniences); and in later figures like Bacon, who opposed science, reason, and modern enlightenment to poetry, fantasy, and ancient wisdom.

In Spenser we find a variant of the evolutionary and the linear views (though different, they tend to fall together) mixed with an often-noted strain of pessimism and melancholy. These attitudes permeate his poetry, and it is pointless to ask whether they are personal or dramatistic—that is, whether they reflect his true feelings, or are deliberately and experimentally assumed. What is to the point is that the mixture produces a tentative and tensional, a continually shifting, perspective on the relations between past and present. This tension is concisely exemplified in the ambiguity of the phrase "plaine antiquitie" (*The Faerie Queene*, VI.Proem.4) as elicited by its context in Books V and VI: The word *plaine* may mean "simple and rude," or "lucid," "apparent," and "simplified." Each of these meanings is itself double-natured. The first, in an historical and social setting, suggests a movement either from natural simplicity to civilized corruption or from primitive to cultivated forms of society. The second meaning suggests the treasury of images, topics, assumptions, and attitudes inherited from the ancients, who saw life more simply and rendered what they saw with a correspondingly classical purity of line. The first meaning apprehends a plain antiquity that is irrevocably behind us, for better or for worse, among the other ragged ruins of time. But in the second sense it is always with us, "deepe within the mynd" (VI.Pr.4), the perennially ideal "image of the antique world" (V.Pr.1) —either (a) our image of antiquity or (b) the image of the world bequeathed to us by the ancients and shaped by their conceptions. Spenser sees that in the mind's tendency to identify (a) with (b) lies the second and more dangerous ambiguity: This image may indeed provide a visionary standard by which the moral imagination judges or improves actuality, but it may also hold forth the temptation of a perfected and changeless simplicity—a vision safely but prematurely insulated from temporal process, and therefore rendered obsolete by passing time—an archaic *locus amoenus* to which the despairing or defeated mind may escape.

It constitutes no great achievement to realize, as Spenser did, that both the optimistic and the pessimistic views of cultural change are mental constructs and that either, taken by itself, may be embraced in the desire to abolish or flee from reality. And it is no great achievement to hold both views in equipoise, believing in the possibility of an ideal world that can adumbrate the true and real, yet remembering that such ideals must change with change, and be not only revisited but also continually revised. Nor is it difficult to perceive that the common bond linking the minds of the past with those of the present is not the particular content of an ideal world, but rather the constructive energy of imagination, the process of seeing and making, reseeing and remaking—the process through which the mind confronts the unruly flux of circumstance and reforms its earlier confrontations in the light of later, more adequate insight and art. It is, I say, no accomplishment simply to come up with a complex idea and attitude, especially since this attitude toward the past is one Spenser could have borrowed from a large number of humanists of the stamp of Erasmus and Valla. The accomplishment lies in the way this complex attitude is translated into the poetry—the incredible fineness of perception and amplitude of conception that attend this embodiment, the added depth of vision and richness of detail. Looking at *The Faerie Queene* through Spenser's historical perspective lens is like looking at a stereoscopical image with both eyes open; to ignore this perspective is to shut one eye. In order to give a very rough indication of the kind of image disclosed in stereoscopical focus, I shall conclude by describing one family of experiences recurrent in Spenser's work.

Again and again we come upon instances of one-sided development in early phases of the career of a character or of a culture and also upon instances of premature union and fulfillment that must be undone, destroyed, or transcended so that they may be re-enacted in more adequate form in a later, more appropriate phase of relationship. Among Spenserian characters, these patterns affect the poet and the lady in *Amoretti/Epithalamion,* Clarion in *Muiopotmos,* the speaker in the *Fowre Hymnes,* Redcross and Una, Guyon (and, in a certain manner, his Palmer), Marinell and Florimell, Scudamour and Amoret, Timias and Belphoebe, the early career of Artegal, and the triumph of Calidore. A number of characters are returned to their

own, or to generic, places of origin so that they may make a new
and better beginning: Satyrane (as an aspect of Redcross), Marinell,
Florimell, Timias, and Calidore. Britomart by the sea (*Faerie Queene,*
III.iv) is a variant of this pattern, whereas a more extended and complicated example is displayed in the way Spenser, from III.xi through
IV.x, recounts the significant points of the relation between Amoret
and Scudamour in reverse order, moving from Amoret's imprisonment
by Busirane (III.xi) through the wedding during which Busirane cap-
tured her (IV.i) to the moment of their first meeting (at the end of
IV.x). Among the symbolically central episodes and locales, the following might be singled out: the harmonious yet limited order of Alma's
House of Temperance (II.ix–x); the premature and one-sidedly feminine fulfillment of the Garden of Adonis (III.vi); the archaic and un-
satisfactory reconciliation of male and female principles, generative
and courtly forms of erotic impulse, pagan and medieval institutions
that are structured into the Temple of Venus (IV.x); the confessedly
antique allegory in the Temple of Isis (V.vii), too exclusively rational
in its symbolism, too pure and sublimated in its ethical disdain of the
unruly energies deriving from passion, blood, and earth; the primitive
modes of harmony and resolution, benign yet rudimentary, exemplified by the satyrs (I.vi) and the Marriage of Rivers (IV.x); finally, in
the minor poems, the idyllic and womblike gardens from which the
youthful poetic spirit must be ejected so that his art and psyche may
face the assaults of actual experience that, if weathered, will transform recreative innocence to mature moral vision (*The Shepheardes
Calender, Muiopotmos, Colin Clouts Come Home Againe*).

This family of instances comprises a subclass of a more general category in which a first or instinctive form of behavior must be experienced, felt as insufficient, then corrected and revised. The second
chance occurs at a later time, in a more sophisticated or complex
phase of poem, career, or culture. The new context and usage confer
on earlier, simpler forms a destiny more inclusive than their own,
a more universal and organic function, allowing them to transcend
themselves in a manner not possible to them in their first isolated
thrust toward the premature fulfillment that they hope will end suffering and pain. The second chance, however, is never construed as the
final resolution, for Spenser sees every triumph as precarious and momentary, and all his happy endings are carefully "unperfited." His
vision is developmental in an evolutionary rather than a progressive
sense, and the development is everywhere tempered or beset by inter-
ruptions, regressions, lapses into despair, and momentary yearnings

toward the vanished glory of an archaic golden age. Yet, if he is more susceptible to archaic charms—and perhaps, therefore, more human— than Bacon, his retrospective vision might well have won the approval of the man for whom "rightly is truth called the daughter of time, not of authority. It is no wonder therefore if those enchantments of antiquity and authority and consent have so bound up men's powers that they have been made impotent (like persons bewitched) to accompany with the nature of things."

## PART ONE

*The Minor Poems*

# The World's Vanity

## *by William Nelson*

With the notable exceptions of *Muiopotmos* and *Mother Hub-berds Tale* Spenser's "complaints and meditations of the worlds vanitie, verie grave and profitable," are not the most attractive of his works. Most of the poems included in the volume entitled *Complaints,* as well as the elegies *Daphnaida* and *Astrophel,* are characterized by a rhetorical lushness and an exaggeratedly emotional utterance that the modern reader is likely to find distasteful, however fashionable these traits were in Elizabethan times. Nevertheless, they repay study if only because they display the range of Spenser's virtuosity in literary construction and because they reflect, in one way or another, the conceptions which underlie his greater works.

A complaint of the world's vanity arises from a sense of the inevitable decay of sublunary things. Although such meditation is to be found in the poetry of every age, there are differences in attitude which mirror differences in intellectual and spiritual temper. Like the Middle Ages, the Renaissance relied in its search for the enduring upon its hope for heaven, and rather more than the Middle Ages upon its faith in the permanence of poetry. While the late medieval concern was primarily with the end to which mankind comes, that dance of death which joins in one charnel house king and bishop, tinker and peasant, the Renaissance was awed by the spectacle of power, fame, and beauty doomed to destruction, death becoming a comment on greatness rather than greatness a comment on death. The literary consequence was a fascination with the strength which is frail, the fame which is fleeting, the beauty which is dust.

Spenser's first exercise in this kind derives from the canzone "Standomi un giorno solo a la fenestra," in which the sorrowing Petrarch

From William Nelson, *The Poetry of Edmund Spenser* (New York: Columbia University Press, 1963), pp. 64–83. Copyright © 1963 by Columbia University Press. Reprinted by permission of the publisher.

tells of six marvelous apparitions: a beautiful creature of the forest, a vessel laden with precious merchandise, a paradisal laurel tree, a sparkling fountain, a phoenix purple and gold, and finally, a graceful, pensive lady. In a moment each of these is destroyed, the lady bitten in the heel by an adder. Indeed, she is not destroyed, for she is sure of heaven:

> Lieta si dipartio, non che secura

But on earth only tears endure.

Inspired by Petrarch's song of the symbols of Laura, Joachim du Bellay added fifteen symbolic visions of Rome under the title "Songe" to *Les Antiquités de Rome,* a sonnet sequence celebrating the glory and lamenting the ruin of the great city. Petrarch's canzone and Du Bellay's "Songe" made their appearance in English in a translation done by the young Spenser for a volume entitled *A Theatre Wherein Be Represented as Wel the Miseries and Calamities That Follow the Voluptuous Worldlings, as Also the Joyes and Pleasures Which the Faithfull Do Enjoy* (1569) compiled by John van der Noot, a wealthy Dutch Calvinist who had found refuge in England. The visions of Petrarch and Du Bellay, illustrated by appropriate woodcuts, here become symbols of the impermanence not of a beautiful woman or of an imperial city but of the world itself. Spenser's translations are in unrhymed verse, doubtless in deference to the humanist contempt for rhyme as a barbaric ornament. In the *Complaints* volume, many years later, Spenser included translations of the rest of *Les Antiquités* and revised versions of the "Songe" and Petrarch's canzone, the principal change consisting in the addition of rhyme. He also wrote a dozen "visions of the worlds vanitie" of his own, giving the form a new turn. In these poems, the weakness of might is manifested by the insignificance of that which overthrows or preserves it: the ant disgraces the elephant, the goose saves Rome. This is also the theme of another poem in the *Complaints,* Spenser's translation of the pseudo-Vergilian *Culex* under the title *Virgils Gnat.*

The logic of Petrarch's canzone moves from mundane transience to the particular case of Laura. *The Ruines of Time,* the first poem of the *Complaints* volume, also treats of the decay of earthly glory both generally and specifically, as the poet declares in his dedicatory letter to the Countess of Pembroke: "I have conceived this small Poeme, intituled by a generall name of the *worlds Ruines:* yet speciallie intended to the renowming of that noble race, from which both you and he [her brother, Sir Philip Sidney] sprong, and to the eternizing of some of the chiefe of them late deceased." [1] The poem is a lament uttered by the spirit of the ancient city of Verulam, or so it begins, for as the complaint proceeds Verulam's spirit seems to be replaced by the poet speaking in his own person. As Rome was empress of the whole world, Verulam declares, "So I of this small Northerne world was Princesse." As in Du Bellay's *Les Antiquités,* the emphasis falls upon the city's vanished greatness:

> High towers, faire temples, goodly theaters,
> Strong walls, rich porches, princelie pallaces,
> Large streetes, brave houses, sacred sepulchers,
> Sure gates, sweete gardens, stately galleries,
> Wrought with faire pillours, and fine imageries,
> All those (O pitie) now are turned to dust,
> And overgrowen with blacke oblivions rust.          (ll. 92–98)

Verulam is gone, but its memory lives thanks to the labors of the historian Camden, "the nourice of antiquitie." Indeed, whether because of Camden's writings or this poem of Spenser's, the ancient city, site of the modern St. Albans, became for Elizabethans a prime figure of the once glorious. Perhaps it was in Shakespeare's mind when he wrote:

> When I have seene by times fell hand defaced
> The rich proud cost of outworne buried age
> When sometime loftie towers I see downe rased,
> And brasse eternall slave to mortall rage

From Verulam, figure of a vanished glory which only literature can preserve, the subject narrows to the departed members of the great Dudley family, especially the Earl of Leicester:

> He now is dead, and all his glorie gone,
> . And all his greatnes vapoured to nought          (ll. 218–19)

and Sir Philip Sidney who has achieved immortality of two kinds:

> So there thou livest, singing evermore,
> And here thou livest, being ever song
> Of us          (ll. 337–39)

The thought of Sidney's victory over death leads to the conclusion that he who wishes to conquer time

---

[1] Spenser's delay in publishing an elegy on Sidney, for which he apologizes in his dedication, may have been the result of a concerted delicacy of sentiment among Sidney's friends that led them to "suppress rather than to publish their expressions of sorrow." See *Nobilis, or a View of the Life and Death of a Sidney,* ed. and tr. Virgil B. Heltzel and Hoyt H. Hudson (San Marino, Calif., 1940), p. 70 and note, p. 112.

on Pegasus must ride,
And with sweete Poets verse be glorifide          (ll. 426–27)

But those who scorn the Muses—the poet's finger points at Cecil—can expect only oblivion. Indeed, all who pride themselves on their worldly glory should note the fate of Verulam.

The poem concludes with two sets of visions of the kind of Du Bellay's "Songe." They are designed to teach "by demonstration" the lesson of the spirit of the dead city. The first set presents images of strength, beauty, and gentility: a stately tower which falls to the ground, a beautiful garden wasted, two white bears, fair and mild, crushed in their cave. The distraught dreamer then hears a mysterious voice:

> Behold (said it) and by ensample see,
> That all is vanitie and griefe of minde,
> Ne other comfort in this world can be,
> But hope of heaven, and heart to God inclinde     (ll. 582–85)

And he dreams again, this time of a singing swan, a harp of gold and ivory floating down a river, a virgin in a stately bridal bed, a knight at arms. The harp, borrowed from Ovid's account of the death of Orpheus, is explicitly that of Sir Philip, "Immortal spirite of Philisides." These precious creations, like those of the first set of visions, reach their earthly end, but they leave to live forever, the swan and the harp as signs in the firmament, the bride in the arms of her Bridegroom, the knight in heaven.

It has been suggested that *The Ruines of Time* may be a patchwork of pieces written at various times and for different purposes, an *ubi sunt* for Verulam ending with a tribute to Camdem; fragments of the *Dreames* and *Pageaunts* mentioned by E. K. and in the Harvey correspondence; and an elegy on Sidney.[2] Whether or not it evolved in this way it stands as an entirely coherent structure. As Petrarch's images are to Laura, so Rome is to Verulam and Verulam in turn to the dead Dudleys. As Verulam endures, despite its destruction, in Camden's imperishable record, so the noble members of that family will live in fame "Above the reach of ruinous decay," glorified by "sweete Poets verse." Spenser describes his poem as a "monument" to the fame of Sir Philip, an enduring one in contrast to the monumental Verulam. But this solution of the problem of oblivion is valid only in a temporal frame of reference, as the concluding visions demonstrate, for heaven

---

[2] *Complaints*, ed. W. L. Renwick, p. 190.

alone is beyond worldly vanity. The poem therefore ends with the injunction to Sidney's sister:

> So unto heaven let your high minde aspire,
> And loath the drosse of sinfull worlds desire.

As if to insist upon the unity of *The Ruines of Time,* Spenser binds the whole together by a numerical device. The main part of the poem consists of seventy stanzas of seven lines each; the two sets of visions are comprised in twenty-eight stanzas, in each set six visions followed by an envoy rejecting the vain world and looking to heaven. Six are the days of this mutable world; on the seventh God rests and change ceases.

*Daphnaida,* another poem in sevens, is a pastoral elegy on the wife of Sir Arthur Gorges, a gentleman poet whom Spenser celebrates under the name of Alcyon in *Colin Clouts Come Home Againe* (ll. 384–91).[8] It is made up of twenty-eight seven-line stanzas and seven "complaints," each seven stanzas long. The narrative closely imitates Chaucer's *Book of the Duchess.* A Man in Black tells of a lost lioness (instead of a queen in chess); the dull inquirer fails to understand the riddle; the revelation, as in Chaucer, is abrupt:

> Daphne thou knewest (quoth he)
> She now is dead

In Chaucer's elegy the interview concludes with

> Is that youre los? Be God, hyt ys routhe!

and the poem itself ends at once. But Spencer's Alcyon falls to the ground in great extremity only to cry out a sevenfold passion of luxuriant rhetoric. It is a strange lamentation, quite contrary to the usual elegiac pattern which begins with weeping and ends with consolation. The death of Daphne is first recognized as a blessed release: "I goe with gladnesse to my wished rest." But the mourner grows more and more inconsolable, hating the world and everything in it, and departs finally

> As if that death he in the face had seene,
> Or hellish hags had met upon the way

Evidently, Spenser strove hard to vary the traditional form. It is not the happiest of his experiments.

If *Daphnaida* is guilty of an excess of passionate declamation, *Astro-*

---

[8] H. E. Sandison, ed., *The Poems of Sir Arthur Gorges* (Oxford, 1953).

*phel,* the poem Spenser composed to serve as an introduction to a group of elegies on Sidney by his sister Mary, Lodowick Bryskett, and others, is often described as lacking in emotional warmth. The shepherd hero is comely, charming, skilled in song and in pastoral sports, solely devoted to his beloved Stella. While slaughtering wild beasts he is wounded by one of them in the thigh. He dies, wept over by Stella, and she dies too in sympathy. The pitying gods transform the pair into a flower, and then the shepherds gather to make their moan. The first to sing is the hero's sister Clorinda.

Spenser, I think, deliberately avoided the personal note in this poem in order to set it apart from the lamentations which it introduces. Astrophel is not Sidney; he is rather a figure for Sidney's character, graceful in person, constant in love, bold in combat. If the shepherd's hurt thigh recalls the wound made by Spanish shot at the battle of Zutphen it also brings to mind the story of Adonis and the wild boar. Stella cannot be Penelope Rich, the Stella of Sidney's sonnets, for the poem is dedicated to Sidney's widow, nor can she be the widow, for instead of dying in sorrow the lady married the Earl of Essex. (In his contribution to the volume, Lodowick Bryskett, too, introduces a weeping Stella.) The Stella of this poem is not a real person at all but a symbol for Sidney's truth in love and the devotion that he inspired in others. *Astrophel* touches its occasion only here and there, enough to make it a fitting frame for the elegies but not enough to compete with them.

The brave beauty of the shepherd Astrophel is destroyed by a cruel, cowardly beast of accursed brood. Ugly Barbarism and brutish Ignorance have silenced the silver music of Helicon and replaced it with *The Teares of the Muses.* In the poem so entitled each of the heavenly sisters recalls her once honored role in the affairs of men, describes the low estate to which she has fallen in the degenerate present, and weeps vociferously. An introduction of nine stanzas leads into the nine complaints, the whole consisting of an even hundred stanzas. The burden of the lamentation is that in the corrupt present men in high places care nothing for virtuous learning but vulgarly seek their private ends. Perhaps this protracted outburst reflects the poet's anger at Lord Burghley as one who should but does not patronize the learned, though there is no pointed allusion to him like the passage condemning the niggardly noble in *The Ruines of Time.* No doubt our failure to sympathize with the plight of the Muses results from our loss of a feeling of urgency in the matter, the issue of the battle between learning and ignorance being no longer in doubt. But the weakness of the poem

is manifest as soon as it is set beside Samuel Daniel's thoughtful, restrained, yet noble treatment of the same subject in *Musophilus.*

With these outpourings on the theme of decay and loss *Muiopotmos
or the Fate of the Butterflie* seems at first to have little to do. It remains
the lightest and most delicious of Spenser's poems even though generations of scholars have attempted to weigh it down with allegorical
significance. Yet it is neither a trifle nor a merely pretty thing. Although the poem is obviously in the mock-heroic vein, the reader does
not laugh at its hero as he does at Chaucer's Chanticleer and Pope's
Belinda, for the butterfly Clarion is too beautiful to be absurd and
though he is little he is not contemptible. Rather, the tragedy of his
end is tempered only by his distance from us.

The opening stanzas echo the beginning of the *Iliad;* the death of
Clarion at the end imitates the death of Vergil's Turnus. The promise
of Spenser's introduction, however, is at odds with the fulfillment of
his tale. The poet declares that he will sing of a deadly battle between
two armed heroes whose mutual hatred led from "small jarre" to open
war. But Clarion and his enemy, the spider Aragnoll, do not meet until
the one falls into the other's web, the hatred is one-sided only, and
there is no encounter between the antagonists that can properly be
called either a "small jarre" or full-scale warfare. As a foreshadowing
of the story this introduction is imprecise and misleading. And to make
matters worse, it closes with the climactic utterance:

> And is there then
> Such rancour in the hearts of mightie men?

There are no "men" in the tale at all.

At the same time, that exclamation tells the reader exactly what
he must know. He is expected to remember that Vergil wrote of Juno's
hatred of the Trojans, "tantaene animis caelestibus irae?" (Can such
resentment dwell in heavenly breasts?) In *The Rape of the Lock* Pope
alludes to Vergil in almost the same way:

> In tasks so bold, can little men engage,
> And in soft bosoms dwells such mighty rage?

But his meaning is very different from Spenser's. Pope's antitheses make
the heroic tasks trivial, the divine rage absurd, very much as the shriek-
ing of Chanticleer's wives becomes laughable when it is compared
with the outcry of the Trojan women. The effect sought by Pope and
Chaucer depends upon the juxtaposition of two realms, the heroic and
the petty. But when Spenser substitutes human breasts for heavenly

ones in Vergil's line he sets against each other not two realms but two
proportions, that between gods and men and that between men and
insects. His equation is exactly the one made by Gloucester in *King
Lear:* "As flies to wanton boys, are we to th'gods." [4] The poet directs
his reader to sit in a godlike seat, to look upon the little world of but-
terflies and spiders so that he may understand how Olympus sees mankind. The stanzas introducing *Muiopotmos* provide, not a prospectus
of the tale itself, but a definition of the viewpoint upon which a comprehension of the tale depends.

In fact, *Muiopotmos* is not one tale but three. The murder of Clarion
by Aragnoll constitutes the principal plot, but the accounts of the
metamorphoses of Clarion's mother, Astery, and of Aragnoll's mother,
Arachne, are not merely decorative digressions. In accordance with
Spenser's usual practice, each part of the poem is designed to illuminate
its theme. In this case, it is the idea that in this corrupt world felicitous
excellence breeds that which destroys it.

No creature could be happier than Clarion. He is the darling son of
a great monarch, young, swift, brave, securely armed, gorgeously beautiful, free to taste all of the world's goods:

> What more felicitie can fall to creature,
> Than to enjoy delight with libertie,
> And to be Lord of all the workes of Nature,
> To raine in th'aire from earth to highest skie,
> To feed on flowres, and weeds[a] of glorious feature,
> To take what ever thing doth please the eie?          (ll. 209–14)

Happy too is his mother Astery, one of Venus' nymphs,

> excelling all the crewe
> In curteous usage, and unstained hewe          (ll. 119–20)

Being nimbler-jointed and more industrious than the others she wins
the goddess's praise for gathering the greatest quantity of flowers.
Arachne's excellence at weaving is world-renowned; she is "The most
fine-fingred workwoman on ground," and Pallas comes down from
heaven to grant her the due reward.

But no earthly happiness is secure,

> For thousand perills lie in close awaite
> About us daylie, to worke our decay          (ll. 221–22)

Astery's downfall is swift and simply told. Her sister nymphs, envying

---

[4] IV.i.38.
[a] weeds: small plants generally.

her success in gathering "the children of the spring," tell Venus that
Cupid has been helping her; the enraged goddess transforms her to a
butterfly. Arachne's fate is of another kind. Her skill with the loom is
so great that even

> Envie pale,
> That al good things with venemous tooth devowres,
> Could not accuse. (ll. 301-3)

But that skill leads Arachne to the presumption of challenging Pallas
herself, and she dares to disgrace the gods by portraying Jove's rape
of Europa. Pallas' answer to this challenge depicts her own competition
with Neptune for the worship of Athens in which her gift of a fruitful
olive tree wins the prize over Neptune's war horse. It is Arachne's
envy of this good and beautiful thing, the "poysonous rancor" within
her, that turns her into a venomous spider. As Iago says of Cassio,
"He has a daily beauty in his life,/That makes me ugly."

Clarion falls because like Astery he arouses envy and like Arachne
he presumes upon his excellence. His race derives from the beauty
of flowers and from jealousy. So beautiful are his wings that ladies
at court, "Beholding them, him secretly envide." Secure in the pride
of his princely freedom he wanders everywhere without suspicion of
friend or fear of foe. Little wonder that fate, or fortune, or an errant
gust of wind blows him into the web of Aragnoll, heir to the poisonous malice of his mother.

Long before Clarion fell into the spider's snare his fate was woven
by Jove's own hand and the image of a butterfly was woven by Pallas
into the web of her tapestry. Mundane felicity inevitably, fatefully,
arouses those dark destructive forces, the "shame of Nature,"

> That none, except a God, or God him guide,
> May them avoyde, or remedie provide. (ll. 223-24)

*Muiopotmos* is a delightful teaching of the tragic lesson that on earth
happiness is its own destruction, that only in heaven or by heavenly
intervention is the fruitful olive victorious over chaos and death.

In contrast with *Muiopotmos* and the other "complaints" the emphasis of *Mother Hubberds Tale* is not on the inevitability of decay
but on the nature of the disease which brings it about. The world which
it portrays is a sick one. The astronomical beginning sets the mood:
August is the month in which the sun enters the sign of Virgo, otherwise known as Astraea, the righteous goddess who fled the earth because of its sinfulness. It is also the month of the dog star, bringer of
pestilence and corruption, and the poet himself is ill.

A disease is known by the state of health which it denies. Much
medieval and Renaissance social comment proceeds from the assumption of a healthy or "natural" condition of the world, not that which
exists or ever has existed save in Eden but that which might exist were
good victorious over evil. In such a world, every plowman would,
like Chaucer's paragon, thresh and ditch and delve "Withouten hire,
if it lay in his myght," and every knight would fight for his lord and
for Christ, not for reward or vainglory. Spenser's contemporary, George
Gascoigne, sees such a world in his mirror:

> Againe I see, within my glasse of Steele,
> But foure estates, to serve eche country Soyle,
> The King, the Knight, the Pesant, and the Priest.
> The King should care for al the subjectes still,
> The Knight should fight, for to defende the same,
> The Peasant he, should labor for their ease,
> And Priests should pray, for them and for themselves.[5]

As with Chaucer, the imagined ideal leads Gascoigne to satiric comparison with the way of the world as it is. This he sees in his steel
glass which reflects the truth without flattery.

Spenser's *Mother Hubberds Tale* is a general satire in this tradition.
Mother Hubberd tells the sick poet a tale of "the Foxe and th'Ape by
him misguided." The pair constitutes a kind of unit, a counterfeit man,
the Ape mocking man in body, the Fox in mind. As the Fox explains
to the Ape when they are arguing about which should be king:

> And where ye claime your selfe for outward shape
> Most like a man, Man is not like an Ape
> In his chiefe parts, that is, in wit and spirite;
> But I therein most like to him doo merite
> For my slie wyles and subtill craftinesse,
> The title of the Kingdome to possesse.          (ll. 1041–46)

In successive episodes, the pair passes itself off as the various kinds
of man, peasant, priest, courtier, and king—just Gascoigne's division.
In each case the consequence is the same: betrayal of responsibility,
damage to the commonwealth, and eventually exposure and expulsion
of the culprits. But in a manner typically Spenserian, each episode is
handled differently.

Ape and Fox are introduced as malcontents, unwilling to lose their

---

[5] *The Steel Glass*, in J. W. Cunliffe, ed., *The Glasse of Government* (Cambridge,
1910), p. 150.

"freedom" by tying themselves to productive labor. The division of
mankind into classes they reject as unjust:

> as we bee sonnes of the world so wide,
> Let us our fathers heritage divide,
> And chalenge to our selves our portions dew
> Of all the patrimonie, which a few
> Now hold in hugger mugger in their hand,
> And all the rest doo rob of good and land.          (ll. 135–40)

Like the egalitarian giant of the Legend of Justice of *The Faerie
Queene* they echo the old cry of the Peasants' Revolt:

> When Adam delved and Eve span
> Who was then the gentleman?

With the protection of a forged passport the Ape pretends to be an
old soldier and the Fox his dog. An unwary Husbandman is fooled
into giving them the ward of his sheep, a kindness they repay by eating
their charges. But the day of reckoning comes and they must fly.

This brief adventure announces the pattern of the rest. Again Ape
and Fox disguise themselves, now with gown and cassock, and again
they provide themselves with a forged license testifying that they are
"Clerkes booke-redd." They encounter a "formall Priest" through
whose advice the Fox secures a benefice while the Ape becomes his
parish clerk. Abuse of their responsibility inevitably leads to the day
of judgment and hasty flight. But the actions of the Ape and Fox
do not bear the weight of the satire in this episode; their tenure in
office is dismissed almost casually. The principal butt is the priest in
form only, as much a counterfeit as they are. He is a false Protestant,
a hypocrite Piers. The simple man cannot read the license, in fact he
cannot read at all, because

> Of such deep learning little had he neede,
> Ne yet of Latine, ne of Greeke, that breede
> Doubts mongst Divines, and difference of texts,
> From whence arise diversitie of sects,
> And hateful heresies, of God abhor'd:
> But this good Sir did follow the plaine word,
> Ne medled with their controversies vaine.          (ll. 385–91)

He scolds the Fox and the Ape for their vagabondage, urging them
to try for advancement in the church,

> In the meane time to live in good estate,
> Loving that love, and hating those that hate;
> Being some honest Curate, or some Vicker
> Content with little in condition sicker.[b]          (ll. 427–30)

When the Ape, rather out of character, fearfully remembers the terrible responsibility of those who are charged with the feeding of men's souls the Priest speciously answers with a text teaching that divine grace alone can justify:

> We are but charg'd to lay the meate before:
> Eate they that list, we need to doo no more.
> But God it is that feedes them with his grace,
> The bread of life powr'd down from heavenly place.
>
>                                                     (ll. 435–38)

Indeed, he has no use for the old Roman Catholic ways, services morning and evening, fasts, haircloth, clerical celibacy. Now there is but one "small devotion" on the Sabbath, and besides,

> we may have lying by our sides
> Our lovely Lasses, or bright shining Brides.
>
>                                                     (ll. 475–76)

It is easy to attain this pleasant life, he explains. All that is necessary is to pretend gravity and saintliness, lie, face, forge, crouch, fee a courtier, or split the income of the living with the lord of the manor.

The adventure at court preserves the scheme and varies it again. The Ape disguises himself as a gentleman

> And his man Reynold with fine counterfesaunce
> Supports his credite and his countenaunce.          (ll. 667–68)

Because he is dressed like a gentleman the court accepts him, he cheats, at length is discovered and banished "by such as sate in justice seate." The substance of the satire appears in Mother Hubberd's contrasting descriptions of the true courtier and the false. A great body of Renaissance literature provides the matter for this contrast. These writings are commonly though inadequately represented by Castiglione's *Il Cortegiano,* a treatise which despite its popularity and its literary excellence is rather more urbane than most of its kind and perhaps lacks their moral dedication and seriousness of purpose.[6] Spenser's true courtier resembles Castiglione's only superficially. He will not abase

---

[b] sicker: secure.

[6] D. L. Aguzzi, "Allegory in the Heroic Poetry of the Renaissance" (unpublished dissertation, Columbia University, 1959), pp. 450ff.

himself, flatter, or traduce a man behind his back. He rides, hunts,
wrestles, recreates himself with "Ladies gentle sports" and with the
Muses, not frivolously but with "wise discourse." He spends his days
in his prince's service, not to win wealth or place but to win honor
"To which he levels all his purposis." He therefore trains himself
both for arms and for counsel

> To learne the enterdeale of Princes strange,
> To marke th'intent of Counsells, and the change
> Of states, and eke of private men somewhile,
> Supplanted by fine falsehood and faire guile;
> Of all the which he gathereth, what is fit
> T'enrich the storehouse of his powerfull wit     (ll. 785–90)

He is Thomas Elyot's Governor rather than Castiglione's Courtier.
The foil for this ideal is the Ape. His sports are dicing and cards; he
plays the poet but only to make divine poetry a servant to base affection; he tries to

> allure
> Chast Ladies eares to fantasies impure.
>                                    (ll. 819–20)

He and his man the Fox cheat simple folk who repose confidence in
those who give the impression of being "on the inside." His only purpose is his own advancement.

The final usurpation is that of the robes and royalty of the Lion,
king of beasts. While the Lion carelessly sleeps, the Ape with the
Fox as his chief counselor acts the role of the tyrant, the anti-king.
In this action, the final judgment cannot be made by a mortal agent.
News of the suffering realm at last reaches

> high Jove, in whose almightie hand
> The care of Kings, and power of Empires stand
>                                    (ll. 1225–26)

Mercury, having confirmed the chaotic injustice of the kingdom, wakes
the Lion who "uncases" the Fox, cuts off the Ape's long tail and pares
his ears, and resumes his rightful rule. There is no description here
of a true king, as there is of a true courtier in the preceding episode.
But the portrait of the tyrant implies the portrait of the king, and
both are the products of a tradition reaching back to the beginnings
of European civilization. Sometimes these portraits are imagined in
literature, or historical fiction, as in Xenophon's *Cyropaedia*, Thomas
Elyot's *Image of Governaunce,* and Shakespeare's *Henry V* and *Richard*

*III;* sometimes they are drawn in didactic treatises like Erasmus' *Education of a Christian Prince.* The characteristics of Spenser's tyrant are by no means exceptional; almost all of them, in fact, can be found in Erasmus' brief description of an evil ruler. In the Ape's first royal act,

> to his Gate he pointed a strong gard,
> That none might enter but with issue hard:
> Then for the safeguard of his personage,
> He did appoint a warlike equipage
> Of forreine beasts, not in the forest bred      (ll. 1115–19)

Says Erasmus: "The tyrant guarantees safety for himself by means of foreign attendants and hired brigands." [7] The Ape makes all the beasts the "vassals of his pleasures"; Erasmus' tyrant keeps his subjects "like slaves." [8] The Ape "enlarg'd his private treasure" with the spoils of his subjects; Erasmus contrasts the tyrant with the king who considers "that his purse is represented by the wealth of his subjects." [9] The Ape rules by fear; Erasmus says, "the tyrant strives to be feared, the king to be loved." [10] The Fox, as chief minister, shares the royal vices and adds some of his own. He keeps low the nobility of the kingdom, the men of arms and letters, just as Erasmus' tyrant uses "every means to reduce the wealth and prestige of any of his subjects, and especially the good men." [11] Here the Fox is an extension of the conventional tyrant; he also plays a separate role as the equally conventional evil minister who gathers all power into his own hands, allows nobody to appeal to the king, and even cheats the king to enrich himself.

Spenser's Fox, in fact, is identical in almost every respect with the butt of John Skelton's *Speak, Parrot; Colin Clout;* and *Why Come Ye Not to Court?* Skelton too rails at a chief minister who acts as though he were sole ruler, handles all business himself and for himself, denies access to the king, builds royal mansions while the commonwealth suffers. In Skelton's satire, the chief minister is Thomas Cardinal Wolsey. Is Spenser's tale of Mother Hubberd a direct attack upon William Cecil, Lord Burghley? The comparison does not lead to easy conclusions. Skelton, like Spenser, draws upon the traditional descriptions of tyrant and tyrannical administrator for his portrait of

---

[7] *The Education of a Christian Prince,* trans. L. K. Born (New York, 1936), p. 163.
[8] *Ibid.,* p. 165.
[9] *Ibid.,* p. 164.
[10] *Ibid.*
[11] *Ibid.,* p. 165.

Wolsey. In fact, he poses as a satirist of vice, not of a vicious individual:

> For no man have I named:
> Wherefore sholde I be blamed? [12]

Nevertheless, he constantly nudges his reader to think of one who rides

> upon a mule
> With golde all betrapped,
> In purple and paule belapped, [13]

of a "braggyng bocher" (Wolsey's father was said to have been a butcher), and unequivocally of the builder of Hampton Court. Puns and topical innuendoes insist upon the identification. This is not the atmosphere of *Mother Hubberds Tale*. Much of the attack upon the Ape and the Fox echoes contemporary attacks upon Cecil, but it also echoes Aristotle, Erasmus, and Skelton. To be sure, the Latin for "ape" is "simia," and Simier was a French ambassador who tried to arrange a marriage between Queen Elizabeth and the Duc d'Alençon. To be sure, Burghley was a "foxy" chief minister who opposed Leicester in favoring the marriage (the Queen, however, called him her "Camel"). But the text of the poem simply will not bear a consistent identification of Ape with Simier and Fox with Burghley.

There are two passages in *Mother Hubberds Tale* which do demand a topical interpretation. One of these is the bitter complaint of the suitor who is disappointed of his promised reward. I have already suggested that these lines were interpolated shortly before the publication of the poem, and that they reflect Spenser's resentment at Burghley's interference with or delay of the reward promised by Elizabeth for *The Faerie Queene*. For the other, which also appears to be a late addition, no satisfactory explanation has been offered and I can present none. To the Ape's inquiry as to which courtiers bear the greatest sway at court the Mule answers:

> Marie (said he) the highest now in grace,
> Be the wilde beasts, that swiftest are in chase;
> For in their speedie course and nimble flight
> The Lyon now doth take the most delight:
> But chieflie, joyes on foote them to beholde,

---

[12] John Skelton, *Colin Clout*, ll. 1113–14.
[13] *Ibid.*, ll. 310–12.

Enchaste with chaine and circulet of golde:
So wilde a beast so tame ytaught to bee,
And buxome to his bands is joy to see.
So well his golden Circlet him beseemeth:
But his late chayne his Liege unmeete esteemeth;
For so brave beasts she loveth best to see,
In the wilde forrest raunging fresh and free.          (ll. 619–30)

At first the Lion seems to be ruler, as he is in the final episode of the
poem. Then the plural "beasts" whom he enjoys seeing turn into a
singular "beast," and finally a feminine "liege"—surely Queen Elizabeth—expresses disapproval of the Lion himself or of one of the other
beasts. Spenser is here extraordinarily recondite or extraordinarily
careless, perhaps both. But apart from these two apparently patched-in
passages, *Mother Hubberds Tale* needs no explanation in terms of
personal or political reference.

However, no writer of power comments on the state of the world
without looking at the world before him. Nor does his audience read
such a comment without reflecting upon contemporary affairs. The
applications of writer and reader do not necessarily coincide: there
may be general agreement about what a tyrant is but little about who
is a tyrant. Evidence outside of the text of the *Tale* suggests that at the
time of its publication Spenser thought Burghley a bad man, and we
may therefore suppose that whatever he intended when he wrote the
poem in the "raw conceipt" of his youth, Burghley came to his mind
as he reconsidered the lines in which he had described an evil minister.
He may have hoped that his readers would think of Burghley too but,
except in his reference to the peer whose grace he lacks, he does not
ask them to do so.[14]

Considered as a story, *Mother Hubberds Tale* suffers from a defect
so obvious that it is hard to understand how a skilled writer could
have overlooked it. The world of the first two episodes is clearly a
world of men into which the shiftless villains can intrude only by
disguising themselves. The setting becomes vague in the third episode,
for although the Ape dresses as a gentleman and the Fox as his groom,
a Mule tells them the tidings of court, a Lion appears to be its king,
and wild beasts his servants. The final episode takes place wholly in

[14] The *Tale* seems to have been interpreted as an attack upon Burghley by the
anonymous author of *A Declaration of the True Causes* (1592) and by Richard
Niccols in *Beggars Ape* (written 1607 and published 1627). See Brice Harris, "The
Ape in Mother Hubberds Tale," *Huntington Library Quarterly*, IV (1940–41), 191–
203, and Harold Stein, *Studies in Spenser's Complaints* (New York, 1934), pp. 79ff.

a world of animals except that the Ape justifies his taking of the Lion's place by explaining that he looks like a man.

The poet's failure to arrive at a clear conception of the circumstances of his story can be explained in either of two ways. It has been suggested that the inconsistencies of *Mother Hubberds Tale* are the result of a hasty and radical revision made after the poem had been laid aside for many years.[15] This is similar to the explanations that have been devised to account for the difference between promise and performance in *Muiopotmos,* the fading away of the spirit of Verulam in *The Ruines of Time,* and the many slips in storytelling that have been detected in *The Faerie Queene.* But the very necessity of explaining so much carelessness demands an understanding of the poet's attitude toward his own fictions. He pays little attention to their consistency and verisimilitude because they are not ends in themselves but servants of idea, of moral intention. In the "complaints" and satires considered in this chapter, as everywhere in Spenser's poetry, the object is to portray the nature of the world in which we live by contrasting it with a state of excellence from which we have declined and to which we may aspire. The decay of the one and the hope for the other therefore constitute a principal theme of his works.

[15] Edwin Greenlaw, *Studies in Spenser's Historical Allegory* (Baltimore, 1932), pp. 115ff.

# The Argument of Spenser's
## *Shepheardes Calender*

### *by A. C. Hamilton*

The critical attention given Spenser's *Shepheardes Calender,* apart from praise of the work as a brilliant poetical exercise, has mainly been to identify certain historical allusions. While the poem is deliberately designed, so it would seem, to provoke from the reader E. K.'s delighted response to "a prety Epanorthosis in these two verses" or "a very Poeticall πάθος," its brilliant rhetorical surface deliberately conceals reference, as E. K. hints many times in his glosses, to certain persons and events. Accordingly, the poem provokes the critic to turn from the display of sheer poetic skill in order to uncover some historical allegory. Yet even a probable identification of Rosalind or Dido or Cuddie does not take one very far into the poem which is read then only as a cipher or intellectual puzzle. The poem was not so read in Spenser's own age. In his *Skialetheia* Guilpin praised "deep Spencer" for "his profound-prickt layes"; to Whetstone, it was "a work of deepe learning, iudgment & witte"; while upon the evidence of the *Calender* alone Nashe upheld "diuine Master *Spencer,* the miracle of wit, to bandie line for line for my life in the honor of *England* gainst *Spaine, France, Italie,* and all the worlde." [1] Unless we dismiss this praise as jingoism, we must allow that the poem has depths of meaning which cannot be probed by removing an allegorical veil. This is to say the obvious, perhaps; yet criticism of the *Shepheardes Calender* has not been much more than footnotes to E. K.'s glosses.

What is so perverse about this effort to identify historical allusions is that Spenser has laboured so carefully to conceal them. Why, then,

From *English Literary History,* XXIII, No. 1 (1956), 171–83. Copyright © 1956 by The Johns Hopkins Press. Reprinted by permission of The Johns Hopkins Press.

[1] Edward Guilpin, *Skialetheia* or, A Shadowe of Truth (London, 1598), E1ʳ; George Whetstone, *Sir Phillip Sidney,* his honorable life . . . (1586), B2ᵛ Margin; Nashe, "Preface to Greene's *Menaphon,*" in G. G. Smith, ed., *Eliz. Crit. Essays* (Oxford, 1904), I, 318.

should the critic turn from what the poet says to what he has left unsaid? Certainly parts of the poem "reflect"—though in no simple one-to-one correspondence—the contemporary historical situation, awareness of which would then provide an added social impact for the contemporary reader; but the poem's substance, its meaning, is not there. Again to say the obvious, Rosalind or Dido or Cuddie is clearly in the poem, while whoever in the age may be doubtfully identified with one of these poetic facts is not, unless we confuse art and life. Spenser conceals private meaning in his poem, it is true; but he does so in order to turn the reader from the particular to the universal. A general moral meaning is dominant throughout the poem: E. K. writes that "the keeping of sheepe . . . is the argument of *all* Aeglogues," and Spenser affirms that his purpose is "to teach the ruder shepheard how to feede his sheepe." Moreover, Spenser insists in the Epilogue that his *Calender* be not confined to any particular historical setting:

> Loe I haue made a Calender for *euery* yeare,
> That steele in strength, and time in durance shall outweare:
> And if I marked well the starres reuolution,
> It shall continewe till the worlds dissolution.

As E. K. paraphrases these lines: "all thinges perish and come to theyr last end, but workes of learned wits and monuments of Poetry abide for euer." [2] Spenser is not writing a history of his time, but prophecy; or rather, as the poet he considers in Sidney's terms not "what is, hath been, or shall be," but ranges "into the diuine consideration of what may be, and should [be." [3]] That Milton read the *Shepheardes Calender* in this way is evident from his comment upon "that false shepherd Palinode in the eclogue of May, under whom the poet lively personates our prelates, whose whole life is a recantation of their pastoral vow, and whose profession to forsake the world, as they use the matter, bogs them deeper into the world. Those our admired Spenser inveighs against, not without some presage of these reforming times." [4] Spenser's intent in choosing "rather to vnfold great matter of argument couertly, then professing it," is not to set up an historical maze, but to seek the universal level of significance. By his time, the pastoral form had become the vehicle for such higher

[2] Gloss on December Emblem. All quotations of the poem are from E. De Selincourt, ed., *Spenser's Minor Poems* (Oxford, 1910).

[3] Philip Sidney, *Apologie for Poetrie*, ed. J. Churton Collins (Oxford, 1907), p. 11.

[4] *Animadversions*, in F. Patterson, ed., *The Student's Milton* (New York, 1933), p. 500.

meaning. Drayton believed that "the most High, and most Noble Matters of the World may bee shaddowed in them," and he held Spenser to be "the prime Pastoralist of England." [5]

My purpose in this paper is to explore the larger meaning of the *Shepheardes Calender*. To state my own position briefly: I believe that the whole poem is integrated through the form of the Calendar; and I shall attempt here to describe the nature of its meaning as a whole, what may be called the poem's argument. It is generally agreed that the poem lacks unity both in form and content;[6] my purpose is to prove otherwise. Only one critic, to my knowledge, treats the poem as a whole. Hallett Smith writes that Elizabethan pastoral poetry illustrates a "pastoral idea" which is "an ideal of the good life, of the state of content and mental self-sufficiency," and that "the pastoral idea, in its various ramifications, *is* the *Calender*." [7] His understanding of Spenser's poem is directly opposed to mine. When he analyzes the poem he does so through the different kinds of eclogues which he sees illustrating the "pastoral idea" and not in terms of the poem's internal structure or developing pattern through which it may possess its own organic unity. My approach, too, differs: being not through what the poem has in common with Elizabethan pastoral poetry, but through what is unique in Spenser's recreation of the pastoral form. The beginning, then, of my discussion of the poem's argument is Spenser's use of the Calendar.

Spenser's contribution to the pastoral form was the Calendar. Its use may have been suggested through Vergil's Fourth Eclogue which celebrates the return of the Golden Age, and the subsequent linking of the pastoral with the Nativity. "In the Angels Song to Shepheards at our Saviours Nativitie," Drayton writes, "Pastorall Poesie seemes consecrated";[8] and in his "General Argument" E. K. justifies the poem's beginning with the month of January because of its association with the Incarnation of Christ "who as then renewing the state of the decayed world, and returning the compasse of expired yeres to theyr former date and first commencement, left to vs his heires a memoriall of his birth." The year with its cycle of seasons determines the form of the poem. The opening lines announce the poet's Exodus

---

[5] "To the Reader of his Pastorals" in *The Works of Michael Drayton*, ed. Hebel (Oxford, 1932), II, 517–18.

[6] Edwin Greenlaw, C. G. Osgood, F. M. Padelford, and others, eds., *The Works of Edmund Spenser: A Variorum Edition*. Vol. I, *The Minor Poems* (Baltimore, 1943), 571–655.

[7] Hallett Smith, *Elizabethan Poetry*, (Cambridge, Mass. 1952), pp. 2, 46.

[8] Drayton, *Works*, II, 517.

as he "led forth his flock, that had bene long ypent," and in the
wilderness of the winter setting he complains of his suffering through
the revolution of the seasons. The contest of the seasons suggests the
sequence of winter–summer–winter that dominates the January–June–
December eclogues, and through them the shape of the whole poem.
The form of the Calendar allows Spenser to return to the ritual origins
of the pastoral seen in Bion's *Lament for Adonis*; only now the lament for the dying God becomes the lament for himself. The poet is
Adonis, the love-wounded God for whom all Nature laments:

> Thou barrein ground, whome winters wrath hath wasted,
> Art made a myrrhour, to behold my plight:
> Whilome thy fresh spring flowrd, and after hasted
> Thy sommer prowde with Daffadillies dight.
> And now is come thy wynters stormy state,
> Thy mantle mard, wherein thou maskedst late.
>
> Such rage as winters, reigneth in my heart,
> My life bloud friesing with vnkindly cold:
> Such stormy stoures do breede my balefull smart,
> As if my yeare were wast, and woxen old.        *(Jan.* 19–28)

The ritual quest for the God becomes the quest for himself, and the
poem's major theme is the effort to "find" himself. The association
of the Calendar with the Nativity adds the life–death–life sequence,
and the mutability of life that brings death within nature is opposed
at the end of the poem by the November eclogue where for the first
time the pagan mood of despair is supplanted by the full Christian
assurance of man's resurrection out of Nature. This assurance, together with the aspiration in October to cast off his shepherd's weeds,
brings him to the resolution of the final eclogue when he lays down
the oaten pipe and emerges as England's heroic poet. The *Calender*
becomes the poet's manifestation, his epiphany to the world. Since
the poem is set within the framework of the Nativity, its moment of
time is when the pagan world violently confronts the Christian, and
the old gods are rejected for the new. The traditional lament, "Pan is
dead" is rendered in Spenser's cry: "Perdie god was he none"; and in
the final eclogue, the pagan pastoral world gives way to the Christian
with the poet's prayer to the greater Pan. Since Christ is the second
Adam whose birth returns "the compasse of expired yeres to theyr
former date and first commencement," the poem is set also in the
framework of the Fall which is constantly echoed and retold throughout.

Within the form of the Calendar, the various eclogues are divided
by E. K. into "three formes orranckes": the Recreative, the Moral, and
the Plaintive. The relationship of these three distinct kinds of eclogues
provides the poem's argument; but first it is necessary to see how they
are distinct. The pastoral world which provides the poem's setting is
traditionally identified with Arcadia, the state of innocence before
the Fall. This "unreal" world, seen in the poem's deliberate artifice
with its conventions of the shepherd life, provides the subject of the
Recreative eclogues: March with its story of Cupid, April's hymn of
praise, and the contest of the shepherds in August. These eclogues
exist in the poem as fragments of an earlier pastoral tradition, the
idyll, that serve to "test" the poet's skill. In each he seeks to "overgo"
the traditional form. When this timeless pastoral world is placed in the
order of time given by the Calendar form, it is seen from the perspective of the Fall caught in perpetual mutability. The pastoral world of
innocence circumscribed by the "real" world of fallen nature becomes
the subject of the moral eclogues with their allegory of the political
and religious conditions of England. The simple pastoral life of en-
joyable ease must then be rejected for the dedicated life where man
does not live according to Nature but seeks escape out of Nature. For
this reason the pastoral life is identified with the antagonists in the
moral eclogues: Cuddie's "flowring youth" (*Feb.*, 31), Palinode's yearn-
ing for "lustihede and wanton meryment" (*May*, 42), the wanton poets
singing "rymes of rybaudrye" (*Oct.*, 76), and Morrell upon the hill
identified with the Garden of Eden where "vsed shepheards all to
feede theyr flocks at will,/Till by his foly one did fall, that all the rest
did spill" (*July*, 65–8). The good shepherds of the moral eclogues, such
as Thomalin, know that since the Fall "shepheardes bene foresayd from
places of delight" (*July*, 69–70). In the moral eclogues the pastoral
conventions become radically allegorical; simple lyricism is replaced
by satire, irony, and open denunciation. The poet's relation to the
simple pastoral world of innocence becomes the subject of the Plaintive
eclogues. Within the pastoral world he is the melancholy shepherd
dominated by the elusive and faithless Rosalind. While Hobbinoll,
the shepherd of the pastoral world, may find Paradise, the poet Colin
Clout must journey through a wilderness:

> O happy *Hobbinoll*, I blesse they state,
> That Paradise hast found, whych *Adam* lost.
> Here wander may thy flock early or late,
> Withouten dreade of Wolues to bene ytost:
> Thy louely layes here mayst thou freely boste.

> But I vnhappy man, whom cruell fate,
> And angry Gods pursue from coste to coste,
> Can nowhere fynd, to shroude my lucklesse pate.

*(June,* 9–16)

(Significantly, the last lines echo Vergil's opening description of Aeneas.) Paradise, tempting man to return to the life of pleasurable ease, is evil; for life lived merely according to Nature, as portrayed through the device of the Calendar, yields eternal death. For this reason the poet withdraws from the pastoral world, signified in the opening eclogue by the act of breaking the shepherd's pipe, and remains disguised until he may find his rightful place in the real world reflected in the moral eclogues. The mode of the plaintive eclogues is the pastoral elegy with its central theme of death and rebirth: hence at the beginning, middle, and end of the poem the poet laments his present "death" until the climax in December: "winter is come, that blowes the balefull breath,/And after Winter commeth timely death" (149–50). At this moment when the year begins to descend through another cycle of seasons, the poet casts off his pastoral disguise, turns from Pan to address the greater Pan, and frees himself from bondage to the pastoral life:

> Adieu delightes, that lulled me asleepe,
> Adieu my deare, whose loue I bought so deare:
> Adieu my little Lambes and loued sheepe,
> Adieu ye Woodes that oft my witnesse were:
>   Adieu good *Hobbinol,* that was so true,
>   Tell *Rosalind,* her *Colin* bids her adieu.

This sudden and climactic resolution coming with full force only in the final line suggests that the poet's release is achieved through the act of writing the poem.

The kinds of eclogues are carefully juxtaposed: in the first half of the poem there is the movement from the opening plaintive eclogue to the moral eclogue and to the recreative eclogue which is repeated, then returning to the moral and to the plaintive eclogue of June; in the second half, there is the same descent from the plaintive to the moral and to the recreative, then returning as before to the moral eclogue which is repeated and to the final plaintive eclogues which resolve the argument of the whole poem.[9] Within this structure Spenser explores

[9] The juxtaposition of the eclogues may be given diagrammatically:

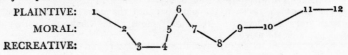

PLAINTIVE:   1      6                    11——12
MORAL:          2   5  7    9——10
RECREATIVE:        3——4     8

the roles of the poet and pastor in society. The subject of the eclogues alternates from the poet to the pastor regularly (the pair of recreative eclogues March and April being taken as one), until October where the poet aspires to fulfil the pastor's role in society. Thus the eclogues form pairs: what is first treated in terms of the poet is then expanded in religious terms. The patterning of the eclogues, as I seek to establish now, provides the developing argument of the poem.

The two opening eclogues serve as prelude to the poem, even as January and February precede the natural year. In January, the poet as Colin is identified with Nature, being at one with Nature, reflected by and reflecting Nature, as he invokes the Nature God Pan. Brought to despair through his vain love for Rosalind, he may only withdraw and break his pipe: "both pype and Muse, shall sore the while abye./ So broke his oaten pype, and downe dyd lye" (71–2). His complaint, "such rage as winters, reigneth in my heart" is expressed in the following eclogue through Cuddie's lament against "rancke Winters rage"; and in reproof Thenot moralizes upon the mutability of the world which must go "from good to badd, and from badde to worse,/From worse vnto that is worst of all,/And then returne to his former fall" (12–14). He illustrates the world's mutability through the fable of the Oak that "had bene an auncient tree,/Sacred with many a mysteree" but later is cut down through the complaints of the ambitious Briar. Whatever particular meaning the fable may hold, the "morall and generall" meaning is dominant, as E. K. declares: it stands as an allegory of the dangers of Reformation, the Oak being the Catholic Church which suffers reform by the Established Church under Elizabeth (the Briar with "colours meete to clothe a mayden Queene").[10] Cutting the tree corresponds to breaking the shepherd's pipe: the January eclogue stands, then, as an allegory of the aspirations of the Renaissance poet. It expresses the desire of England's "new Poete," the successor of the old Poet Chaucer, to escape the pastoral form.[11] The poem becomes his "retracciouns" of "many a song and many a leccherous lay"—his Dreams, Legends, Courts of Cupid, and his Dying Pelican—and the record of his dedication to the higher argument of the heroic form.

"The yeare beginneth in March," and "proportioned" to that season is a recreative eclogue describing the pastoral world of Flora, who

---

[10] See Greenlaw, in *Minor Poems,* I, 603.

[11] The antithesis between the old poet and the new is carefully made in the Epistle: "the new Poete . . . the olde famous Poete Chaucer . . . that good old Poete . . . this our new Poete."

"bids make ready *Maias* bowre" and leads the shepherds to "sporten in delight,/And learne with Lettice to wexe light" (17, 19–20). The fable of the discovery of Cupid whose wound, the shepherd complains, "ranckleth more and more,/And inwardly it festreth sore" (100–1) presents allegorically the state of human nature within the natural world. The eclogue defines the world out of which the poet seeks escape. E. K. writes in the "Epistle" that the poet's purpose in his poem is to warn others against his folly, for "his vnstayed yougth had long wandred in the common Labyrinth of Loue." In the following eclogue the poet as Colin is described as one who "doth forbeare/His wonted songs" for "Loue hath wounded [him] with a deadly darte" (22). This account is juxtaposed to the intensely lyrical hymn of praise to the Queen who appears as Flora attended with her nymphs, being crowned with flowers and surrounded by "this beuie of Ladies bright" (118). She inspires him to song, and he dedicates to her his poetic labours:

> To her will I offer a milkwhite Lamb:
> She is my goddesse plaine,
> And I her shepherds swayne,
> Albee forswonck and forswatt I am.                    (96–99)

The counterpart of April is the May eclogue: here Palinode the dedicated shepherd-pastor delivers his hymn of praise to Lady Flora who is a parody of the Virgin Queen, being the companion of "a lusty Tabrere" (22). (The two eclogues are companion pieces on the themes of sacred and profane love.) As the shepherds in March are led by Flora to "sporten in delight," so Palinode lusts after the "great sport" of Lady Flora and her Nymphs. The protagonist, Piers, reproves Palinode's recantation of the dedicated life for "shepheard must walke another way,/Sike worldly souenance he must foresay" (81–2), and denounces any temporizing between them. Piers' declaration completes the first part of the poem's argument: by withdrawing from the pastoral life the poet need not be, as Palinode, a "worldes childe" but may lead a dedicated life within but not of the world. Milton understood that the eclogue shows how one must "learn first to renounce the world and so give himself to God, and not therefore give himself to God, that he may close the better with the world." [12] Hence with June the poet returns to the pastoral setting being now prepared to forsake the pastoral Paradise for a dedicated life. His poetical ambitions are expressed through Hobbinoll's advice to leave the pastoral world for

[12] *Animadversions*, p. 500.

the court. But he dare not as yet aspire to a higher muse, though he hopes to be baptized by Chaucer, and rejects the ambition that would lead him to "presume to *Parnasse* hyll" (70). Thus the first part of the poem treats of the individual self and points forward to the truly dedicated life. There remains the problem treated in the second part, how one may lead the dedicated life within the fallen world. In July, the companion eclogue to June, the same theme of aspiration is given for the shepherd-pastor. Morrell, the proud and ambitious pastor inhabits the hill which is identified with seven different hills (signifying the seven hills of Rome and therefore the fallen world) including Eden and Parnassus. As the poet in June would not climb Parnassus, so the good pastor Thomalin scorns the hill and loves the low degree.

The August eclogue is a recreative interlude displaying the poet's skill through the traditional singing-contest in which the shepherds' praise of love is significantly opposed by his lament upon love. Renwick calls the eclogue an "allegory of the new poetry: the simple swains sing merrily enough, but a grave, elaborate, Italianate song of *Colin's* hushes them in admiration, their simple impromptu is overshadowed." [13] The September and October eclogues conclude the debate upon the role of the poet-pastor in society. In September, the allegorical veil is removed and Diggon denounces openly the corruption of pastors in England. His denunciation summarizes the attacks made previously against the shepherds who "bene ydle and still,/And ledde of theyr sheepe, what way they wyll" (as Palinode), those who "bene false, and full of couetise,/And casten to compasse many wrong emprise" (such as Morrell), and those represented by the Briar who "ne in good nor goodnes taken delight:/But kindle coales of conteck and yre" (80–7). Corrupt pastors ("badde is the best") corrupt the sheep who do not listen to their voice but "wander at wil, and stray at pleasure,/And to theyr foldes yead at their owne leasure" (144–5). October presents a similar complaint against the corrupt age; and at this moment of crisis the poet aspires to become the heroic poet who may fulfil the role of the pastor and through his work move the infected will:

> O what an honor is it, to restraine
> The lust of lawlesse youth with good aduice:
> Or pricke them forth with pleasaunce of thy vaine,
> Whereto thou list their trayned willes entice.           (21–4)

In the May eclogue Piers upheld the dedicated life within the world;

[13] W. L. Renwick, ed., *The Shepherd's Calendar* (London, 1930), p. 206.

now he advocates the life of service dedicated to the Queen. He urges the poet to "lyft vp thy selfe out of the lowly dust," and Colin is inspired by that love which "lyftes him vp out of the loathsome myre" and may "rayse [his] mynd aboue the starry skie" (92, 4). That man may be lifted out of the lowly dust and raised above the starry sky becomes the theme of the November eclogue which treats the death and resurrection of Dido. E. K.'s claim that this eclogue surpasses all others in the book is a measure of its significance. Here, for the first time, is shown the ultimate defeat of Nature with man's release from the state of mutability. The assurance of resurrection out of the state of Nature resolves, as it does for Milton in *Lycidas,* the problems which led to writing the poem. Then with the return to the pastoral setting in the concluding eclogue, the poet prays to the greater Pan who is Christ: to him he addresses his complaint against life confined to the state of Nature, and at the end abandons the pastoral world.

The argument of the *Shepheardes Calender* is, then, the rejection of the pastoral life for the truly dedicated life in the world. For Spenser, this life is that of the heroic poet whose high religious calling is to serve the Queen by inspiring her people to all virtuous action. Upon the level of merely private allusion, the poem may refer covertly to Spenser's circle of friends, to local gossip and other topical matters; but such allusion is carefully submerged, being occasional, digressive, and extrinsic to the poem's organic unity. Upon another level, the personal, the poem records Spenser's progress from his apprenticeship to pastoral poetry towards the heroic poem. Like the Red Cross Knight, he is a "clownishe younge man" described in the "Letter to Ralegh" who "rested him on the floore, vnfitte through his rusticity for a better place" until the Faery Queen appoints him his task. (A year after the *Calender* appeared, Spenser started to write *The Faerie Queene.*) This level of meaning is transmuted through the pastoral conventions and the Calendar form into an allegory of human life within the order of Nature. Through the device of the Calendar, human life is seen in the perspective of the Fall and the Nativity: the one bringing the state of death out of which man must escape through rejecting the pastoral Paradise, the other promising rebirth which he may gain through seeking the truly dedicated life in the world.

# Spenser's "Sweete *Themmes*":
# Of Time and the River

## by M. L. Wine

The final verse of the refrain to Spenser's *Prothalamion* has never wanted admirers, even among those who, feeling that they have to make a choice for some reason, prefer the *Epithalamion*. Sir Sidney Lee, for instance, considered the former poem "hardly a whit inferior to" the latter: "Its far-famed refrain . . . sounds indeed a sweeter note than the refrain of answering woods and ringing echoes in the earlier ode. It leaves an ineffaceable impression of musical grace and simplicity. It was Spenser's fit farewell to his Muse." [1] Saintsbury, too, thought that the *Prothalamion* was "even more beautiful than the *Epithalamion* itself in the gravity and delicate management of the refrain." [2] Miss Ing, calling attention to the function of the refrain in both poems "of persistently reminding the reader of the idea of singing," describes "Sweete *Themmes* runne softly, till I end my Song" as "unchangingly beautiful." [3]

Others, however, though probably not deaf to the "musical grace and simplicity" of the line, have felt, not without reason, that the entire refrain at times forced Spenser into creating some strangely incongruous and awkward stanzas. Edward Marsh, who thought little of the poem in the first place, observed: "Spenser has so little control over the refrain which ends every stanza that he lets it force him into wishing his two young couples 'fruitful issue *upon their Brydale day,*' regardless of the inconvenience and even scandal which would result. But it is difficult to believe that even in this mood he would speak of making brides brides against their bridal day." [4] Dan Norton justified

From *Studies in English Literature*, II, No. 1 (1962), 111–17. Copyright © 1962 by Rice University Press. Reprinted by permission of *Studies in English Literature*.

[1] Sidney Lee, *Great Englishmen of the Sixteenth Century* (London, 1907), pp. 186–189. The *Prothalamion* was Spenser's last published poem during his lifetime.
[2] George Saintsbury, *A History of English Prosody* (London, 1923), I, 362.
[3] Catherine Ing, *Elizabethan Lyrics* (London, 1951), p. 216.
[4] Edward Marsh, "An Emendation in Spenser's *Prothalamium* [*sic*]," *London Mercury*, IX (1924), 300.

what may seem like a "clumsily forced" conclusion to the ninth
stanza—

> And great *Elisaes* glorious name may ring
> Through al the world, fil'd with thy wide Alarmes,
> Which some braue muse may sing
> To ages following,
> Vpon the Brydale day, which is not long:
> Sweete *Themmes* runne softly, till I end my Song[5]—

by finding in "the Brydale day" an "anagogic" reference to the Accession Day of Queen Elizabeth, "the virgin bride of England." [6] One
might add that some justification also seems needed for the conclusion
of the final stanza:

> They two forth pacing to the Riuers side,
> Receiued those two faire Brides, their Loues delight,
> Which at th'appointed tyde,
> Each one did make his Bryde,
> Against their Brydale day, which is not long:
> Sweete *Themmes* runne softly, till I end my Song.

Surely Spenser did not intend to imply that the bridegrooms married
their brides-to-be even before "their Brydale day."

Probably no one would deny the sheer musical appeal of the refrain;
yet, if we are not to believe that the refrain forced Spenser into a
strait jacket, we must reconsider its function in the poem. What has
not been observed is that the effect of the refrain in *every* stanza—and
this may be one of the reasons for its appeal—is somewhat ambivalent,
and in this ambivalence may lie the clue to the much vexed problem
of the poem's organization and meaning.[7] Most explications tend to be
biographical and historical in nature, with the implication in most of
them that the poem fails to achieve unity because its "intention" (or
the poet's in the poem) is divided between the celebration of the forthcoming nuptials which occasion the poem and a frustrated bid for
patronage. Although studies have revealed a unity of theme, imagery,
and setting within the poem, the division between allegory and realism

[5] All quotations from the *Prothalamion* follow the text in Edwin Greenlaw, C. G.
Osgood, F. M. Padelford, and others, eds., *The Works of Edmund Spenser: A
Variorum Edition* (Baltimore, 1932–49). Vol. II, *The Minor Poems.*

[6] Dan S. Norton, "Queen Elizabeth's 'Brydal Day,'" *Modern Language Quarterly*,
V (1944), 149–54.

[7] I am indebted to Professor Robert D. Mayo, who, in discussions of the poem,
first raised the question of the meaning of the refrain that I am trying to answer
here.

still remains to be explained. On the face of it, the charge leveled by
John Hughes in his prefatory "Essay on Allegorical Poetry" in the
first eighteenth-century edition of Spenser's works—that "The Allegory
breaks before the Reader is prepar'd for it"—may not seem altogether
unjust; but by his handling of the refrain Spenser did invent, as
Hughes thought he ought to have, "some probable means of coming
out of" the allegory.[8]

The variations played upon the initial refrain—

> Against the Brydale day, which is not long:
> Sweete *Themmes* runne softly, till I end my Song—

are slight, but in the following nine repetitions the variant "was not
long" appears five times in the first line. That the bridal day "is not
long" or "was not long" obviously means, in a poem which is "a
spousall verse," that the day of marriage *is* expected to take place not
long after the publication of the poem or that it *was* not far in the
future when the poet had the experience he writes about. But the effect of the variants *is* and *was* is to create ambivalent readings: does
the refrain suggest that the day itself is, indeed, not long and, in the
nature of things, cannot be?

Moreover, the second line of the refrain evidently implies some
contrast. The poet seems to be coaxing, even praying to, "sweete
*Themmes*" to "runne softly" till he ends his song. What will happen
when he *does* end his song? Are we to assume that the river ordinarily
runs loudly, that is, rapidly, threateningly, and that the "sweete
*Themmes*" the poet is addressing is something extraordinary for the
moment? The very beginning of the poem suggests that even the day
he is singing about is an unusual one:

> Calme was the day, and through the trembling ayre,
> Sweet breathing *Zephyrus* did softly play
> A gentle spirit, that lightly did delay
> Hot *Titans* beames, which then did glyster fayre.

The first word of the poem immediately suggests by the unspoken but
implied contrast that this was a special day; and the stress that the in-
verted foot gives to *Calme* emphasizes how rare, like the softly running
river, was the mood of the moment. As in the refrain, the forces of
nature are personified; and the gentle west wind, Zephyrus, softly (like

[8] John Hughes, *The Works of Mr. Edmund Spenser* (London, 1715), I, xlix. See
variorum notes under "Allegory" in *The Minor Poems*, II, 666–67, and also Jay L.
Halio, " 'Prothalamion,' 'Ulysses,' and Intention in Poetry," *College English*, XXII
(1961), 390–4.

the river) playing through the leaves only *delays* (not nearly so force-ful a verb as *allays*) hot Titan's beams, the full force of which seems inevitably in the offing. The "trembling ayre" is fraught with brooding expectation; the scene itself contrasts to the poet's own state, but na-ture at this moment, like "sweete *Themmes*," is only tenuously in harmony with the occasion of the "song."

The implied contrast in these opening lines and in the refrain be-tween nature and the poet's condition becomes more meaningful when we examine the time scheme of the poem, for it then appears that *Themmes* is associated in the poet's mind with time and muta-bility; as it rushes along, what it carries on its "brode aged backe" (stanza eight) is the decay and destruction of human beauty and dig-nity.[9] The poem celebrates the "spousall" of two couples whose bridal day has yet to take place. The central situation of the poem—the pas-sage of the swans and their reception as brides-to-be by their prospec-tive bridegrooms—is an event in the past. Yet the poet sings in the present ("Sweete *Themmes* runne softly, till I end my Song"), recol-lecting, so to speak, an emotion in a moment of tranquillity.

Within individual stanzas the time scheme is even more compli-cated as the poet alternates between describing his own present state of "sullein care" and the vision of loveliness he has and the feelings this vision arouses in him. Thus, in the first stanza, he describes the calm day in the past when he walked along the river to ease the pain of his discontent; but he interjects that his vain expectation of idle hopes "still doe fly away, / Like empty shaddowes." Then immediately back in the past tense he tells how he found the beautiful bankside

> Fit to decke maydens bowres,
> And crowne their Paramours,
> Against the Brydale day, which *is* not long:[10]
> Sweete *Themmes* runne softly, till I end my Song.

Except for the refrain in the sixth stanza, "sung" by one of the nymphs herself, the first line of the refrain reads thereafter, until the eighth stanza where the next elegiac passage of personal disillusion occurs, "which *was* not long." From the eighth stanza to the final one, the

---

[9] One would like to see in the spelling *Themmes* for Thames a paronomasia or "elegant pun"—like several in the poem—on the name of the river and *tempus*, "time." The spelling for the river is consistent throughout the poem, and nowhere else in Spenser's works does this spelling occur. Unfortunately, the printer of *Prothalamion* is unknown, and we cannot determine whether this is a compositor's spelling.

[10] My italics.

phrase is again in the present tense although the last stanza still describes a past event.

The *is* of the last three stanzas (eight to ten) has implications of future time, and the eighth stanza itself may be taken as a turning point in the poem; for here the poet abandons the swan allegory, and in the ninth stanza he gives us an actual human example of splendor and dignity as embodied in "a noble Peer, / Great *Englands* glory and the Worlds wide wonder." Thus the ninth stanza serves as a transition to the tenth, where the swans of the allegory have become transformed into real brides.[11] What makes this change possible is the dramatic development of the poem, based, in part, on the shifts in time. Although the poet never says so, the allegory of the swans, always described in the past tense, resembles a vision: there is no transition from a waking to a dream state as in the typical medieval dream vision poem, but the sight has all the appearances of a dream or vision allegory: "There, in a Meadow, by the Riuers side, / A Flocke of *Nymphes* I chaunced to espy. . . ."

*Chaunced to espy!* The world this vision evokes is not natural, or it is nature very much adorned by art. We can more easily picture it as a tapestry. The "rutty Bancke . . . / Was *paynted* all with various flowers," "all the meades *adornd* with *daintie gemmes*" (my italics). Even the vocabulary in this section is artificial; Spenser is purposely using words that were "antique" in his own day, such as "feateously," "Paramours." [12] In this world the nymphs are natural, and the celestial imagery indicates how transcendent a vision this is. It is a vision of a golden age where, it is implied, gods associate with men; and the fifth stanza clearly invites comparison with the bucolic landscapes of classical pastoral poetry.

In the poet's world, however, the world of the present, the world implied in the urgency of the refrain, there are no nymphs. The vision of loveliness is bounded by two elegiac passages of personal disillusion (stanzas one and eight) and, of course, by the ever-recurring refrain. Yet even within the vision itself warning signs of what the real world is like intrude. In the sixth stanza, the one Marsh so strongly objected to, one of the nymphs sings a "lay" to the swans, the brides-to-be, which not only includes the refrain of the poem (in the present tense) but also, like the refrain, is something of a prayer that "this happie

---

[11] Spenser's punning on the frequent Elizabethan spelling *birdes* for *brides* (see *Oxford English Dictionary*) helps make this metathesis seem natural.

[12] See Veré L. Rubel, *Poetic Diction in the English Renaissance from Skelton through Spenser* (New York, 1941) pp. 263–264.

hower" may lead to "endlesse Peace" and plenty and "fruitfull issue" to bring the couples joy and confound their foes. The lay looks to the future, to the world the poet knows so well.

In the eighth stanza, the procession of swans having come "To mery *London*," the contrast between the poet's present fortune in that city ("my freendles case") and the happy childhood he recalls there ("my most kyndly Nurse") so intensifies his original elegiac mood that he has trouble sustaining his joyful one. Furthermore, the contrast between what the river once bore (the Templar Knights who "decayd through pride") and what it now bears (the unheroic studious lawyers) adds to his disenchantment. But only momentarily, for the "ioyes" of the vision do manage to sustain him; and the prospect of the forthcoming marriage, of men like the "noble Peer" (stanza nine) who redeem the lost glory of the Templar Knights, turns vision into reality, so that in the concluding stanza the swans are, indeed, brides; and the same celestial imagery of the vision now figures in making the reality transcendent. The song is ended, and the poet has triumphed over "sweete *Themmes*."

The poem does end, however, on the refrain; and the bridal day still "is not long," even though the concluding lines before the final refrain tell us that the two knights, the bridegrooms, "Receiued those two faire Brides, their Loues delight, / Which at th'appointed tyde, / Each one did make his Bryde." Even the praise of the "noble Peer" that serves as a transition between vision and reality is, like the "lay" the nymph sang to the swans, actually a prayer that time *return* to a golden age of chivalry. Like the nymph's prayer for the swans, the poet's prayer is also for "endlesse happinesse" and the confounding of the nation's foes by the peer's "prowesse and victorious armes." Thus one understands why *Prothalamion* brought tears to Coleridge's eyes: even at its most elevated and triumphant moments, the burden of the "undersong" checks the visionary with its melancholy implication that all bridal days and all bridal joys are brief, that time brings with it decay.[13]

Nevertheless, it is also in time that time is conquered, for it is "sweete *Themmes*" after all that runs softly to allow the poet to sing his song and to recall a vision of loveliness—although, perhaps, the

[13] The refrain, therefore, with its persistently recurrent hint that the poem is about mutability, stands, as it were, outside the immediate context of any given stanza. It is not, as Marsh suggests, that "Spenser has so little control over the refrain," but rather that he subtly employs the refrain to integrate all elements of the poem—the personal passages, the swan allegory, the praise of the peer, the celebration of the "spousall."

poet's song enchants the river to run softly; for in the refrain Spenser proclaims his abiding faith in "song" to "delay" and even overcome the threat of mutability.[14] *Themmes* can run loudly now, but the song is here to proclaim this vision "to ages following," just as "some braue muse may sing / To ages following" the deeds of the noble peer; for by such visions of loveliness—fleeting though they may be—men achieve dignity and a sense of permanence and the will to endure. The poet's vision, Spenser seems to be saying, is a necessary balance to life's "empty shaddowes." Like the fame of heroic deeds and the "fruitfull issue" of marriage, song recalls man's worthiness in a universe of transition, in a universe where man's worthiness is meaningful only because of transition. A world of ruinous decay gives marriage and fame and song their brilliance and desirability; love and noble deeds and art being most godlike and most enduring, they make a brazen world golden.

[14] That the Prothalamion is not a mere occasional piece, but a poem about mutability, should not seem strange, particularly after Professor A. Kent Hieatt has so recently demonstrated in his *Short Time's Endless Monument* (New York, 1960) that Spenser took the occasion of his own marriage to produce in the *Epithalamion* both "a marriage ode and a register of time," "a celebration of life and short time" and a "celebration of eternity" (pp. 51–52).

# The Triumph Over Hasty Accidents:
# A Note on the Symbolic Mode of
# the *Epithalamion*

## *by Richard Neuse*

Spenser's *Epithalamion* has recently been shown to be of greater complexity as a poetic artifact than had been suspected. The number symbolism which A. K. Hieatt has, to my mind convincingly, demonstrated for the poem,[1] indicates the care with which Spenser composed his poem, the great importance he apparently attached to it. One of the puzzles raised by Mr. Hieatt's discovery is why Spenser should have done so: what in the nature of the poem warranted this expenditure of energy and ingenuity?

I attempt an answer to this question by dealing first with a part of the poem that has always seemed very puzzling to me: the envoy. No critical account I have seen does justice to the obscurities of the envoy, and the hypothesis which this essay proposes is intended to resolve at least some of these. At the same time it has necessitated another hypothesis, that of a continuity between *Amoretti* and *Epithalamion*. In short, I am proposing that the envoy represents the climax of a deliberate progression that moves from the sonnets to the marriage song. And it is in terms of this progression, and the *Epithalamion's* special place in it, that I think much of its unusual complexity can be understood.

In general terms, the progression is one from romantic to conjugal love and all that this implies; in aesthetic terms it involves the transi-

From *The Modern Language Review*, LXI, No. 2 (1966), 163–74. Copyright © 1966 by The Modern Humanities Research Association. Reprinted by permission of The Modern Humanities Research Association and of the Editors.

[1] See Hieatt's *Short Time's Endless Monument: The Symbolism of the Numbers in Edmund Spenser's Epithalamion* (New York, 1960). And see his "The Daughters of Horus: Order in the Stanzas of *Epithalamion*," in W. Nelson, ed., *Form and Convention in the Poetry of Edmund Spenser* (New York, 1961), pp. 103–21. Spenser citations are from *Spenser's Minor Poems*, ed. E. De Selincourt (Oxford, 1910).

tion from an essentially Platonic to a sacramental mode of symboliza-
tion. But the word *progression* is misleading here insofar as it connotes
a straightforward linear development. On the surface, indeed, a series
of love poems culminating in a marriage song looks straightforward,
not to say conventional (even if at Spenser's time it was not). But the
envoy itself helps to warn us that the appearances are deceptive: it
reminds us that the lovers are not merely (or primarily) figures of
literary convention but also actual persons subject to the vicissitudes
and discontinuities of actual experience. Finally, it seems to indicate
that the *Epithalamion* is the poet's personal response to such discontinuities: more than a "mere" epithalamium, in other words, it must
test and extend the very nature and function of such a poem.

Whereas in the previous stanzas the poet invoked the powers of
heaven and earth to set off his wedding day as special and auspicious,
in the envoy he addresses his poem itself:

> Song made in lieu of many ornaments,
> With which my loue should duly haue bene dect,
> Which cutting off through hasty accidents,
> Ye would not stay your dew time to expect,
> But promist both to recompens,
> Be vnto her a goodly ornament,
> And for short time an endlesse moniment.           (ll. 427–33)

Some of the questions that present themselves here may be stated as
follows. Why is the envoy there at all? What function does it serve?
What are the many ornaments with which his love should have been
decked? What the hasty accidents? What is the due time? What are the
antecedents of "which" in the third line, and of "both" in the fifth?

Obviously, first of all, the envoy functions to state the special purpose which the poem is intended to serve. By breaking with the formal
rhythm of the preceding stanzas, it pulls the reader up short and invites him to contemplate the meaning of the ornament-monument
which the poet is presenting to his bride. Further, as we shall try to
show, the envoy serves to place the wedding song in the context of the
personal drama which began with the sonnet sequence.

That the "many ornaments" refer to poems [2] is suggested by the idea
of poem-as-ornament in the envoy itself and in the beginning of the
*Epithalamion* ("Ye learned sisters which haue oftentime/beene to me
ayding, others to adorne. . . ."). The poet, in that case, feels he should
have adorned his love with many poems, but that the *Epithalamion,*

---

[2] See A. C. Judson, *The Life of Edmund Spenser* (Baltimore, 1945), p. 172.

"cutting off" these many, is now to serve as the single ornament-poem in their stead. For it has "promist both to recompens," that is, to make up for the "many ornaments" and the "hasty accidents."

The meaning of these ornaments and accidents becomes clearer if we invoke our second hypothesis, namely that the *Amoretti* and *Epithalamion*, published together in 1595, constitute a unit.[3] Now one of the striking features of the sonnet sequence is that it stops abruptly —as if "through hasty accidents"—with the separation of the lovers. The "many ornaments" of the envoy, I therefore suggest, refer to those sonnets that should "duly" have been written to celebrate the happy reunion of the lovers. These were never, in fact, composed, and in their stead the *Epithalamion* shaped itself in the poet's imagination.

This idea is reinforced by a major element of continuity between sonnet sequence and wedding song: an overarching time scheme plotted in the *Amoretti* and leading into the "dew time" of the *Epithalamion*. For the due time the latter would not stay to await is, I think, precisely the time which it celebrates: the actual wedding day. In a partly witty but obscure way, therefore, the envoy seems to say that though the poem was written for a special occasion, it is not merely occasional or conventional, but the product of an imperious inner impulse.

The "incompleteness" of the *Amoretti*, as well as their continuity with the *Epithalamion*, is intimated in a number of ways. Thus the love affair follows a well-defined time sequence: New Year (Sonnet 4), Spring (19), one year (60), a second New Year (62), Easter (68), and Spring (70); but with the separation of the lovers the seasonal progression breaks off on a note of wintry desolation:

> Lyke as the Culuer on the bared bough,
> Sits mourning for the absence of her mate:
> and in her songs sends many a wishfull vow,
> for his returne that seemes to linger late.
> So I alone now left disconsolate,
> Mourne to my selfe the absence of my loue.        (Sonnet 89)

The *Epithalamion*'s opening address to the Muses alludes to the conclusion of the *Amoretti*:

> Helpe me mine owne loues prayses to resound,
> Ne let the same of any be enuide:
> So Orpheus did for his own bride,

[3] The intervening anacreontics may serve as a way of making the break between *Amoretti* and *Epithalamion*, on which see below.

> *So I unto my selfe alone will sing,*
> The woods shall to me answer and my Eccho ring.
>
> (ll. 14–18. My italics)

The poem is born of a sense of privation, and the Orpheus simile indicates what is to be its major task: to invoke, by the magic of its music, the presence of the bride. And here we see another way in which the wedding song brings to fulfilment what has been a "failure" in the sonnet sequence. The image of the beloved that the sonneteer cultivates in his own soul—"Her temple fayre is built within my mind,/ in which her glorious image placed is,/on which my thoughts do day and night attend" (22)—reflects in its development his growth in love.[4] But at the point when he needs it most to sustain him, the image fails him. The crisis, foreshadowed in Sonnet 78, comes to a climax in Sonnet 88, where, with the absence of the Lady, the interior image dissolves because it is utterly unconsoling:

> Ne ought I see, though in the clearest day,
> when others gaze vpon theyr shadowes vayne:
> but th'onely image of that heauenly ray,
> whereof some glance doth in mine eie remayne.
> Of which beholding the Idaea playne,
> through contemplation of my purest part:
> with light thereof I doe my selfe sustayne,
> and thereon feed my loue-affamisht hart.
> But with such brightnesse whylest I fill my mind,
> I starue my body and mine eyes doe blynd.

The precise nature of this crisis is and must remain obscure. But we may imagine it as followed by a period during which the lover meditates on the relationship which the sonnets have celebrated and the claims his love will have upon him as a person without the mask of the poet in a world of accidents and impermanent feelings. From the meditation there emerges the *Epithalamion;* "promist both to recompens," it will deal with and make up for the predicament on which the *Amoretti* had "foundered." It will assert an image of the bride that will outlive the night of separation and the vagaries of time. How can it do so when the sonnets have already declared the inadequacy of the image? It will do so by means of a poetic mode especially

---

[4] See Ficino: "amans amati figuram suo sculpit in animo. Fit itaque amantis animus speculum in quo amati relucet imago." *Commentarium in Convivium,* in *Opera Omnia* (Facsimile edition, Turin, 1959), Vol. II, Tomus I, 1329. Also A. Chastel, *Marsile Ficin et l'Art* (Geneva and Lille, 1954), p. 119. Other sonnets involving the inner image are numbers 8, 45, 51, and 61.

designed to come to terms with, if not to "conquer," Time. On this point above all, I believe, Spenser brought to bear the full resources of his imagination, and the resultant strategy can best be understood in terms of the Pythagorism of sixteenth-century Humanist aesthetics.[5]

Here Mr. Hieatt's discovery of a complex symbolism in the *Epithalamion's* stanza and line numbers is of capital importance. He has shown that its numbers—corresponding to the hours of the day, the days of the year, and so forth—make the poem into a symbol of all time, "a Calendar for euery yeare." Now this framework of an ideal time fits in exactly with a cardinal feature of the Pythagorean aesthetic, namely the hidden or implicit harmony which the artist was supposed to impose upon his work. Thus the numerical-symbolic structure of the *Epithalamion* serves, in Pythagorean fashion, to express its secret affinity with the mathematical order of the universe and functions as a means of invoking quasi-magical powers.

For combined with its demand for an abstract structure or pattern, Humanist Pythagorism had a conception of artistic production as a kind of magical *ars ministra naturae*.[6] The artist's imagination must enter into, become identified with Nature's generative course, and produce images as by her agency. This is the same idea as Pico's natural magic which, "in calling forth into the light as if from their hiding places the powers scattered and sown in the world by the loving kindness of God, does not so much work wonders as diligently serve a wonder-working nature." The magician, says Pico,

> Having more searchingly examined into the harmony of the universe, which the Greeks with greater significance call συμπάθεια, and having clearly perceived the reciprocal affinity of natures, . . . brings forth into the open the miracles concealed in the recesses of the world, in the depths of nature, . . . just as if she herself were their maker; and, as the farmer weds his elms to vines, even so does the *magus* wed earth to heaven, that is, he weds lower things to the endowments and powers of higher things.[7]

[5] See R. Klein, "La Forme et L'Intelligible," in E. Castelli, ed., *Umanesimo et Simbolismo* (Padua, 1958), pp. 102–21; also A. Chastel, *Art et Humanisme à Florence au Temps de Laurent le Magnifique* (Paris, 1959), pp. 99ff. For the manipulation of time in Renaissance poetry, see L. Nelson, *Baroque Lyric Poetry* (New Haven, 1961).

[6] See Klein, especially pp. 104f., 111.

[7] Giovanni Pico della Mirandola, *Oration on the Dignity of Man*, E. Cassirer and others, eds., (Chicago, 1959), pp. 248–9. For the poet's imitation of Nature in her inner drive (*natura naturans*) see further H. S. Wilson, "Some Meanings of 'Nature' in Renaissance Literary Theory," *Journal of the History of Ideas*, II (1941), 434ff.; and compare the use of *energeia* by Puttenham, *Elizabethan Critical Essays*, G. G. Smith, ed., (Oxford, 1904), II, 148 and n. 419); Scaliger's *efficacia* is echoed by Sidney (*Eliz. Crit. Ess.*, I, 157 and n., 386).

The embodiment of this Humanist dream of man's power over nature was the poet-magician Orpheus.[8] To this figure, it will be remembered, Spenser relates himself in the first stanza and it is indeed with an Orphic voice that he sings his epithalamium. He knows that natural magic commands nature by obeying it, that he "conquers" time by submitting to it (thus fashioning a "short time's endless monument"). Hence in demanding of the sun "let this one day be myne" (l. 125) the poet at the same time through the very form of his poem gives the progress of the sun its due, translating the rhythm of nature into the poem's numbers, for these are also the hours through which the sun moves (cf. ll. 278ff.). The zodiacal motion in the poet's wit is in harmony with that of the heavens.

That time is thus of the essence in the *Epithalamion* appears not only from the poem's temporal structure but also from the basically temporal nature of its major symbols. Following Mr. Hieatt's lead, we have seen how the sun, and its movement (*sol temporis auctor:* Macrobius), serves as paradigm for the poem's movement. Night, out of which the sun emerges and to which it returns, plays an analogous though more complex role, and may serve as our first and principal example of the *Epithalamion*'s symbolic mode. Much of the imagery, it may be noted in passing, which in the *Amoretti* served as part of the metaphoric play of the sonnet conceit, is taken up again in the *Epithalamion*. There it is used, characteristically, to point simultaneously to an external reality in time and to the inward activity of the mind, establishing a sense of mysterious congruence between them.

The *Amoretti* ended in a metaphoric night, the *Epithalamion* begins in a literal night: in terms of the day whose progression the poem imitates, it is still night when the poem opens (and night again in its final stanzas). Night is thus, as it were, the source of the day which the poet tries to make his own, but it also comes to be felt as its potential negation. "I wander as in darknesse of the night," the poet had said in Sonnet 88, and the associations of this statement linger on in the *Epithalamion*. They have been well described by Thomas Greene:

> The poem is unconventional in the repeated expression it gives to the ominous elements associated with night, the elements which might potentially destroy the joy of the wedding and even the marriage. The induction refers to mishaps raised by "death or love or fortune's wreck" in the

[8] See A. Chastel, *Art et Humanisme,* p. 272; and in his *Marsile Ficin et l'Art* see "Prométhée et Orphée," especially pp. 175–6, and "Connaissance Orphique et Magie," pp. 71ff., 94f.

lives of those who have appeared earlier in Spenser's poems. The second stanza refers to the vicissitudes of the courtship dramatized in the *Amoretti*, the "pains and sorrows past," and the Muses are asked to sing of "solace" as well as of joy to the bride. At nightfall the appearance of Hesperus . . . occasions unconventional praise of the star for its guidance of lovers "through the night's sad dread." This "sad dread" is elaborated two stanzas below in the invocation to night. . . .

The ominous associations of darkness are evoked again, . . . in the last stanza, where the stars are described as torches in the temple of heaven

> that to us wretched earthly clods
> In dreadful darkness lend desired light.

Here it is not only the marriage but the whole of human experience which is menaced by the night's sad dread. Thus the threat of disaster, the irrational fear of vaguely specified suffering, hovers faintly over the poem, lending particular urgency to the concluding prayers. It is perhaps not too fanciful to relate the wolves of the fourth stanza to this cluster of night associations and to find in the decorative invocation to the "light-foot maids" an added symbolic nuance. . . .[9]

This excellent account of Night in its negative, threatening aspects, needs only to be extended and made more specific in one particular point. The "fear of vaguely specified suffering" can be linked with the poet's anguish described in the last sonnets of the *Amoretti*. Remembering the images of night and darkness with which the *Amoretti* concluded, and the Orpheus image in the first stanza of the *Epithalamion,* we can add: it is out of this very night that the wedding must be evoked; in the face of its hostile, almost demonic, forces the wedding day's resplendent actuality must be asserted.

A suggestion of this is to be found in the description of the sunrise, with the continued appeal to the Muses, in stanza 2:

> Early before the worlds light giuing lampe,
> His golden beame vpon the hils doth spred,
> Hauing disperst the nights vnchearefull dampe,
> Doe ye awake, and with fresh lusty hed,
> Go to the bowre of my beloued loue,
> My truest turtle doue,
> Bid her awake. . . .                                   (ll. 19–25)

The sun rising and dispersing the night's dampness is, as the wording seems to imply, a repetition of the first "Let there be light"; and the

[9] Thomas Greene, "Spenser and the Epithalamic Convention," *Comparative Literature,* IX (1957), 226–7.

poem, an analogous creative act, intends what the Muses are called upon to do: to rouse the bride out of the night of absence and separation.

But the negative is only part of Night's symbolic significance in the poem. It is balanced by a positive role such as appears in the sixth stanza, for instance. As parent, with Day, of the Hours, Night is shown to be also an integral element in the creative dynamism at the heart of the poem's design:

> But first come ye fayre houres which were begot
> In loues sweet paradice, of Day and Night,
> Which doe the seasons of the yeare allot,
> And al that euer in this world is fayre
> Doe make and still repayre.                    (ll. 98–102)

The Hours are the Horai of Greek mythology, identified variously with the seasons, as givers of fertility, ripeness, and so forth. But they are also the twenty-four segments of the day, and thus point to the conception of time as an essentially generative process. The other, destructive role of time is also hinted at, however, in the word *repayre*. We may conclude that the creative and destructive are here seen as dual aspects of time dialectically related; or that in the temporal process there is a negative element, nothingness, into which things pass but out of which they also come into being.

It is in the latter part of the poem that Night's dual role is emphatically restated:

> Now welcome night, thou night so long expected,
> That long daies labour doest at last defray,
> And all my cares, which cruell loue collected,
> Hast sumd in one, and cancelled for aye;
> Spread thy broad wing ouer my loue and me,
> That no man may vs see,
> And in thy sable mantle vs enwrap,
> From feare of perrill and foule horror free,
> Let no false treason seeke vs to entrap, . . .
> But let the night be calme and quietsome,
> Without tempestuous storms or sad afray:
> Lyke as when Ioue with great Alcmena lay,
> When he begot the great Tirynthian groome·
> Or lyke as when he with thy selfe did lie,
> And begot Maiesty.                              (ll. 315–31)

Night as the sum of all "cares" (griefs and fears) embodies the negative role of an antagonistic, destructive force. It symbolizes the source of chaos, of hasty accidents wreaking havoc with human existence, of time the destroyer, with which, as we saw, the poet had to come to terms. The *Epithalamion* was his way of doing so, and the degree to which it has succeeded in its task and wrought a redemption of time, is here symbolically asserted: through this same night all the cares are now "cancelled for aye."

The role of Jove (embodiment of power and a kind of grace) hinted at in this and the preceding stanza, represents a striking parallel to that of the poet. Thus the bride is compared to Maia, "when as Ioue her tooke/In Tempe, lying on the flowry gras,/*Twixt sleepe and wake*" (ll. 307–9, my italics); and as Jove descends and takes Maia, so the poet has conjured the Muses, and through them the bride, out of "sleep" and awakened her to life in his soul as in his poem.

With Alcmena Jove momentarily made time stand still as he extended one night into three (and made it fruitful). The poet has performed a similar if lesser feat in incorporating the wedding day—his day—in the timely-timeless structure of his poem. Finally, Jove lying with Night and begetting Majesty, *quae mundum temperat omnem* (*Fasti,* v, 25), sums up most fully the genesis of the poem.

Majestic is surely the one adjective to apply to bride and poem, both in the traditional and mythic Ovidian sense. But if we understand the mythological imagery in an internal, spiritual sense, then night points to a state like that self absorption of the soul when, as Dante describes it, the senses are extinguished and it is ready for the grace of inspiration: into the soul's darkness there enters the "light formed in heaven" ("Purgatorio," xvii, 17). So Jove cohabiting with Night would parallel the sunrise (described in stanza 2) seen as the light dawning upon the landscape of the soul. In both cases, it may be thought, the majesty of the visible world of day is engendered.

Aside from encompassing the ambivalence of Time's process, Night accordingly expresses an ecstatic, timeless moment by which the imagination is enabled to divine the creative ground at the source of this process.[10] As such it is perhaps the most complex figure, but its opera-

---

[10] For the "intuition of becoming" see G. Poulet, *Studies in Human Time,* trans. E. Coleman (New York, 1959), pp. 31–3. Also, Augustine's discussion of Time, *Confessions,* XI, xxvii ff.; J. F. Callahan, *Four Views of Time in Ancient Philosophy* (Cambridge, Mass., 1948), Chapter 4, especially pp. 177ff.; and Plotinus, *Enneads,* III, vii, 13. There is a multiplicity of sources, from Hesiod's *Theogony* and the Orphic Hymn to Night to George Chapman's *The Shadow of Night* (London, 1594), for Night as an ambivalent figure at once demonic and a creative source. For Chapman's association of Night with "rapture," see M. C. Bradbrook, *The School of Night: A Study of the Literary Relationships of Sir Walter Raleigh* (Cambridge, 1936), pp. 134, 136.

tion can be paralleled by the other major symbols of the poem. In stanza 2, for instance, we are told that

> Hymen is awake,
> And long since ready forth his maske to moue,
> With his bright Tead that flames with many a flake,
> And many a bachelor to waite on him. . . .                    (ll. 25–8)

The figure of Hymen reflects the image of the sun (at the beginning of this stanza) waiting in the dark to move over the rim of the horizon. It is set in dance-like motion as the performer of the day's ceremonial, and this motion echoes the larger rhythm of the day and of the sun, so that lower things are again wedded to the endowments of higher things.

At the same time Hymen with his masque is none other than the epithalamium, the embodied symbol of the poem itself. The Muses, Nymphs, Graces, and Hours, therefore, come to be seen as participants in this masque, as if sprung from its "Invention." But just as the processional masque of the sixteenth century created its setting by transforming the actual social scene into an integral part of its symbolic ritual, so the figures of the *Epithalamion* become more than allegories or symbols: each in turn and in its way is made to unfold its traditional associations, thus fashioning a scene for the wedding.

The movement is from convention outward to the establishment of a natural and social context, and the poetic principle involved is that of echo. This, as the refrain indicates, is also the poem's fundamental device, and the Muses' role is paradigmatic in this respect. Traditionally, they can "teach the woods and waters to lament" (l. 10), so that the pastoral song finds its resonance from without: "The woods shall to you answer and your Eccho ring." So as the poet invokes the various figures, they come forth as an echo to his command or song; he rediscovers them, as it were, out there, with their multiple associations and functions. The echo is thus truly incremental: in response to the (initially) single voice there is created a regular polyphony of voices which, interpenetrating, form an expanding context for the rite to be enacted.

By the end of the poem the image of Hymen's torch has undergone enormous expansion to encompass the host of "other stars":

> And ye high heauens, the temple of the gods,
> In which a thousand torches flaming bright
> Doe burne, that to vs wretched earthly clods,
> In dreadful darkness lend desired light. . . .          (ll. 409–12)

The image of the cosmic temple framing earthly existence here is itself the culmination of a development that has its antecedents in the *Amoretti*. There the temple occurs as part of the metaphorics of the sonnet: the Lady's "temple fayre is built within my mind. . . ." (Sonnet 22). A similar imagery is applied to the bride in the *Epithalamion*, but no longer with merely internal reference:

> . . . all her body like a pallace fayre,
> Ascending vppe with many a stately stayre,
> To honors seat and chastities sweet bowre.          (ll. 178–80)

The ascent from physical to spiritual and moral, into the inner chamber to see "that which no eyes can see,/The inward beauty of her liuely spright" (ll. 185–6), is moreover, directly paralleled to the entry into the actual temple:

> Open the temple gates vnto my loue,
> Open them wide that she may enter in, . . .
> And all the pillours deck with girlands trim,
> For to recyue this Saynt with honour dew,
> That commeth in to you.
> With trembling steps and humble reuerence,
> She commeth in, before th'almighties vew,
> Of her ye virgins learn obedience,
> When so ye come into these holy places,
> To humble your proud faces. . . .          (ll. 204–14)

Palace, royal throne of the mind (l. 194), and temple images fuse into the image of the bride as at once real woman and saint in her own temple, a physical, moral, and spiritual exemplar in one.

The command in the temple: "*all the posts* adorne as doth behoue,/ And all the pillours deck . . ." (ll. 206–7) is echoed by that after the temple ceremony, at home: "Sprinkle *all the postes* and wals with wine . . ." (l. 253). We can say that we have moved from one "holy place" to another: for Bacchic feast and holy day (stanzas 14 and 15) sanctify even the home. Or else the temple and its ceremony have expanded to include the home and its feast, just as by the end of the poem the temple image has expanded to encompass the cosmos in a hallowing of all space: "And ye high heauens, the temple of the gods,/ In which a thousand torches flaming bright. . . ." (ll. 409–10).

The kind of symbolism that the poem achieves may best be called typological as this term is now used in Dante criticism.[11] At the least,

---

[11] See J. Chydenius, *The Typological Problem in Dante: A Study in the History of Medieval Ideas* (Copenhagen, 1958). Another term would be "figural": see E.

it represents an extension of the typological principle insofar as it combines the visionary with the sense or authority of a literal reality (thought to be) revealed by scripture or similarly sacred tradition. Thus we might speak here of a twofold typological symbolism, of which one is essentially Biblical: the temple imagery, that is, draws upon the Solomonic temple and the pleromatic temple of the New Jerusalem (Revelation, 21), and the architectural (and other) imagery applied to the bride in stanza 10 is based upon the "epithalamium" of the Song of Songs.[12] The second kind consists of the typology of the day or time and is essentially liturgical, though it might also draw on a text like Ephesians 5:13–16:

> For whatsoever is manifest, that same is light. Wherfore he sayth: Awake thou that slepest, and stond vppe from deeth, and Christ shall geve the light.
> Take hede therfore that ye walke circumspectly: not as foles: but as wyse redemynge the tyme: for the dayes are evyll. (Tyndale's translation, 1534)

Poetically it is achieved through the interpenetration of images, by which the images of the imagination are wedded to the typical, the diurnally repeated phenomenon. Thus Hymen, invoked for the unique occasion of this particular day, comes to participate in the reality and power of the sun's daily passage from night to day. In this sense, it is another way of looking upon the event of dawn.[13]

The concept of typological symbolism was introduced in part because I think that if we combine it with the poem's ritual, incantatory manner we may be justified in seeing the *Epithalamion* as a poetic analogue to the religious sacrament whose signs "function to transform man and the world on a supernatural level." [14] Like the sacrament,

---

Auerbach, "Figura," *Scenes from the Drama of European Literature* (New York, 1959), pp. 11–76. Spenser employed this kind of symbolism earlier in Book I of *The Faerie Queene.*

[12] See Israel Baroway, "The Imagery of Spenser and the *Song of Songs," J.E.G.P.,* XXXIII (1934), 23–45. For the sacramental and typological importance of Canticles, see Jean Daniélou, *The Bible and the Liturgy* (Notre Dame, Ind. 1956), pp. 193ff.

[13] Both kinds of symbolism, biblical and diurnal, are combined in the bride, who rises in a gradual birth out of darkness: ll. 93ff., 148ff. As type of rising evening star, moon, sun (ll. 151, 154ff.) she participates in the celestial masque of Hymen. At the same time, the bride's existence as real woman is established by the realistic social context projected: ll. 159ff.

[14] Sister M. Laurentia Digges, Congregation of St. Joseph, *Transfigured World: Design, Theme and Symbol in Worship* (New York, 1957), p. 25. See J. Daniélou, *The Bible and the Liturgy,* p. 3, and Hooker's Anglican view of the Sacraments, *Of the Laws of Ecclesiastical Polity,* V, lvii (Everyman edition, II, 236). Spenser

the poem may itself be regarded as a dramatic performance taking place in the poet's soul, in such a way that "the meaning of the symbolic words, acts, . . . are not only brought to mind but are effected, caused, actually happen" there.[15]

For further illustration let us consider the typology of the solstitial holy day, which culminates with the boldest stroke of literal realism. At the homeward procession, the poet exclaims: "Make feast . . . now all this liue long day,/This day for euer to me holy is" (ll. 248–9). Next he proclaims it a holiday, calling for a general cessation from profane labors:

> Ring ye the bels, ye yong men of the towne,
> And leaue your wonted labors for this day:
> This day is holy; doe ye write it down,
> That ye for euer it remember may.          (ll. 261–4)

And finally comes the triumphant assertion that this is literally a calendrical holiday:

> This day the sunne is in his chiefest hight,
> With Barnaby the bright,
> From whence declining daily by degrees,
> He somewhat loseth of his heat and light,
> When once the Crab behind his back he sees.
>
> (ll. 265–9)

Here the poem has achieved its greatest expansion: its symbols momentarily become transparent, as it were, to the real sun and to real time. This is perhaps the closest the poet can come in his mimesis of the sacrament whose signs "effect what they signify."

The day of the solstice itself is, then, the most perfect embodiment or analogue of the poem. It signifies the apex of Time's plenitude, and as a turning point in the annual calendar when the sun (and thus time) seems temporarily to stand still, it represents an ecstatic moment which, to men of earlier societies, afforded an extraordinary perspective on the very rhythm of nature and the eternal pattern or powers controlling its course. As in the poem, therefore, men experienced their existence as participating simultaneously in a timeless, eternal order and in a temporal one. This conjunction may be the essence of the

---

was familiar with and made poetic use of traditional medieval (Catholic) sacramentalism, as Beatrice Ricks shows: "Catholic Sacramentals and Symbolism in Spenser's *Faerie Queene*," *J.E.G.P.*, LII (1953), 322–31.

[15] Digges, p. 26. See the ancient Greek concept of *mousiké* and the comments on the poem as "performance" in Nelson, *Baroque Lyric Poetry*, pp. 71ff.

holy; it signified a highly intensified mode of life in which existence was felt to be charged with and taken out of itself by celestial vigor. These feelings found formal expression in the festival, which enacted the cosmic event by participation, as it were. Through ritual release from the profane time of everyday, the celebrants returned to a "mythical dream-time . . . located simultaneously at the *beginning* and *outside* of evolution." [16] The ritual varied, but had two typical features: Dionysian revelry, excess; and ceremonial gesture, invocation, dance.

The solstitial holiday heightens the festal nature of the wedding and gives it an added dimension. The Dionysian excess in stanza 14, "Poure out the wine without restraint or stay,/Poure not by cups, but by the belly full . . ." (ll. 250–1) implies release and festive immersion in the beneficent fullness of life corresponding to the "height" of solar power of the next stanza. And there the singing and dancing about bonfires—a standard feature of Midsummer festivals[17]—points to ritual participation in the plenitude of the sun's energy.

Now, in terms both of the year and day, the sun is "declining . . . by degrees" from "his chiefest hight." And the poet-lover impatiently urges it on its way: "Hast thee O fayrest Planet to thy home/Within the Westerne fome. . . ." (ll. 282–3). And with nightfall he dissolves the masque which has been his wedding song: "Now ceasse ye damsels"

---

[16] R. Caillois, *Man and the Sacred*, trans. M. Barash (Glencoe, Ill. 1959), p. 103. For the importance of seasonal festivals in Elizabethan literature, see C. L. Barber, *Shakespeare's Festive Comedy: A Study of Dramatic Form and its Relation to Social Custom* (Princeton, 1959). For his key terms, "release" and "clarification," see Chapter I, "The Saturnalian Pattern."

[17] This custom appears to be the chief Midsummer ceremony. See Thomas Naogeorgus (Kirchmaier), "Popular and Popish Superstitions and Customs on Saints-Days and Holy-Days . . . being the Fourth Booke of *The Popish Kingdome* . . . englyshed by Barnabe Googe . . . 1570," in F. J. Furnivall, ed., *Phillip Stubbes's Anatomy of the Abuses in England* (London, 1877–82), Part I, p. 339, ll. 769ff. An unresolved problem is the customary dating of Midsummer on John the Baptist's Day, June 24; however, many ceremonies were associated with more than one day, and according to one tradition Barnabas' had a broad designation: "The author of the *Festa Anglo Romana* says, p. 72, 'This Barnaby-day, or thereabout, is the summer solstice . . . being the longest day of the year, about the 11th or 12th of June; it is taken for the whole time, when the days appear not for fourteen days together either to lengthen or shorten.'" (John Brand, *Observations on the Popular Antiquities of Great Britain*, enlarged by Sir Henry Ellis [London, 1890], I, 294.) In other words, Spenser's day might be one in and for a number of days, like Jove's three nights in one with Alcmena.

Despite its obvious importance, I pass over the possible *liturgical* organization of the *Epithalamion*. (The poem might be seen, for example, as the wedding framed by Matins and Vespers—the "reformed" Hours of the Book of Common Prayer.) See H. C. White, *The Tudor Books of Private Devotion* (Madison, Wis. 1951).

(merchants' daughters? Muses? Nymphs? *All* "these glad many," l. 294)

> your delights forepast;
> Enough is it, that all the day was youres:
> Now day is doen. . . .                    (ll. 296–8)

The very thing the poet had striven to make his—"this one day"—
he now surrenders as, Prospero-like, he dismisses the revels and their
cast:

> Now it is night ye damsels may be gon,
> And leaue my loue alone,
> And leaue likewise your former lay to sing:
> The woods no more shal answere, nor your echo ring.

> (ll. 311–14)

With the return of night we sense again an inward movement of the
imagination, as indicated by the poet's withdrawal from the damsels
and the change to the negative refrain. With significant variations,[18]
the symbolic-reflexive mode of the beginning of the poem reappears,
and it is as though the poem has, in circular fashion, turned in upon
itself. The poet's sacrament, generated out of the night, having passed
through the circling hours of the day, finds its conclusion where it
began, rediscovers its source, but a source clarified and transformed.

The transformation is signalized by the change of pronoun from
*You* (as in the dismissal of the damsels: *"your* delights forepast")
to *We* in the final stanzas, where it becomes part of the refrain to
form *"our* song." The poem thus has moved from the single *I* of the
first refrain to the personal plural. And in the course of this movement
it, or the poet's self, has discovered that it was never really alone in
the radical, singular meaning of the term. What has been clarified is
the nature of the self as containing the love which is both the subject
of the poem and its generative law. For Spenser this love leads forward as well as upward, into the future symbolized in the poem by
the generations of a "large posterity" (l. 417), but also into a realm
before which his art finally abdicates. The envoy deliberately breaks
with the symmetrical structure of the *Epithalamion,* as the poet offers
up the poem on which he has expended the full resources of his imagination to the greater reality of his bride to be.

In *this* realm—*outside* the poem—his song is to be no more than
ornament for the woman. And yet in this one point art and life do
meet again: the ornamental function of poetry as an enrichment of

---

[18] See L. W. Hyman, "Structure and Meaning in Spenser's *Epithalamion," Ten-
nessee Studies in Literature,* 3 (1958), 40, 41.

existence. More: art is also paying back its debt to life; for it was through the real woman, his relationship to her, that the poet found his true self *in relation* to the "short time" which in the redemptive transformation of the *Epithalamion* has become the infinitely precious moment of human existence. The stage at which he has arrived has a perfect gloss in the thought of Kierkegaard:[19]

> Time, where the aesthete gets stranded, is important. The Judge [in *Either/Or*] asserts this by an aesthetic analogy. He says that the better an art knows how to express its theme in time, the higher it stands. The highest of all arts is the art of living and time is its medium, as it is with music. Marriage belongs to the art of living and therefore time is its medium too. He who recognizes the value of time lives as a Person; i.e. as a *persona* in a play where God is both Playwright and Prompter. This play has time as its real element. The person in the play has a history. It is the history imparted to him by God and his own reflective will. As Kierkegaard puts it elsewhere, "Time is taken into the service of an ethically existing individual."

Interwined with the time element, whose invisible arc extends from the *Amoretti* to the *Epithalamion,* the poet's personal history has been in the background all along. Thus the consciousness of time is there from the outset: to a limited extent it affects and controls the more or less extravagant play of attitudes and images of the *Amoretti*. But the latter ended inconclusively, even despairingly, in the face of time's hasty accidents.

In the ensuing crisis the mind resolves its perplexity: still speaking in Kierkegaard's terms, it makes a leap from the aesthetic to the ethical, from romantic to conjugal love. The leap does not mean an abandonment of the aesthetic-romantic ideality and inwardness (or even its theatrical playfulness); instead, these are transfigured in the ethical-sacramental perspective of the *Epithalamion,* whose magical mode achieved a kind of identity between its aesthetic time and real time by divining the eternal centre in mutability. In the envoy, therefore, the poet's Self can shed all poetic disguises and renew its history on the stage where all are merely players for the short time allotted to them. The part he must play is revealed: his poem is its "endlesse moniment."

[19] T. H. Croxall, *Kierkegaard Commentary* (New York, 1956), p. 118. See also Kierkegaard's *Either/Or,* trans. David F. Swenson and Lillian Marvin Swenson (New York, 1959) for the aesthetic-ethical distinction mentioned below.

# Plowman and Knight:
# The Hero's Dual Identity

### *by Donald Cheney*

The opening lines of *The Faerie Queene,* echoing as they do the introduction to the *Aeneid* as the Renaissance knew it,[1] explicitly turn from pastoral poetry to the higher demands of an epic subject:

> Lo I the man, whose Muse whilome did maske,
>     As time her taught in lowly Shepheards weeds,
>     Am now enforst a far vnfitter taske,
>     For trumpets sterne to chaunge mine Oaten reeds,
>     And sing of Knights and Ladies gentle deeds;
>     Whose prayses hauing slept in silence long,
>     Me, all too meane, the sacred Muse areeds
>     To blazon broad emongst her learned throng:
> Fierce warres and faithfull loues shall moralize my song.
>
> (I.Pr.1)

The poet of the *Shepheardes Calender,* like Vergil before him, sees himself as reaching poetic maturity only when he faces the realities of his own world and ceases to linger in an imagined paradise of rural simplicity. It may be objected that such a development is in fact an argument of pastoral poetry itself: that Colin Clout has already seen his year come full cycle and, in the "December" eclogue, has resignedly hung up his pipes after experiencing all the torments of his pastoral life.[2] But what is more to the point here is that the pastoral poet's

From Donald Cheney, *Spenser's Image of Nature: Wild Man, and Shepherd in "The Faerie Queene"* (New Haven, Yale University Press, 1966). Copyright © 1966 by Yale University Press. Reprinted by permission of the publisher.

[1] Merritt Y. Hughes, *Virgil and Spenser,* University of California Publications in English, 2 (Berkeley, 1929), 318.

[2] A. C. Hamilton, "The Argument of Spenser's *Shepheardes Calender,*" *English Literary History,* XXIII, No. 3 (1956), 171–82 [See pp. 30–39 above—ED.]; S. K. Heninger, "The Implications of Form for *The Shepheardes Calender,*" *Studies in the Renaissance,* IX (1962), 309–21.

conclusion is the epic poet's premise. If the pastoral impulse leads the poet to mask himself in humble garb and flee to a simplified world which then, on closer examination, is revealed to be a microcosm of the world of daily involvement he had abandoned, epic proposes to follow an opposite course. The poet, with due apology for his weak wit and dull tongue, petitions the Muse for a "high" style with which he can confront his bewilderingly complex world from its full historical and topographical perspective.

In Spenser's poem, however, it is not only the poet or narrator who is represented as abandoning the pastoral mode; it is the hero as well. Perhaps a parallelism of narrator and protagonist is not surprising in a poem which repeatedly evokes the quality of a dream vision, with its unnamed or riddlingly named figures in a self-referential landscape: many of Spenser's most eloquent passages gain their fullest effects from a fluid setting in which more naturalistic criteria of decorum are abandoned and characters dissolve into one another as they face similar crises or explore avenues of choice ignored by earlier heroes. But this lack of naturalism must be distinguished from that of a naïve allegory[3] concerned simply with a discursive anatomizing of the author's (and reader's) world. Here, by contrast, we have a poem which explores the relationship of that "real" world to projected worlds of desire and fear; and it is in the context of such a relationship that the Proem and opening stanzas of Book I enunciate Spenser's subject matter.

At the beginning, then, *The Faerie Queene* juxtaposes the pastoral masks of the early Spenser and the naïve rusticity of the youthful St. George. "Immerito," the anonymous "new Poete" of the *Shepheardes Calender,* becomes the narrator of a poem whose hero (as the Letter to Ralegh informs us) had himself first appeared at Gloriana's court in the guise of "a tall clownishe younge man" and had "rested him on the floore, vnfitte through his rusticity for a better place." It is only after Una has seen him dressed in the armor of a Christian knight, which she has brought with her to Fairyland, that he seems "the goodliest man in all that company" and wins her approval as the champion of her cause. In fact, it is at once apparent from the poem itself, with-

---

[3] A better term might be "naïvely read allegory": I am not eager to measure Spenser's poem against any of the traditional examples of allegory—*Everyman* or *Pilgrim's Progress,* for instance—since all can be read more or less profitably as works of fiction. It is not necessary to find a scapegoat, however; perhaps none in fact exists. What does exist is the habit of reading works reductively, or precipitating a didactic content which is then taken to be the sole "meaning."

out reference to Spenser's letter, that the symbolic appropriateness of the armor to its wearer has yet to be fully established:

> A Gentle Knight was pricking on the plaine,
>   Y cladd in mightie armes and siluer shielde,
>   Wherein old dints of deepe wounds did remaine,
>   The cruell markes of many' a bloudy fielde;
>   Yet armes till that time did he neuer wield:
>   His angry steede did chide his foming bitt,
>   As much disdayning to the curbe to yield:
>   Full iolly knight he seemd, and faire did sitt,
> As one for knightly giusts and fierce encounters fitt.
>
>     . . .
>
>   Right faithful true he was in deede and word,
>   But of his cheere did seeme too solemne sad;
>   Yet nothing did he dread, but euer was ydrad.          (I.i.1–2)

The knight is known only in terms of this armor until the tenth canto, when at the House of Holiness he learns that he is English and hears his name of George attributed to his childhood upbringing "in ploughmans state" (I.x.66). To be sure, there is no question of a mystery as to his identity: the reader is surely expected to recognize the tableau of knight, lady, ass, and lamb described in the first stanzas of the Book. But the tableau, like the red cross which identifies the knight for the rest of the poem, is not a riddle to be solved and then discarded by the reader; rather, it is what the Renaissance found in the Egyptian hieroglyph and tried to create through its chivalric imprese: a means of stressing the visual image as the unit of poetic discourse and of arresting the tendency of language to translate image into metaphor and metaphor into dead metaphor or "name." Even when for the sake of convenience we refer to the knight as "Redcross," we are naming him where Spenser characteristically points to him, giving him only as much of an epithet as identifies him or serves the emphases of the moment: "the youthfull Knight," "that Elfin knight," "that Redcrosse knight." Spenser's periphrastic treatment of Redcross is an extreme instance of a tendency shown elsewhere in the poem, whereby he repeatedly gives his characters names symbolic of their roles but announces those names only after showing them in action, so that the names themselves become capsule summaries or mottoes. His more extended emphasis on Redcross's anonymity is directly related to the plot of Book I, however, which in seeking to define Holiness is concerned with the nature of the hero and the sources of his strength. As an unproved knight, Redcross is therefore only potentially St. George: Book I traces the steps by which he is to gain his identity. The ambiguities of Redcross's position, and the resultant tension between the sense that his armor is at first a mere protection, or even a disguise, and the promise that it may come to be an image of his inner nature, are presented by means of the poem's opening incidents, in which the ambiguities of natural settings are stressed. An extended analysis of the first part of Book I will show the ways in which Spenser defines his poem's problems—and tries to protect himself against the reductive reading which he has too frequently received. If the following remarks seem at times to dwell in tedious detail on the minutiae of tonal ironies, it is because Spenser has been widely criticized (or more damningly, praised) for a relaxed, ornamental style which evades any direct confrontation of the complexities of life. Or, alternatively, as a sage and serious preceptor he has seemed constitutionally incapable of that manipulation of imagery more readily attributed to the Metaphysical poets. The corrective to these assumptions must come from an examination of Spenser's poem in the order of its presentation, for the individual concerns of commentators have too often led them to reassemble motifs from various parts of the poem and to neglect those elements of meaning which depend upon the poem's own sequence.

The first challenge to Redcross comes as a consequence of a sudden shower which drives the knight and lady into the Wood of Error. Though the storm is called a "tempest dred" in stanza 8, possibly in an ironic allusion to the knight who dreads nothing (stanza 2), its suddenness and its bluster are set against the ominous, prideful security of the wood:

> . . . Thus as they past,
> The day with cloudes was suddeine ouercast,
> And angry *Ioue* an hideous storme of raine
> Did poure into his Lemans lap so fast,
> That euery wight to shrowd it did constrain,
> And this faire couple eke to shroud themselues were fain.
>
> Enforst to seeke some couert nigh at hand,
> A shadie groue not far away they spide,
> That promist ayde the tempest to withstand:
> Whose loftie trees yclad with sommers pride,
> Did spred so broad, that heauens light did hide,
> Not perceable with power of any starre:

> And all within were pathes and alleies wide,
> With footing worne, and leading inward farre:
> Faire harbour that them seemes; so in they entred arre.     (I.i.6-7)

In fleeing the shower, they have abandoned one kind of nature for another. On the plain they are exposed to the elements and almost ludicrously unprepared to confront them. To see how far this is from the "tempest" of epic or tragedy—in the sense of the hostile environment which tests man's capacity to endure—one need only compare this shower with the storm which confronts Aeneas in Book I of the *Aeneid*. Spenser makes no attempt here to develop a theme of divine wrath—his allusion to "angry *Ioue*" seems the shallowest of epithets for the darkened sky—and the abruptness of the rain is such that everyone has fled before the question of any possible resistance to it can arise. If there is any similarity here to a Vergilian storm, it is more likely to the shower that drives Dido and Aeneas together,[4] for in Vergil too the absence of any extended description of that later storm suggests the instinctive nature of the lovers' flight from it. Redcross and Una do not hesitate to take cover, and they find themselves in a wood which they seem to know all too well: wilfully shrouding themselves from the light as well as the rain, they praise the trees in a catalogue which reflects man's confident moral dissection of his universe. In such a context it is ominously appropriate that the foliage of the trees should be their "sommers pride," and that the birds whose song "seemd . . . to scorne the cruell sky" provide the background for the human praise of the trees: man seems to share with the lower creatures this false sense of a security which ignores the changing seasons. The catalogue does not merely provide another link with Chaucer through the similar catalogue in the *Parlement of Foules,* establishing Spenser's position in the English tradition; it finds its deeper and more resonant origins in the Dantesque dark wood of a narrow preoccupation with the things of this world to the exclusion of broader concerns.[5]

---

[4] *Aeneid* 4.16off.

[5] William Nelson, *The Poetry of Edmund Spenser* (New York, 1963), p. 159, discusses the relationship of Spenser's wood to the allegorical glosses on Vergil's *sylva* (especially as found in the *Aeneid* 1 and 6) proposed by Servius and his Renaissance followers. A. C. Hamilton, *The Structure of Allegory in "The Faerie Queen"* (Oxford 1961), pp. 30-43, discusses the episode as an initiatory "shrouding" of the knight. E. R. Curtis, *European Literature and the Latin Middle Ages*, trans. W. R. Trask, Bollingen Series, 36 (New York, 1953), 194-5, classifies examples of this "mixed forest" as a subspecies of the idealized landscape, while recognizing that they may belong instead under the heading of the Homeric or Hesiodic "catalogue." This *topos* does in fact bring together a number of classical forms; and to these

Since they have abandoned the sunlight as well as the storms of the plain, it is significant that Una and her knight together "beguile the way" in describing the functions of the individual elements in the wood. It is only when they have realized that they are lost, and have come upon the hollow cave of Error, that Una belatedly recognizes their position. Until then, they are content to identify the trees and append the appropriate moral or emblematic tags to each: "The sayling Pine, the Cedar proud and tall,/ The vine-prop Elme." Each of these epithets presupposes a congruence between man's world and that of nature. Even when the allusion is to the violence and suffering of man's world, as with "The mirrhe sweet bleeding in the bitter wound," the pain has been beguilingly transformed by such a sense of congruence. Only the final Alexandrine strikes a discordant note with its mention of "the Maple seeldom inward sound," where the sense of anticlimax is turned against the presumption of the human compilers of such a catalogue.

The entire first canto in fact depends for much of its irony upon a careless stockpiling of aphorisms which, for all their individual merits, tend when taken together to dissipate the hero's understanding of his position in a given episode. Thus when Una urges caution at the mouth of Error's den, such an accumulation of proverbs is nicely suggestive of perplexity:

> Be well aware, quoth then that Ladie milde,
>> Least suddaine mischiefe ye too rash prouoke:
>> The danger hid, the place vnknowne and wilde,
>> Breedes dreadfull doubts: Oft fire is without smoke,
>> And perill without show: therefore your stroke
>> Sir knight with-hold, till further triall made.
>> Ah Ladie (said he) shame were to reuoke
>> The forward footing for an hidden shade:
> Vertue giues her selfe light, through darkenesse for to wade.
>
> (I.i.12)

The rapid exchange of comments, with each aphorism generating its own imagery without reference to its neighbors' and with the syntax and verbal echoes contributing to a sense of frenzy, reaches its climax when the Dwarf is moved to interject his own comment: "Fly fly (quoth then/ The fearfull Dwarfe:) this is no place for liuing men."

---

may be added in Spenser's case a possible echo of Genesis 2:9, "And out of the ground made the Lord God grow every tree that is pleasant to the sight, and good for food; the tree of life also in the midst of the garden, and the tree of knowledge of good and evil."

It is an ironic comment on the knight's confidence in the illumination cast by his virtue that when he looks into the cavern's mouth,

> . . . his glistring armor made
> A litle glooming light much like a shade,
> By which he saw the vgly monster plaine . . .
>
> (I.i.14)

Such a transition from complacent philosophizing to a frantic search for the appropriate tag-ends of philosophy makes abundantly clear the nature of the Error which Redcross defeats at this first trial. It is the sort of Error which the knight's glooming light is capable of discerning plainly, Error in its crudest and most obviously repellent form: "Most lothsom, filthie, foule, and full of vile disdaine." Her serpentine form—her most potent weapon, since her method of attack is that of the boa constrictor—recalls the labyrinthine paths of moral commentary that have led the knight to her; and though she must be fought on her own terms, she can be overcome only when faith reinforces the knight's human powers: "Add faith vnto your force," Una urges, "and be not faint:/ Strangle her, else she sure will strangle thee" (I.i.19).

Various elements in the description of Error are suggestive of broader contexts. As a combination of woman and serpent, she anticipates Duessa's foul nether parts and may point toward Adam's fall.[6] At the same time, and with more obvious relevance to the structure of Book I, she provides Redcross with practice for his climactic battle with the dragon. With respect to all these relationships, it is important to note how the present incident serves to define more closely the range of the Book's action. Error is handily defeated by Redcross with Una's assistance; her offspring die quickly when they drink her poisonous blood in a vain effort at "Making her death their life, and eke her hurt their good." Error's limitations are apparent from this grotesque parody of the traditional comparison of Christ to the dying pelican, giving mankind eternal life through His blood. No such communion is possible to the creatures of Error: in fact, the only way of destroying them definitively is through a resolute attack on their poisonous source.

The crudity of Spenser's characterization of Error may seem to discourage too prolonged a meditation on her implications; perhaps it would be sufficient to read the incident, with Ruskin, as a straight-

[6] Virgil K. Whitaker, "The Theological Structure of *The Faerie Queen*, Book I," in W. R. Mueller and D. C. Allen, eds., *That Soueraine Light* (Baltimore, 1952), p. 75. See John M. Steadman, "Spenser's *Errour* and the Renaissance Allegorical Tradition," *Neuphilologische Mitteilungen*, 62 (1961), 22–38.

forward statement that "Reverence and Religion must always vanquish . . . this first open and palpable form of Error." [7] The importance of this battle for the present study, however, lies in its relationship to the wandering wood of discontinuous meanings which lead
the knight and his lady to Error's den. Their inability to see the
forest for the trees—more specifically, for the isolated virtues which
they ascribe to each of the trees—is here a prelude to crisis. Their delight in praising the trees as emblems of various virtues becomes suggestive of a human weakness as soon as it leads them to a degree of
involvement in this *selva oscura* from which honorable retreat is impossible. They must go forward with no sounder criterion than their
decision to follow the beaten path; and it is only after defeating the
monster that Redcross can follow this same beaten path back to the
light.

If this wandering wood is suggestive of a naïve and disjunctive reading of nature, it remains to ask how much it presents an obstacle definitively overcome and how much a continuing threat to hero and lady.
On the one hand, Error is clearly dead, the more clearly so since her
brood die with her, by the very terms of their being. But her setting,
the dark wood, and her mixture of human and subhuman forms contribute to overtones of menace which continue in subsequent incidents.
The hazards of natural settings, and of physical appearances in general, become the focus of the scene which immediately follows, when
the knight passes from his open challenge by Error to the hidden menace of Archimago. Once again in this second part of the first canto,
the two take refuge in a pastoral setting; and here it is Una who per-
suades Redcross to take this dangerous rest:

> Now (sayd the Lady) draweth toward night,
> And well I wote, that of your later fight
> Ye all forwearied be: for what so strong,
> But wanting rest will also want of might?
> The Sunne that measures heauen all day long,
> At night doth baite his steedes the *Ocean* waues emong.

> Then with the Sunne take Sir, your timely rest,
> And with new day new worke at once begin:
> Vntroubled night they say giues counsell best.          (I.i.32–33)

Throughout Book I the night will be felt as a time of menace, when
the powers of darkness assert their dominance; and in urging Redcross to imitate the sun in going beneath the waves, Una is introducing

---

[7] *Stones of Venice* (3 vols., London, 1851–3), quoted in *Variorum* I, 422.

in all innocence an image which will become increasingly evocative both of spiritual danger and of the need to confront that danger through symbolic death. Her reference to the ocean waves in connection with sleep is immediately echoed in the description of the hermitage's setting—"Thereby a Christall streame did gently play,/ Which from a sacred fountaine welled forth alway"—and by the repeated association of water with oblivion, isolation from care, and sensual surrender in the stanzas which follow. Redcross and Una are "drownd in deadly sleepe" when Archimago begins his enchantment. Una's last recorded word to Redcross before their separation, the aphorism quoted above, seems conspicuously inappropriate in view of the troubles which this night is to bring. Archimago is quick to support Una, adding with a fine ambiguity that "the way to win/ Is wisely to aduise" (I.i.33). Dinner at the hermitage becomes, then, a combination of temperate diet and smooth pieties:

> Arriued there, the little house they fill,
>     Ne looke for entertainement, where none was:
>     Rest is their feast, and all things at their will;
>     The noblest mind the best contentment has.
>     With fair discourse the euening so they pas:
>     For that old man of pleasing wordes had store,
>     And well could file his tongue as smooth as glas;
>     He told of Saintes and Popes, and euermore
> He strowd an *Aue-Mary* after and before.          (I.i.35)

The narrator's tone and his insistence on Archimago's Romish habits make the hypocrisy clear enough to the reader;[8] but Redcross and Una go to their sleep suspecting nothing, lulled by easy platitudes and the appearance of a cloistered virtue.

Archimago's temptations bring into clear focus the present state of Redcross's spiritual health: the combination of strength and weakness implicit in his active conscience and his dependence on reason and the evidence of his senses. It is helpful here to examine these temptations in some detail. Morpheus, the source of Archimago's erotic dream, is first seen like Redcross himself "drowned deepe/ In drowsie fit" (I.i.40), in an atmosphere which combines the elements of darkness, water, and careless isolation already associated with the hero's sleep:

> And low, where dawning day doth neuer peepe,
>     His dwelling is; there *Tethys* his wet bed

---

[8] C. S. Lewis, *The Allegory of Love* (London, 1936), pp. 321–4.

> Doth euer wash, and *Cynthia* still doth steepe
> In siluer deaw his euer-drouping hed,
> Whiles sad Night ouer him her mantle black doth spred.
>
> . . .
>
> And more, to lull him in his slumber soft,
>   A trickling streame from high rocke tumbling downe
> And euer-drizling raine vpon the loft,
>   Mixt with a murmuring winde, much like the sowne
>   Of swarming Bees, did cast him in a swowne:
>   No other noyse, nor peoples troublous cryes,
>   As still are wont t'annoy the walled towne,
> Might there be heard: but careless Quiet lyes,
> Wrapt in eternall silence farre from enemyes.          (I.i.39–41)

This passage has been justly praised for its assimilation of traditional presentations of Sleep, its use of onomatopoeia and personification, and its realistic humor in describing the grumbling sleepiness of Morpheus; but what must be stressed here is its relevance to the condition of Redcross. Morpheus, wholly removed from the world of day, is in a condition of passivity which seems diametrically opposed to the active commitment of Redcross seen earlier in the poem. Against the energy which had gone into numbering the trees of Error's wood is set a negative *vis inertiae* which determinedly banishes Care and "takes keepe" of nothing. The dreamless sleep which Morpheus seeks and to which he returns after satisfying Archimago's demands is seen as the pole toward which the water imagery is directed; a sleep troubled by dreams is significantly associated with a "dryer braine." [9] The water here takes the forms of trickling stream and drizzling rain, providing an hypnotic murmur to lull the sleeper and to drown out the "troublous cryes" of others.

Yet even for Morpheus total oblivion is impossible, as the presence of these troubling and troubled cries suggests to the reader (the image of the walled town further hints that the disturbance is as likely to be within the walls as without, and hence that there is no clear boundary between dreamer and dream), and as his rude awakening makes explicit. Spenser has been careful in his presentation of sleep to insist on the "wakeful dogges" which protect Morpheus, as well as the other forms of care which are devoted to ensuring his carefree rest. The humor in this personification of Morpheus is ultimately related, therefore, to the ironic sense that not even the god of Sleep can get an uninterrupted night's rest, for all the effort directed toward this goal.

---

[9] R. E. Neil Dodge (*Variorum* I, 195) relates the passage to traditional physiology.

And, more generally, it is seen that in the world of sleep dreams reflect the cares of day rather as the moon reflects the sun: indirectly and changeably. In the case of Redcross, the images which come in his sleep are a direct challenge to his interpretation of his waking world. The chaste Una first appears, to complain "how that false winged boy,/ Her chast hart had subdewd, to learne Dame pleasures toy." Venus seems to bring her to his bed, accompanied by the full machinery of a pastoral vision like that of Calidore in Book VI:

> And eke the *Graces* seemed all to sing,
> *Hymen ı̄ō Hymen,* dauncing all around,
> Whilst freshest Flora her with Yuie girlond crownd.
>
> (I.i.48)

The image of the pastoral garland will be repeated throughout the Book as a mocking reminder of an erotic motive which lies hidden beneath the conscious level of the quest—a motive which is accommodated only at the end when Una is crowned, "twixt earnest and twixt game," at the time of her betrothal to Redcross (I.xii.8). Against this first, dreaming vision, when "nigh his manly hart did melt away,/ Bathed in wanton blis and wicked ioy," Redcross is able to oppose his active will. But the source of his rescue is ambiguous: he wakes in a "great passion of vnwonted lust,/ Or wonted feare of doing ought amis." Either he is shocked out of sleep by the novelty of this lust or he forces himself to consciousness in an habitual response to his scrupulous conscience. As the sequence of his temptations makes clear, these alternatives are more closely related than might appear at first. Both are expressions of that excessive solemnity alluded to in the first lines of the canto: the singleminded concentration on the narrow demands of his quest which blinds him to its broader implications. It is in this sense that he has yet to make his armor fully meaningful, fully a part of himself. His naïve dependence on a literal reading of the *visibilia* of his experience makes him an easy victim not only of the deceptive visions fashioned by Archimago, but also of the conflicting responses provoked by a single image—here that of his lady.

In this instance, it is in the former area that Redcross succumbs: not until his surrender to Duessa in Canto vii will he let himself "melt away" under the influence of the enervating fountain, where he will be found by Orgoglio "Pourd out in loosnesse" (I.vii.7). For the moment, his manly heart resists the explicit incitement to lust which he finds in his dream. The second stage of his temptation takes the form of a waking vision of the false Una created by Archimago, and here he is able to temper his first impulse of anger at her "shamelesse guise," and to hear her complaint. Ominously, though, he is chiefly concerned "To proue his sense"; it is in this continuing dependence on the evidence of his senses that his susceptibility to Archimago consists. When he chooses to put the more honorable construction on the false Una's confession of love, it becomes apparent how closely related are his scrupulousness and his sexual innocence. What faith in his lady remains at this point seems largely a result of his willed effort to repress the sexual overtones of the speech he has just heard. When he returns to bed to muse on her apparent lightness, it is clear that, although he may be no closer to succumbing to lust, he is substantially closer to repudiating Una. Significantly he is chiefly bothered by this evidence of unworthiness in someone "For whose defence he was to shed his blood" (I.i.55).

It is supremely appropriate that Archimago's assault should be directed toward the sexual sphere, for here the very solemnity of the young knight's preoccupation with his quest becomes at once his strength and his weakness. His naïve idealism is most effectively challenged in an area where his faith in a reality contrary to appearance is most difficult. He has overcome Error by following Una's advice to add faith to his force; but when in the third and final phase of his temptation Archimago presents him with the apparent evidence of Una embracing a "young Squire," such a faith becomes impossible, since it would mean denying not only the objective evidence of his senses but also (as subsequent events verify) the subjective evidence of a motive he has not yet reckoned with. The final stage in his fall comes when he yields himself totally to Duessa and presents to Orgoglio the compromising spectacle which Archimago now prepares for his sight: the image of this false Una in the arms of her companion sprite,

> Like a young Squire, in loues and lusty-hed
> His wanton dayes that euer loosely led,
> Without regard of armes and dreaded fight.          (I.ii.3)

As is so often the case in *The Faerie Queene* (Verdant in Acrasia's bower is the most conspicuous example), lust is here presented as primarily a dereliction of chivalric duties, a "looseness" which is opposed to the rigors of the quest. For the present, Redcross's response to this spectacle is merely described, rather ambiguously, as "bitter anguish of his guiltie sight"; he is driven to fly "from his thoughts and gealous feare;/ Will was his guide, and griefe led him astray" (I.ii.6,12). Spenser is less concerned here with rendering realistically his hero's psychological state than with suggesting the implications of the split between

Redcross and Una. But the terms of this schism are such as to invite (though not wholly to support) an interpretation of Redcross as an adolescent squire who is diverted from his quest by an inability to reconcile his idealistic goals with the demands of his senses, with the limitations of his fallen human nature.

The chief faults of such a psychological reading lie in its tendency to focus on Redcross to the exclusion of Una and to exaggerate the sexual element in Redcross's fall.[10] The distracted departure of Redcross at this point is only incidentally related, if at all, to a fear of his own sexuality. But, although he is fleeing the imagined lust of his chaste lady, he runs unhesitatingly toward an erotic involvement of his own with Duessa. Spenser's technique here as elsewhere in the poem is one of symbolic counterpoint: the parallel stories of Una and Redcross complement each other and together define the "divided personality" produced by the separation of knight and lady. In the present discussion I hope to demonstrate that the motion of Book I is toward a meaningful return to the tableau shown at the beginning of the first canto: a return symbolized by the killing of the dragon (the formal "blazoning" of the knight's armor) and by the betrothal scene (the solemnization of the union of knight and lady). Such actions are possible only after the natural world, with all its limitations, has been reconciled with the transcendent goals of the quest.

The necessity for such a reconciliation gives particular meaning to Una's earlier advice to Redcross, when she had impressed upon him the need for "Untroubled rest." In the terms of the imagery of Book I, it is more than a commonplace to say that one cannot fight well without sleep. Throughout the poem a recurrent theme is the human need for rest: the heroes of the poem repeatedly succumb to this need (Redcross and Guyon in the seventh cantos of their respective Books), and the inevitable dangers of such relaxation indicate that without assistance man cannot maintain the eternal wakefulness demanded of him. Sooner or later the forces of darkness will catch him in an unguarded moment. In the case of Book I, with its emphasis on the integrated individual (holiness being seen less as a distinct virtue than as a more generalized spiritual health or wholeness), the moment will come when Redcross has exhausted the resources of this intense preoccupation with his chivalric career. The pattern of Book I stresses the repetition of scenes in which he overcomes a clear and present threat only to fall

---

[10] Such tendencies seem present in the otherwise helpful articles by Linwood E. Orange, "Sensual Beauty in Book I of *The Faerie Queene*," *Journal of English and Germanic Philology*, LXI (1962), 555–61, and John W. Schroeder, "Spenser's Erotic Drama: The Orgoglio Episode," *English Literary History*, XXIX (1962), 140–59.

prey to a hidden danger. In the first canto he overcomes Error but is fooled by Archimago's deceptive appeal to the evidence of his senses. In the second, he can vanquish the clearly labeled Sans Foy (rising to the full strength of his "natiue vertue" when the Saracen curses the Cross), but at the same time uncritically accepts Duessa when she calls herself Fidessa.

Throughout the first half of Book I repeated emphasis is placed on the youth and naïveté of Redcross. When he leaves Una he moves into a world of artifice where he is ludicrously unprepared to read images that are immediately recognizable to the narrator and the reader. Duessa seems to him no scarlet lady but an irresistible object of admiration; her elaborate account of her sufferings is scarcely needed since he barely listens, "More busying his quicke eyes, her face to view,/ Then his dull eares, to heare what she did tell" (I.ii.26). His response to her provides a clear example of the tone with which Spenser presents him in these cantos:

> Henceforth in safe assuraunce may ye rest,
>    Hauing both found a new friend you to aid,
>    And lost an old foe, that did you molest:
>    Better new friend then an old foe is said.
>    With chaunge of cheare the seeming simple maid
>    Let fall her eyen, as shamefast to the earth,
>    And yeelding soft, in that she nought gain-said,
>    So forth they rode, he feining seemely merth,
> And she coy lookes: so dainty they say maketh derth.
>
>                                                           (I.ii.27)

The narrator's proverb in the last line wryly caps Redcross's attempt to sum up the situation in the first half of the stanza: "they say" echoes the inanity of "is said," while the metrical awkwardnesses and verbal repetitions of the fourth and ninth lines direct attention to the feebleness of the knight's aphorisms. And Redcross's desire to please Duessa drives him to a "seemely merth" which, in view of his characteristic solemnity, is as much a product of artifice as Duessa's modest glances. Even the apparent aimlessness of Redcross during these central cantos is in keeping with the picture of him as a naïve knight, too preoccupied with the details of chivalric behavior to meditate on his own abandoned quest.

The extent to which Redcross has lost what limited defenses he first possessed may be measured by his response to Fradubio, whose grove resembles the Wood of Error in offering an apparent escape from the rigors of the quest. But here it is explicitly the heat of day rather than

a sudden shower which drives the knight and his lady to seek refuge,
and this grove is described in terms of a menace which the humbler
shepherd can avoid:

> Long time they thus together traueiled,
> Till weary of their way, they came at last,
> Where grew two goodly trees, that faire did spred
> Their armes abroad, with gray mosse ouercast,
> And their greene leaues trembling with euery blast,
> Made a calme shadow far in compasse round:
> The fearfull Shepheard often there aghast
> Vnder them neuer sat, ne wont there sound
> His mery oaten pipe, but shund th'vnlucky ground.

(I.ii.28)

The apparent non sequitur in the seventh line demands a reconsidera-
tion of the contrast between the green, trembling leaves and the calm
shadow which they throw; and in the implication that one man's
pastoral refuge may be another's prison is introduced the first in a
series of reassessments of the natural setting. The elaborate antitheses
of Fradubio's speech—he is one of Spenser's most euphuistic characters
—dramatize the sense of stalemate, of a helpless subjection to contradictory insights, which his name implies. He groans for "My tender
sides in this rough rynd embard"; he is acutely aware that in the very
act of providing shade for others he is himself exposed "in open
plaines" to the sun and the north wind, "For though a tree I seeme,
yet cold and heat me paines." In telling his story, he displays mixed
emotions toward Fraelissa, "my dear loue,/ O too deare loue, loue
bought with death too deare," and his two views of Duessa are juxtaposed through the unfolding of a single phrase: "a like faire Lady by
his side,/ Like a faire Lady, but did fowle *Duessa* hyde" (I.ii.31–35).
The verbal style of Fradubio's narrative expresses a sense of paradox
far removed from the simplistic moral readings given to the trees in
the Wood of Error, or from the naïve aphorisms characteristic of the
knight to this point. When one of the trees speaks for itself, it demonstrates an Ovidian sensitivity to the poetic justice of its metamorphosis.
Fradubio's human reason is the first to fail him when he chooses
Duessa; and after learning his error, he further fails to use his animal
faculty of motion, being content to "refraine, in minde to slip away,/
Soone as appeard safe oportunitie" (I.ii.41). What remains is a vegetative state which contains its own punishment.

Fradubio's role as an emblem of man trapped by the flesh has been
generally recognized by readers, and more recently critics have adduced

a variety of analogous uses of the tree image which point suggestively toward the incident's position in the plot of Book I. The figure of "Despair," who sings from an oak tree during Elizabeth's entertainment at Woodstock in 1575, reinforces our sense of Fradubio's continuing relevance to Redcross's condition through all the stages of his decline until his arrival at the House of Holiness.[11] Suggestions of Adam's fallen condition are implicit throughout the episode, emerging most clearly in Fradubio's statement that he and Fraelissa cannot be liberated from this "death" until they are "bathed in a liuing well." [12] Fradubio's relationship to Redcross is far from simple. It is at this point that Redcross has made a first gesture toward enacting the scenes of his erotic visions at Archimago's house, in preparing for Duessa a pastoral crown like the one Flora had placed on the false Una's head:

> And in his falsed fancy he her takes
> To be the fairest wight, that liued yit;
> Which to expresse, he bends his gentle wit,
> And thinking of those braunches greene to frame
> A girlond for her dainty forehead fit,
> He pluckt a bough . . .                                    (I.ii.30)

The limbs of Duessa's earlier victim make a fitter garland than Redcross is able to realize. The details of Fradubio's narrative both assert his resemblance to Redcross and by so doing help to clarify the reader's sense of the direction in which the other is moving. Fradubio has won Duessa in battle, and his award of a "Rosy girlond" to her in preference to Fraelissa represents an explicit choice of false beauty over true. Like Redcross, he is barely restrained from killing his true love in a fit of revulsion, and he is induced to leave her "where she now is turnd to treen mould." And, again like Redcross, he is "drownd in sleepie night" when Duessa works her final change on him.

From his prison Fradubio speaks with an acute awareness of his condition. But knowledge, far from setting him free, is an index of his inability to act. His name, his manner of speaking, and his history all emphasize the extent to which his contradictory impulses have negated one another. It is toward this emphasis that the differences between him and Redcross are directed. He is first seen as the typical young knight,

---

[11] Nelson, *The Poetry of Edmund Spenser,* p. 162; see also Frances A. Yates, "Elizabethan Chivalry: The Romance of the Accession Day Tilts," *Journal of the Warburg and Courtauld Institutes,* XX (1957), 12–13.

[12] Nelson, *ibid.;* Hamilton, *The Structure of Allegory,* p. 66.

> In prime of youthly yeares, when corage hot
> The fire of loue and ioy of cheualree
> First kindled in my brest . . .　　　　　　(I.ii.35)

But though he lacks the excessive solemnity of Redcross and rejoices in the erotic aspects of the chivalric life, he is all the more rapidly driven to a crisis which the other reaches only after much indirection. When Fradubio is challenged by Duessa's champion, the challenge is explicitly formulated in erotic terms. When he has won the pyrrhic victory which brings Duessa as a more insidious challenge to his faith in Fraelissa's beauty, he recognizes within himself the challenging doubt which had previously appeared outside him, where it could be overcome more easily. Finding himself now "So doubly lou'd of Ladies vnlike faire," he cannot resist the temptation to compare the two ladies. And it is because in his eyes the choice hangs in "doubtfull ballaunce" that Fradubio finds himself caught between an extreme loathing for Fraelissa and a subsequent, equivalent loathing for Duessa. It is significant that Fradubio is imprisoned not within a complacent sensuality (the animalism of Gryll in Book II, for example), but within a cycle of sexual attraction and revulsion. The two states of loathing suggest clearly enough that he is first blinded by lust to Fraelissa's "shining ray" (easily dimmed by Duessa's "foggy mist"), and then later brought in due time to a recognition of the beastliness of his new mistress. When he views the disfigured Duessa, he responds intuitively:

> Her neather partes misshapen, monstruous,
> Were hidd in water, that I could not see,
> But they did seeme more foule and hideous,
> Then womans shape man would beleeue to bee.
>
> 　　　　　　　　　　　　　　　(I.ii.41)

Fradubio's besetting sin (if such a term is relevant here) is that of Lechery; and the description of that sin in the procession at the House of Pride (I.iv.24–26) similarly emphasizes the "greene gowne" of vegetative function which covers the inconstant spirit filled with "reproachful paine." In this respect Fradubio is contrasted with Redcross, who is moving toward a more inclusive Pride in his self-centered concern for his quest and the glory which attends its fulfillment. In serving as an antithesis to the hero as well as a token of the hero's fate, Fradubio's role becomes all the more evocative of the inevitability of crisis. In subsequent episodes the immediate causes of Redcross's downfall will be associated with his prideful joylessness: images of Sans Joy, Lucifera, Hippolytus, and Orgoglio will illuminate the specific weaknesses of his character. Yet the point is not that Una should have chosen a less solemn champion, one who, like Fradubio, might have been less resistant to Archimago's earlier incitements to lust. It is rather that any champion from Gloriana's court would have fallen as surely as does Redcross, though he would have fallen to different forces.

What seems to be involved here ultimately is Spenser's evaluation of the chivalric milieu within which his action is set. As I shall try to show in the second chapter, Spenser borrows from the Italians the concept of an ironic projection of human impulses into a simplified world of chivalric values as a means both of demonstrating the inadequacy of those values when naïvely formulated and of suggesting the extent to which the contradictions inherent in those values may, in the long run, be their most valuable asset, since they lead back to illuminate the dialectical process operative in the unsimplified world of poet and reader. And it is toward such a repudiation of "naïve allegory" that Spenser's technique of "symbolic parody" [13] is directed: toward the sense that all images, and all actions in fact, are ambivalent and demand an ability not only to comprehend their various implications but, when necessary, to step outside such a comprehension in order to take a decisive action.

In the present case the dual emphasis of the chivalric ethic upon both love and glory is at the heart of the combined image of Redcross and Fradubio. The latter seems to have responded to this ethic on a relatively low level of abstraction. His interest is focused on his lady, and his role as knight seems largely directed toward defending her beauty as an extension of his own reputation. For him the lady is not a symbol but an object sought in and for herself. Consequently, his "faith" is subject to a challenge on the level of his faith in her beauty. Fraelissa is frail in the sense that all flesh is frail: it is subject to the varying desires of the beholder. Redcross, in contrast, conceives his quest on a far higher level of abstraction; the repeated superlatives in the following quotation emphasize the transcendent terms in which he views his goal:

> Vpon a great aduenture he was bond,
>> That greatest *Gloriana* to him gaue,
>> That greatest Glorious Queene of *Faerie* lond,
>> To winne him worship, and her grace to haue,
>> Which of all earthly things he most did craue;

[13] Northrop Frye, "The Structure of Imagery in *The Faerie Queene*," *UTQ*, XXX (1961), 109–27.

> And euer as he rode, his hart did earne
> To proue his puissance in battell braue
> Vpon his foe, and his new force to learne;
> Vpon his foe, a Dragon horrible and stearne.          (I.i.3)

Such transcendence implies a consequent lack of concrete definition. A recent discussion of the poem remarks upon the abruptness with which Spenser introduces the betrothal of Redcross and Una, when their relationship until the twelfth canto has shown Una as simply "the pure object of his assigned championship." [14] Far from indicating any slackness in Spenser's control over his narrative, however, this is clearly designed to indicate the knight's limited understanding of the meaning of his quest. From the beginning he is prepared to view his armor as symbolic, but it is the extent of the symbolism which he has not yet grasped. Where he differs from Fradubio is in viewing "faith" in broad, abstract terms: not simply—or even primarily—as faith in his lady, for he has already abandoned her before he tilts against Sans Foy. Accordingly, it is not the person of Una but the abstraction— faith—which is challenged by the knight; and Duessa presents herself as "Fidessa" and adapts her tale to echo Una's.

Yet a further ironic complication becomes apparent at this stage in the narrative. Duessa's tale falls on deaf ears, since Redcross's very act of separation from Una has brought him closer to Fradubio's condi- tion; the same force which makes him flee the tarnished ideal which he sees in Una drives him to a new receptivity to sensual temptation. For the moment Duessa's wiles seem a step behind the changes in Redcross himself, as he feigns mirth and sets out to court his temptress. Even the cautionary tale of Fradubio's undoing is powerless to halt him. The canto ends with a stanza whose verbal antitheses are reminiscent of Fradubio's own and whose ambiguities of reference dramatize the implications of the kiss being described:

> Her seeming dead he found with feigned feare,
>     As all vnweeting of that well she knew,
>     And paynd himselfe with busie care to reare
> Her out of carelesse swowne. Her eylids blew
> And dimmed sight with pale and deadly hew
> At last she vp gan lift: with trembling cheare
> Her vp he tooke, too simple and too trew,
>     And oft her kist. At length all passed feare,
> He set her on her steede, and forward forth did beare.

>                                                        (I.ii.45)

---

[14] Graham Hough, *A Preface to "The Faerie Queene"* (London, 1962), p. 141.

Redcross has turned away from the tree, thrusting the bleeding bough into the ground and stopping the wound with clay, "That from the bloud he might be innocent." The gesture is one of piety, yet it also suggests the repression of unwelcome knowledge. The naïve "innocence" which he seeks will bring its own guilty knowledge; the busy care with which he tries to wake Duessa will bring him to a careless swoon; her hue is "deadly" in two senses; his "trembling cheare" is an echo of Fradubio's own emotional state, seen earlier in his trembling leaves; it is not clear who is "too simple and too trew" as the two kiss.

These ambiguities reverberate throughout the poem, for Redcross is here close to assuming the role of an Adonis: compare the relevant passage in Shakespeare's version of the myth (*Venus and Adonis,* 463ff.). In terms of the quest of Books I and II, these versions of Adonis appear as fatal temptations, destructive of that integrity of the individual which Holiness and Temperance assert in their respective ways. For Shakespeare and Spenser, as for Ovid and his Renaissance commentators, the story of Adonis represents a myth of man's precipitation through lust into the world of time, into the combination of personal mortality and racial immortality which is man's fate as a part of nature. Only by recognizing the full force of his human condition, only by falling through the successive stages of his decay, can Redcross come to an understanding of the logical impossibility of independently fulfilling his quest, and thereby to a recognition of the true meaning of the armor which Una has given him. In kissing Duessa he is like Adonis unconsciously committing himself to a pattern of fall and transformation, though his later career will show that he is unlike Adonis (and unlike the elves of Spenser's fairyland) in being fortunately fallen out of Eden and into a Christian dispensation.

Yet, although the movement of Redcross toward the House of Pride is clear enough at this point, the pattern of the poem's development echoes the episodic counterpoint of the chivalric poem. Spenser interrupts the story of his hero to turn to Una's experiences. These experiences, which occupy the third and sixth cantos in their entirety, have received relatively little attention from recent critics. There are probably several reasons for this neglect. Una seems to belong to a different level of reality than Redcross. As her name suggests, she is not subject to change and hence to the developmental history seen in the adventures of the young hero. Although the full range of her significance is progressively displayed to the reader through a series of oppositional relationships,[15] it is through these relationships that she functions as a

[15] Edwin Honig, *Dark Conceit: The Making of Allegory* (Evanston, 1959), p. 63; Hamilton, *The Structure of Allegory,* p. 88.

touchstone by which the nature of the hero is to be further examined.[16] Throughout her wanderings she is continually in the position of a heroine in search of her knight; and it is chiefly instructive to observe the variety and nature of the substitutes for Redcross which present themselves to her. For it is as a means of illuminating those characteristics of Redcross which eventually permit him to slay the dragon—his combination of clownish plowman and Christian knight—that Spenser shows Una exploring the resources of a natural setting, "in wildernesse and wastful deserts strayd,/ To seeke her knight" (I.iii.3). As she works her way back to Redcross, she is successively dependent on a lion, a band of satyrs, Satyrane, and Arthur.

Her first defender, the lion, is explicitly compared to Redcross as a symbol of the proud beast mastered by beauty. Una's meditation on this emblem of "yielded pride and proud submission" stresses the defect of Redcross's love which has separated the two:

> The Lyon Lord of euerie beast in field,
>> Quoth she, his princely puissance doth abate,
>> And mightie proud to humble weake does yield,
>> Forgetfull of the hungry rage, which late
>> Him prickt, in pittie of my sad estate:
>> But he my Lyon, and my noble Lord,
>> How does he find in cruell hart to hate
>> Her that him lou'd, and euer most adord,
> As the God of my life? why hath he me abhord?     (I.iii.7)

The metaphoric sense in which Redcross is Una's "Lion" gives particular relevance to the historical allusion which is presumably implicit in this episode. Redcross is too little the lion: he possesses the proud rage but lacks the intuitive capacity to recognize and pay homage to virginity. As a rational being he is divorced from those same intuitive powers which would have defended him against Archimago's lying visions. Henry VIII, by contrast, the first English champion of the Protestant faith, is in a sense too much of a lion. Given the obvious abuses of Corceca, Abessa, and Kirkrapine, he can act forcefully and decisively against the powers of hypocrisy and false piety by suppressing corrupt institutions and helping Una as she "Marres blind Deuotions mart" (I.iii.Arg.). But the lion is frail in two senses: he is as incapable of recognizing Archimago's new deceits as Una herself, and as Redcross had been the night before (when the Roman church had

[16] M. Pauline Parker, *The Allegory of "The Faerie Queene"* (Oxford, 1961), pp. 69ff. Note that Una is called "true as touch" at I.iii.2.

masked itself in Archimago's glib pieties and had avoided the bestial obviousness visible during this second night); and he is, finally, a victim to Sans Loy. Henry VIII sets in motion a violence which, from an Elizabethan perspective, lacks the guiding intelligence of a statecraft which can consolidate its achievements. The champion of Protestantism must ultimately be prepared to cope with a Saracen enemy whose bestial lust, like that of Sans Loy, is informed by an understanding of "feates of armes." In appealing to his audience's sense of recent history, Spenser underscores the necessity of a holiness which goes beyond the natural piety of an instinctive alliance to virtue.

\* \* \*

Una, the helpless maiden wandering in the wilderness, is subject to the alternation of menace and assistance which she finds in the savage figures who confront her. In the third canto we see one such cycle completed when the friendly lion is killed by Sans Loy; the end of the canto falls as she is carried off by this new, inimical figure of bestial lust. The two cantos that describe her adventures frame the fourth and fifth cantos, in which Redcross visits the House of Pride and encounters Sans Joy; the gentle maiden's experiences in an uncivilized setting thus provide a backdrop for her youthful knight's similarly passive role in a sophisticated world. Lucifera's relationship to the chivalric norm is clear enough to the reader: her house is built on the sands, and her diabolic ancestry is seen in her name and retinue. But while the reader is being shown the operations of a Pride which dominates all other sins and is in turn upheld by them, Redcross is responding with tragic naïveté to a social situation which he reads as a naturalistic imitation of courtly life. His only negative responses to Lucifera's court are ironic tokens of his own pride:

> Yet the stout Faerie mongst the middest crowd
> Thought all their glorie vaine in knightly vew,
> And that great Princesse too exceeding prowd,
> That to strange knight no better countenance allowd.

> (I.iv.15)

When Lucifera and her counselors go out "To take the solace of the open aire," Redcross again stands on his dignity, disdaining to leave the House of Pride, "Him selfe estraunging from their ioyaunce vaine,/ Whose fellowship seemd far vnfit for warlike swaine" (I.iv.37). It is no wonder that the third of the Saracen brothers arrives at this point.

Sans Joy is repeatedly presented in terms which suggest his similarities to Redcross. Both knights are fighting for Sans Foy's shield (a curious emblem for Redcross to defend), and their battle is described in a weaving alternation of phrases (I.v.7: "The Sarazin was stout, and wondrous strong . . . The knight was fiers, and full of youthly heat . . . Both stricken strike, and beaten both do beat.") which obscure distinctions while pretending to stress them. The repeated phrase, "So th'one for wrong, the other striues for right," is mocked by the simile of griffin and dragon competing for "rightfull rauine" (I.v.8). It is at this point that Redcross is seen most clearly to be fatally misguided in his concern for the acquisition of glory through chivalric combat. Duessa's visit to Sans Joy on the eve of battle seems to echo the false Una's appearance to Redcross earlier; and, like Redcross, Sans Joy is confident in his unassisted powers as he sends her back to bed. In so ambiguous a conflict it is appropriate that Redcross should win his limited victory after misinterpreting Duessa's shout of encouragement, and that the descent into the underworld to cure Sans Joy should present elements of considerable relevance to Redcross's own situation.

Sans Joy is brought to Aesculapius, whom Jove has cast into hell for reassembling and reviving Hippolytus' dismembered body. Such a punishment may at first seem an arbitrary act of jealousy by a deity who fears encroachment:

> Such wondrous science in mans wit to raine
> When *Ioue* auizd, that could the dead reuiue,
> And fates expired could renew againe,
> Of endlesse life he might him not depriue,
> But vnto hell did thrust him downe aliue,
> With flashing thunderbolt ywounded sore:
> Where long remaining, he did alwaies striue
> Himselfe with salues to health for to restore,
> And slake the heauenly fire, that raged euermore.
>
> (I.v.40)

Yet Aesculapius' punishment is an ironic commentary on the nature of his offense. By destroying the powers of death, he has prepared for himself an endlessly painful life against which his salves are of no avail. His condition is similar to that in which Prometheus, the creator of the faery race, finds himself as a consequence of his similar interference with divine prerogative (II.x.70): in both cases Jove has simply presided over what might be called the merely human condition, the condition of man in the natural order. Both Aesculapius and Prome-

theus are painfully fixed in time, divorced from the natural cycle. In
the stanza quoted above, Spenser seems to be aware that Aesculapius
was eventually to return from the world of the dead. His familiar association with the emblem of the serpent, moreover, links him to the
many serpents figured in Book I, among them that of Fidelia at the
House of Holiness. Similarly, Prometheus' imprisonment was to end
eventually through the heroic intercession of Hercules; but for the
moment the world of fairyland is unredeemed by its creator.[17] In the
present instance Aesculapius is to be seen in the context of the other
figures in Book I—Fradubio, Despair, the Deadly Sins themselves—
who are trapped within a sense of paradox. His decision to revive
Sans Joy is a dramatization of his own raging pain: Duessa urges him to
"shew thy famous might" precisely because he has no hope left, because "heauens king/ From hope of heauen hath thee excluded quight"
(I.v.43). His despairing gesture of defiance is like that of Satan, but as
a curative, redemptive act it comes so close to an imitation of Christ
that it could serve as a warning to Redcross of the ambiguity of his
own quest.

Similarly, the story of Hippolytus has a particular relevance to the
state of the proud young knight:

> *Hippolytus* a iolly huntsman was,
>     That wont in charet chace the foming Bore;
>     He all his Peeres in beautie did surpas,
>     But Ladies loue as losse of time forbore . . .            (I.v.37)

Once again Spenser provides a picture of imbalance. On the literal
level Hippolytus is merely the innocent victim of his stepmother's
lust, but metaphorically he invites nemesis by turning all his energies
to a single goal; and the form of his death seems to express this failure
to control his various conscious and unconscious motives. In this
variation on the image of Redcross/Sans Joy, however, the emphasis
begins to move toward the larger problems of the cycle of fertility and
the various possibilities of immortality. The mention of the boar anticipates the figure of Adonis, and the curious insistence on his failure

---

[17] Frye, "The Structure of Imagery"; Hughes' remarks on Spenser's transformations
of the Dantesque and Vergilian underworlds are relevant: "Spenser's hell is Dante's
inferno atrophied . . . a pale dying gleam of the tragic medieval conception of
hell as a place where life's seemingly deathless glories are whelmed in a real immortality of pain" (*Virgil and Spenser*, pp. 376–7). I would differ from Hughes,
however, in attributing this unalloyed gloom not to the poet's immature vision, but
to the special conditions of the Spenserian context. It is not the knight who visits
this underworld but only his joylessness, so to speak; his own view of history is to
be revealed in Canto x.

to leave a "moniment" explains the need for his "rebirth" at the hands of Aesculapius.[18]

> His goodly corps on ragged cliffs yrent,
> Was quite dismembred, and his members chast
> Scattered on euery mountaine, as he went,
> That of *Hippolytus* was left no moniment.        (I.v.38)

The monsters that rise from the sea to fulfill a paternal wrath contrast with the more familiar beast that Hippolytus has hunted in the same chariot. The motifs gathered from the daytime quests of the poem acquire confusingly ironic overtones in this infernal setting; but in general the descent to the underworld seems designed—here as in other epics—to dramatize the challenge of mortality to the hero's quest for identity. The story of Hippolytus' fall has a special relevance for a knight whose naïve literalism has limited him to purely nominal victories over his foes and has blinded him to Una's pertinence to his quest. But it is a function of this same literal imagination that Redcross should be deprived of the vision of hell given to the reader: his own vision is sufficient to rescue him from the House of Pride, but it leaves him vulnerable to a new figure of pride who is more "natural" and "monstrous." [19] Reason (to employ momentarily the conventional interpretation of the Dwarf) is able to protect Redcross from the "civilized" world of Lucifera; and the panorama of victims in her dungeons is precisely the sort of underworld vision that the Dwarf can reveal to his master: there, Old Testament names flow into a list of Romans, "The antique ruines of the *Romaines* fall" (I.v.49), which suggest through their epithets ("Stout . . . stubborne . . . sterne . . . High minded") that the stoic virtues on which Redcross is currently depending are no better than synonyms for pride. In Spenser's poem nemesis takes the form of a balancing force that reasserts the validity of the natural cycles of time: Redcross leaves the House of Pride only to fall in weariness before the enervating fountain (commemorating, ironically, the weary nymph of Diana) where all his energetic resistance will be mocked as he falls prey to Orgoglio.

[18] If Spenser is drawing on the *Aeneid* 7.761–82, as well as on Boccaccio, *Genealogia Deorum* 10.50, he is more likely to have borne in mind Hippolytus' later name Virbius ("twice-born" in Servius' gloss), with its Christian overtones. See H. G. Lotspeich, *Classical Mythology in the Poetry of Edmund Spenser*, Princeton Studies in English, 9 (Princeton, 1932), 69–70. Douglas Bush, *Mythology and the Renaissance Tradition in English Poetry* (Minneapolis, 1932), p. 112n., sees Seneca's Hippolytus as the main source.

[19] S. K. Heninger, Jr., "The Orgoglio Episode in *The Faerie Queene*," *English Literary History*, XXVI (1959), 171–87.

# The Fall of Guyon

## *by Maurice Evans*

Book II of *The Faerie Queene* has been more variously interpreted than any other section of the poem. Professor Kermode refers to some of these interpretations in his recent chapter on the Cave of Mammon,[1] and he himself offers an explanation of the canto which, if it is accepted, must affect the interpretation of the entire book. Starting from the resemblance which has often been noticed between Guyon's passage through the Cave and Christ's temptation in the desert, Professor Kermode argues that Guyon, like Christ, chooses to undergo temptation in order that his virtue may be strengthened. The temptation with which Mammon faces him is a total one, involving not only the seductions of worldliness but of forbidden knowledge also, and when he has come through the ordeal, like Christ he receives the ministration of angels. The whole sequence is interpreted as an initiation, voluntarily chosen and triumphantly undergone, through which Guyon prepares himself for the role of a hero.

Professor Kermode's analysis of the temptations which assail Guyon is very convincing, but his interpretation of the episode as a whole is open to question. In particular, he ignores the chain of events which leads Guyon into the Cave in the first place, and he does not take into account the highly controversial faint which strikes Guyon down as soon as he escapes. The questions which this episode of the poem has always provoked still remain to be answered. Should Guyon have gone into the Cave at all? Was this Occasion for temptation a proper one to be embraced, or one which the Palmer would have counselled him to avoid? Does the outcome suggest the victory of Christ, or the Fall of Adam?

To me, the answers seem to lie in a proper understanding of the Palmer. Spenser always describes him as a guide:

From *English Literary History*, XXVIII, No. 3 (1961), 215–24. Copyright © 1961 by The Johns Hopkins Press. Reprinted by permission of The Johns Hopkins Press.

[1] F. Kermode, *Elizabethan Poetry*, Stratford-upon-Avon Studies, No. 2, (London, 1960), Chap. VIII.

> Then Guyon forward gan his voyage make,
> With his blacke Palmer, that him guided still.
> Still he him guided over dale and hill, . . .          (II.i.34)

That is how we first see him, and in Canto XII he is still stiffly steering
Guyon past those deceptions of Acrasia which Alma's boatman is un-
able to circumvent by his own unaided vigor. The bodily health which
Alma's man symbolizes may make us instinctively recoil from the Gulfe
of Greedinesse or the Whirlepoole of Decay, but it takes a more deliberate kind of virtue to survive the song of the syrens or the fog of
horrible imaginings. The Palmer represents our reason in its special
capacity to distinguish between right and wrong; he is the power,
which God of his grace restored to Adam after the Fall, enabling him
still to retain a glimpse of the divine truth. The Palmer's rod, like that
of Cambina, is made of the same wood as Mercury's Caduceus (II.xii.
41), and Mercury was the leader of the Graces and master of the
sacred Hermetic knowledge.[2] Steering by the Palmer is steering by
"a stedfast starre," and without him Guyon, for all his skill, is like a
mariner

> When foggy mistes, or cloudy tempests have
> The faithfull light of that faire lampe yblent,
> And cover'd heaven with hideous dreriment, . . .

Spenser habitually describes the eclipse of reason and virtue in terms
of mists and clouds which obscure the light, and when Guyon's light
is hidden by them, he has to make do with the inferior guidance of his
map and compass:

> Upon his card and compass firmes his eye,
> The maisters of his long experiment, . . .          (II.vii.1)

The distinction is clearly between that knowledge which comes from
an authentic glimpse of the divine truths and that which results from
studying the record of human experience and learning the lessons of
past actions. For this reason Spenser tells us that Guyon, "having lost
his trusty guide," goes on his way feeding himself with comfort

> Of his own vertues, and prayse-worthy deedes.
>                                                          (II.vii.2)

The memory of these is all he has to steer by, and we shall see that his
mistakes are mainly caused by this fact. The Palmer is the judge par
excellence of what is a good or a bad Occasion, and the fact that he

---

[2] Edgar Wind, *Pagan Mysteries of the Renaissance* (London, 1958), pp. 106–8.

accompanies Guyon neither on the Idle Lake nor into the Cave of Mammon is a fair indication that Guyon is out of his true way.

Guyon's behavior in the absence of his Palmer bears this out. From the moment that a little idle mirth separates him from his guide, he is very uncertain in his moral judgments. It is generally assumed, for example, that Guyon resists the temptations of Phaedria, but this does not seem to me to be wholly true. Certainly Guyon is not attracted by her; the "great contentment" which her "light behaviour and loose dalliance" gives to Cymochles is not for him, and he goes ashore as soon as he can. Nevertheless he has made a compromise with her; he is careful to be polite to her, not to seem

> . . . so rude, and thewed ill,
> As to despise so courteous seeming part . . .
>
> (II.vi.26)

He allows himself to be persuaded to a peace with Cymochles, and when he leaves the boat he "to that damsell thankes gave for reward." Guyon is, in fact, trying to steer his course by the map of his own past virtues, and having learned in his previous adventure to avoid the Occasion of Fury, he mistakenly tries to overcome the temptations of pleasure by the same means. He is studiously mild when the proper virtue would have been the virtuous and merciless wrath which Arthur shows against Cymochles in Canto VIII, or the contempt which the Palmer himself pours on Phaedria when they meet her on the way to the Bower of Blisse. By giving way to Phaedria's amorous pleas and sparing Cymochles, Guyon has taken on something of Cymochles's wavering nature and is in part defiled.

Spenser gives us the clearest warning of the dangers involved in the little boat when it first comes to shore:

> A little Gondelay, bedecked trim
> With boughes and arbours woven cunningly,
> That like a little forrest seemed outwardly . . .
>
> (II.vii.2)

It is so slight and charming, straight out of the popular Romances, and a fitting featherweight symbol for the momentary pleasures of an idle joke; yet it is constructed with the same cunning art as the Bower of Blisse, and it is an outpost of the great forest in whose shade all the bestial passions, the lustful foresters and evil cave dwellers of *The Faerie Queene* have their being. Guyon is not in a position, as we are, to recognize the symbolism and so he goes on towards his fall. In consequence there is no Palmer waiting for him when he comes ashore, and his journey onward to the Cave of Mammon is both misguided and fruitless:

> Long so he rode, yet no adventure found,
> Which fame of her shrill trompet worthy reedes:
> For still he traveild through wide wastfull ground,
> That nought but desert widernesse shew'd all around.
> At last he came unto a gloomy glade,
> Cover'd with boughes and shrubs from heaven's light . . .
>
> (II.vii.2–3)

The little forest of the Gondelay has led him into a much larger forest of temptation.

Guyon enters the Cave of Mammon of his own free will, and Mr. Berger [3] accuses him of the sin of inordinate curiosity, whereas Professor Kermode praises him for the desire to test and strengthen his virtue. The two interpretations are not incompatible. Guyon goes in, conscious of his role as a temperate man and anxious to discover whether there can be a virtuous mean in regard to what Mammon has to offer; that is why he looks into everything and wants to know whether the gold is "well got." His earlier training in virtue has given him all the answers to the rather conventional temptations which he encounters, and he rejects everything with an almost ascetic contempt. His victory over temptation is as complete as that of Christ over Satan —with this difference, however, that Guyon is not Christ and he has therefore to pay the penalty for driving his virtue so hard that it has itself become almost a form of excess. A human being has only so much resistance and Guyon's three-day Marathon absorbs it all. The physical exhaustion produced by the strain of his prolonged vigilance is the cause of the attack by Pyrochles and Cymochles which he is now too weak to resist.

His fall is due to Pride: he has failed to realize the limitations of human strength and, as we have seen, he is overconfident in his own virtues and praiseworthy deeds, so that he squanders his virtue in seeking out occasions for its exercise which he would have been wiser to avoid. It is not until he has visited the House of Alma and understood the subtle interdependence of physical and spiritual fitness that he finally learns the wisdom of avoiding unnecessary trials. He crosses the sea to the Bower of Blisse in safety only because he knows when to steer away from temptation, so that he may conserve his energies for those temptations from within which have to be resisted.

[3] Harry Berger, *The Allegorical Temper* (New Haven, 1957), pp. 18–24.

It is important to realize that Guyon in his fall follows the general pattern of Spenser's heroes. They are all able to resist the head-on attack of temptation but they fall immediately after they have resisted it and because they have done so. Redcross resists all the allurements of Lucifera but falls as soon as he escapes from her palace through very pride in his own powers of resistance; Amoret holds out against all the temptations of illicit love which Busyrane can force upon her, only to be seized by lust when under the protection of Britomart—in other words, when she is virtuously married. Arthegall defeats Radegund but is betrayed by an impulse of misplaced mercy at the moment of his triumph, and Calidore is deflected from his quest not by a vice but by the dream of an unfallen world which the pastoral idyll seems to offer him. The triumph of our virtue either makes us vainglorious or makes us relax into unwariness, or, as in the case of Guyon, exhausts our stock of resistance. If we drive sin out of the front door it creeps in at the back again and attacks us from another direction. This is the point which Spenser is making in his account of the fight between Arthur and Maleger. Maleger begins with a direct attack on the five senses, but when this fails he fights by running away, and as Arthur rushes in pursuit, he is seized from behind by Impotence and Impatience. Maleger has used a sort of moral jujitsu to trip Arthur up by the very force of his own resistance, and this is exactly how Guyon falls. The resemblance is underlined by the fact that both knights "began to faint and life decay."

Seen in its entirety, therefore, the adventure with Mammon is an allegory not of heroism but of human weakness, and Guyon has to learn what Arthur by his very nature always knew, that the only answer to the subtleties of sin is divine Grace. Arthur is twice saved by Grace alone in his fight with Maleger, and Canto VIII makes the same point in relation to Guyon and to mankind in general. The canto is concerned with Redemption. Guyon's faint clearly symbolizes the Fall of Adam. The Palmer talks of Guyon as if he were actually dead:

> Certes, Sir Knight, ye bene too much to blame,
> Thus for to blot the honour of the dead, . . .        (II.viii.13)

and he is continually described in language which suggests his complete degradation:

> For why should a dead dog be deckt in armour bright?
>
> (II.viii.15)

Even Arthur agrees that such degradation goes beyond Guyon himself
and extends to all his issue, both direct and indirect:

> Indeed (then said the Prince) the evill donne
> Dyes not, when breath the bodie first doth leave,
> But from the grandsyre to the Nephewes sonne,
> And all his seed the curse doth often cleave,
> Till vengeance utterly the guilt bereave: . . .     (II.viii.29)

The reference is obviously to Original Sin, and Cymochles demands
the full penalty for the sin of Adam:

> Why should not that dead carrion satisfie
> The guilt, which if he lived had thus long,
> His life for due revenge should deare abie?     (II.viii.28)

Arthur, however, pleads for mercy, and Guyon receives mercy although
he has not merited it. Spenser, as Vergil K. Whitaker has shown, followed the Anglican interpretation of the doctrine of Justification.[4]
Like Milton he believed the Fall to be only partial since God immediately restored to Adam and his seed a modicum of that reason
which had been forfeited through sin—not enough to control the cor-
rupted will but enough, at least, to enable man to recognize good from
evil and to desire the good. As a further act of Grace, God sent his son
to pay the penalty that Adam had incurred and to offer redemption
to those who choose to believe in him. This is the traditional scheme
of Grace which Milton outlines in Book III of *Paradise Lost,* and it is
the theme which dictates the allegory of Canto VIII. As soon as Guyon
faints, Grace descends to him in the form of the Angel:

> . . . But O th'exceeding grace
> Of highest God, that loves his creatures so, . . .
>
>                                              (II.viii.1)

The angel does not, however, save Guyon himself; instead, he restores
to him his reason—the Palmer hears the voice and comes to his master.
It is a reason weakened by the Fall: The Palmer is no longer a match
for Pyrochles and he cannot help Guyon to tie up Occasion as he has
in the past. He can, however, call on Arthur for help, and Arthur in
rescuing Guyon symbolizes Christ the Redeemer. That is why Spenser
makes him win the fight with the help of Guyon's sword which the
Palmer hands to him, his own having been stolen; it is with man's

---

[4] Virgil K. Whitaker, *The Religious Basis of Spenser's Thought* (Stanford, 1950),
pp. 34–49.

weapons that Arthur triumphs and it was as a man that Christ redeemed mankind. It is no accident that Pyrochles, seeing death approaching, cries out "Harrow and well away," like the devil in the old
play. As soon as the knights of intemperance are destroyed, Guyon
rises up fresh and new, redeemed from his sin by his rational capacity
to believe in his Redeemer and accept the proffered grace of God. He
turns to Arthur "with reverence dew" and, thanking him for the life
which his "great graces" have preserved, swears to be ever bound to
him (II.viii.55). Professor Kermode is surely wrong in comparing the
angel who succors Guyon to the angels who ministered to Christ after
his temptation in the desert. The true parallel to the angels of Christ
is the servants of Alma by whom Arthur is tended, after his fight with
Maleger.

> Where many Groomes and Squiers readie were,
> To take him from his steed full tenderly,
> And eke the fairest Alma met him there
> With balme and wine and costly spicery
> To comfort him in his infirmity:                         (II.xi.49)

Cantos VI, VII, and VIII, therefore, are of crucial importance in the
education of Guyon, since they show his discovery not only of human
weakness but of the Christian answer to it. In this respect I disagree
with Mr. Berger who finds no such development.[5] To him, Book II is
a study in contrast between the Aristotelian and the Christian conceptions of temperance, the former based on self sufficiency, the latter
rising from a profounder sense of human weakness. Guyon is the
knight of the one, Arthur of the other, and they go their separate ways
meeting the temptations proper to their natures, but operating in
entirely separate spheres of experience. Guyon does not stay to fight
Maleger because he himself, with his ideal of rational control, is in-
different to the sort of physical weaknesses of which Maleger is the
source. In the Bower of Blisse he becomes, for the first time, uneasily
aware that such weaknesses do exist within his own nature, and hence
the excessive anger with which he smashes the Bower; but for Mr.
Berger there is no question of Guyon ever abandoning the classic for
the Christian ideal.

Such an interpretation is contrary to the general pattern of the
other books of *The Faerie Queene,* all of which are concerned with
the education of a single hero in his special virtue, while Arthur
demonstrates the perfection of that same virtue. Mr. Berger is right

---

[5] *The Allegorical Temper, loc. cit.*

in seeing Guyon as the embodiment of Aristotelian virtue when he sets out; his armor is perfect and undinted, his horsemanship is assured and his allegiance to the rather academic temperance of Medina's household is complete. Yet from the start he is placed in situations which suggest with some irony the human weakness of which he is still ignorant. The procession in Canto II, for example, when Guyon carries the sullied armor of Mordaunt and the Palmer follows with the bloody-handed babe, might almost be an emblem of Original Sin, and to cap it, Guyon finds his horse stolen: The best horseman of them all without a horse on which to demonstrate his peculiar excellence—this is the imperfect life which Guyon hopes to govern by reason alone. His fall is gradual and the culmination of all that has gone before. The only difference after his rescue by Arthur is that he knows that he is liable to fall but he has also learned, like Redcross, that no fall need be final. He has learned how easily his Palmer may be lost, but also the heavenly strength which lies within the Palmer. He therefore goes on to face the same temptations as Arthur has already faced in defense of the house of Alma; the owls, the hounds and the snails which besiege the citadel, each one embodying the excess of a particular sense, are only an allegorical expression of the sensuous temptations which assail the ears and eyes of Guyon in the Bower. On this occasion he resists with the help of his restored reason, but another time he may fail as Redcross will fail; neither he nor his Palmer is strong enough to convert Gryll from his hoggishness. Yet the final message is one of hope; Acrasia's latest victim is rescued, and the name Verdant in place of the earlier Mordaunt is symbolic of the hope of Grace. Verdant is only the "few green ears" of Herbert's poem, but he contains the ultimate hope of the ring which Spenser must have expressed by the marriage of Una and Redcross if he had completed the poem.

Book II then shows the Christianization of Guyon and in this it embodies at greater length the historical allegory which Mr. Berger traces through the Chronicle of British Kings.[6] As the Pagan gives way to the Christian in British history, so Medina gives way to Arthur in Guyon, and so too in Book I Una leaves the classical temperance of Satyrane for the Christian protection of Arthur. This analogy between Books I and II is yet another of the innumerable parallels which exist between the two books, the reason for which has never been fully explained. Why did Spenser make his two heroes go through such precisely parallel sequences of adventures? An answer perhaps lies in the fact that the two books are dealing with complementary aspects of the

6 *The Allegorical Temper,* pp. 89–114.

same theological scheme. Salvation demands both faith in the grace
and mercy of God as manifested through the Redeemer, and reason
by which to choose and follow that faith through an act of free will.
Both halves of this circle of love are necessary; heaven only stoops to us
provided that we struggle upwards to the extent of our limited powers.
In the words of Hooker:

> His prayer must not exclude our labour. . . . Surely if we look to stand
> in the faith of the sons of God, we must hourly, continually, be providing
> and setting ourselves to strive. It was not the meaning of our Lord and
> Saviour in saying "Father, keep them in thy name," that we should be
> careless to keep ourselves. To our own safety, our sedulity is required.[7]

Both books embody the whole double process, but the emphasis in
Book I is on faith, and in Book II, on reason. Book I is the book of
rescues; Book II that of the human struggle. As Redcross is rescued
from Orgoglio, the Law, and from Despair and the Dragon of Sin by
the promise of the Gospels, so Guyon learns never to slacken in his
quest:

> Before her gate high God did Sweat ordaine,
> And wakefull watches ever to abide: . . .          (II.iii.41)

If Book I corresponds to the Scheme of Redemption which God pro-
pounds in the third book of *Paradise Lost,* Book II presents the successful struggle of Adam and Eve after the Fall to avail themselves of
the offered Grace. The two processes are inseparable and the two
knights represent the same humanity looked at from different angles.
Together they make up the full story of Christian Redemption.

[7] Sermon on the Certainty & Perpetuity of Faith in the Elect, in *The Works of
R. H. Hooker,* arranged by J. Keble (Oxford, 1865), III, 480.

# Venus and Diana:
# Some Uses of Myth in
## *The Faerie Queene*

### *by Kathleen Williams*

The aim of this paper is to suggest and examine some of the ways
in which the resources of classical mythology are used by Spenser in
the third and fourth books of *The Faerie Queene*. Any such attempt
must be made with some misgiving, for definitions can convey little
of the deep responsiveness with which such a poet as Spenser apprehends his myths, and of the richness and fullness of meaning which
they have for him. The present study is limited, therefore, to an aspect
which I think it is possible to isolate in terms of the main themes of
these two books: the relating of material, through myth, so as to out-
line what Spenser calls the "general intention." Even so limited a
treatment must distort, by the drastic omission which is necessarily involved, but that organizing function of Spenser's myths which I shall
try to isolate is, at least, one which should suffer less than others from
the hazard of definition.

In the more recent of the many partial explications of *The Faerie
Queene,* the third and fourth books have been, comparatively, little
treated, except as they help to reveal the meaning of other books, as
in the now time-honored association of the Garden of Adonis with
Guyon's Bower of Bliss. The most favored books of late have been
those Of Holiness and Of Temperance, and though many details are
still arguable and are likely to remain so we have been made aware
of the precision with which these books operate within the framework
of their intellectual systems, theological and moral. Whatever the
theoretical relationship of these systems, they are present as a scheme

From *English Literary History,* XXVIII, No. 2 (1961), 101–21. Copyright © 1961
by The Johns Hopkins Press. Reprinted by permission of The Johns Hopkins Press.
A revised version of this essay is included in Miss Williams' *Spenser's World of
Glass* (Berkeley and Los Angeles: University of California Press, 1966).

which supports a clearly outlined narrative structure: temptations are encountered and a quest achieved. The scheme helps, moreover, to guide our interpretations, including interpretations of the meanings contributed by classical myth, both where it is used directly and where it enters in the allusive form of an original adaptation, as in the case of the Circe-like enchantress Acrasia. So, for example, when Guyon encounters Tantalus in the depths of Mammon's cave, we relate him to the moral error which is here under consideration, and recognize that he is present primarily as the moralized Tantalus, signifying that avarice which is the less satisfied the more it acquires. Myth defines meanings but is in its turn defined, as to its central and particular meaning, by the precision of its context. Similarly, in the House of Pride, Lucifera's name alone would be enough to suggest, when she is compared to Phaeton, what the chief point of the comparison is to be. Lucifer, the star who fell, the light bearer whose light turned to destructive fire, is paralleled by Phaeton who inflamed the sky "with fire not made to burne, but fairely for to shyne" (I.iv.9). Phaeton, appearing in connection with pride and with Lucifer who fell through pride, is related to a specific sin. Of course, this guidance is further enforced by the particular and local wording, as well as by the context of the book as a whole; for example, by the repetition which makes the transition from Lucifera to Phaeton in terms of excess:

> Yet her bright blazing beautie did assay
> To dim the brightnesse of her glorious throne,
> As envying her selfe, that too exceeding shone.

> Exceeding shone, like *Phœbus* fairest childe.                          (iv.8–9)

In both these examples, mythological figures are referred to directly and briefly, but the same particularity of relationship is found in the more allusive use of myth and legend, where the original story echoes through the adventure of the knight. Guyon's voyage to Acrasia's Bower is like the voyage of Ulysses because Ulysses was a type of temperate wisdom; both he and Guyon undertook an adventure constantly repeated in the life of moral man, as Redcross achieved the unending quest of the Christian soul. The infinite resonance of the ancient and familiar stories is heard of course through Spenser's words—the steadfast toil of Ulysses, the pathos and waste of Phaeton's fall as of Lucifer's, the horror of Tantalus, and this is a great part of their significance. But in each case the point of contact between the myth and Spenser's narrative is exactly placed in relation to the book's central meaning, although that meaning does not comprehend the full significance for him, or the full effect upon us, of the comparison or the allusion.

Thus the first two books have, from the nature of their subjects, a kind of precision which in general it is not too difficult to tabulate. Structure and meaning are interdependent, and illustrative or enriching mythological material can be seen as exact in its primary function, so far as that can be differentiated from the aura of indefinable association which necessarily accompanies and develops it. In the third and fourth books this is, I believe, still true; but the structure, unsupported by a traditional or logical series of temptations and a final victory over dragon or enchantress, is of a different kind, and mythology is used more pervasively and perhaps with more complication. Indeed myth here is itself, in a sense, an element of structure, in that the meanings are in part built up by connections between a few mythological situations and, especially, mythological or legendary personages, who appear in some cases as themselves and also as elements in the characters of Spenser's invention. Thus the characters are interrelated by their relation to a common center, and the shaping of the material depends to a considerable degree upon this common reference.

In such an arrangement, the myths and legends have to work rather harder, and must often have more than one such central and definable function. One of their tasks approximates to that of the Ulysses story in Book II. Marinell recalls very clearly certain episodes in the life of Achilles, while Artegall no less clearly recalls both Achilles and Hercules. But even here the use of mythology is less straightforward. As a type of the just hero, using his strength to overthrow injustice and inhumanity, Hercules is relevant to Artegall as was Ulysses to Guyon. But whereas in the second book other aspects of Ulysses' character are not relevant, and we are given no opportunity to consider them—his reputation for craftiness, or for the betrayal of his comrades—in Artegall's case we are led, by the choice of incidents, to remember that Hercules had other characteristics as well as an unusual facility in destroying monsters. His labors as a whole properly represented the exercise of justice, but he was known also for his uncontrolled temper and for his readiness to submit to the feminine tyranny of Omphale, or as Spenser has it, of Iole, who showed her power over the hero by making him sit at her spinning wheel. Similarly the fierce and wrathful warrior Achilles possessed a streak of feminine softness which in the centuries after Homer had been more fully treated by the narrators of new versions of the fall of Troy. The moralization of myth here takes second place to the paradoxical elements in the figures of classical story; different aspects are developed which establish meanings through their relation either within one character or between two characters. Spenser's attitude to the myths and legends is, rightly, arbitrary; as Diodorus Siculus advises, he "takes out of them that which is to the purpose, and is in the form of a similitude." Arbitrary, but never, I think, unjustifiable. The use he makes of them is always genuinely, if embryonically, present in the myth, is usually traditional, and is pointed to in Spenser's text. And through the deliberate playing of these "similitudes" against one another, a considerable complexity of meaning is established in perhaps the most economical of all possible ways, that of contrast.

That Spenser makes much use of contrast within likeness has of course long been recognized, and parallelism between two complete books, Holiness and Temperance, has lately been rewardingly explored by Mr. A. C. Hamilton. But in the books which I propose to consider, the method is especially marked and works in a particular way. The figures of myth constitute a firm center of reference, and the paradoxical quality suggested by a character such as Achilles can then be developed through similarities within difference, and differences within similarity, in a series of related persons. The structure and the meaning which is inseparable from structure here depend chiefly upon such relationships and not upon a progressive narrative. The contrasts, moreover, are now arranged so as to establish the meaning of characters rather than of events. Both, of course, are still important; but whereas in the preceding books one main figure has to encounter a number of different situations, here several more or less main figures have to encounter rather similar situations, and the most important point of differentiation is in their varying reactions. In the first and second books, it is important to know as exactly as we can what the cave of Mammon or the dungeons of Orgoglio are. In the third and fourth, it is at least as important to differentiate between the main figures themselves, within the context suggested by their relation to Achilles, Diana, and the rest, as it is to differentiate between the hyenas, giants, wild men or foul fosters who throng their paths. Certain places, indeed, are in themselves important, as are the houses of Malecasta and Busyrane, the Temple of Venus, or Isis Church, which though it occurs in the fifth book has relevance to preceding stories. But even these contribute to the system of parallel and contrast between persons: Implicit in them is an unavoidable comparison in behavior.

The stories of the chief invented characters, therefore, have a certain rough similarity. Of Amoret, Florimell, and Britomart, each is separated from or searching for a particular knight, but in every case the behavior of the characters is different. Arthur, seeking Gloriana, is another parallel with a difference, and he here serves to bring out further aspects of the theme. Belphoebe, as twin sister of Amoret, is an important part of the whole system of comparison. But Britomart, being both a knight and a woman in search of a knight, is related by likeness and difference to most of the others. They are the faulty attempts at solving the problems set by the figures of myth: she is the complete success. In this sense Britomart dominates the third book as fully as Redcross and Guyon do theirs. In Book IV she takes part, and powerfully, in the action, but there is here no one dominant knight. Instead we have, appropriately to the theme, a dominant group of knights, Cambel and the three sons of Agape, set in symmetrical relationship and forming, in themselves, a unity, a unity which is emphasized by another tournament which stands over against theirs, the tournament for Florimell's girdle, a scene of pointless and chaotic strife. As Britomart presents the theme of Book III in its aspect of success and of completeness, so does this close-knit group present the theme of Book IV. But the themes are two aspects of the same thing, and to speak of the books as one is usual and, I think, legitimate. Technically entitled the Legends of Chastity and of Friendship, they examine the same subject, love, with slightly differing emphasis; love is a kind of friendship, friendship a kind of love. For this reason, the troubled adventures of Amoret and Scudamour, Florimell and Marinell, Britomart and Artegall, are continued in the Book Of Friendship and indeed beyond that book.

The series of relationships which builds up both books is repeated in little, and in much more schematic form, within the dominant group of Book IV. First, the three sons of Agape unfold, it has been said, the nature of Agape itself. The differences between the three warrior brothers are real, but complementary, and contribute to a common unity:

> Like three faire branches budding farre and wide,
> That from one roote deriv'd their vitall sap.        (IV.ii.43)

When two brothers are killed by Cambel, the third, Triamond, possesses both their souls, and all is knit together by a marriage between the two pairs of brother and sister. Thus the group presents an example of the workings of strife and friendship, and of love as an aspect of friendship; an example of concord, schematically shown through the relations not only of two warriors but of the two warriors and the ladies who restrain and accord them, the wedding of force with gentleness, enmity with love. This is a dominant theme of both books; both might be called the Legend of Concord, for the idea of concord in its Renaissance signification underlies the whole structure of likeness and difference, of inadequacy overcome by the conjunction of opposites which, when alone, are useless or even harmful. The subjects of chastity and of friendship are both developed in relation to true and false *concordia*.

The most precise and particular statement of the nature of concord is that given in Scudamour's description of the Temple of Venus. Outside the Temple stand two young men,

> Both strongly arm'd, as fearing one another;
> Yet were they brethren both of halfe the blood,
> Begotten by two fathers of one mother,
> Though of contrarie natures each to other:
> The one of them hight Love, the other Hate.          (IV.x.32)

Between them stands Concord, tempering them so well that she forces them to join hands, just as she keeps the world steady by holding "with her blessed hands" air and fire, lands and waters. Concord involves opposition accorded, an equilibrium of opposing principles expressed, in another familiar version of the same conception, by the birth of Harmonia from the union of Mars and Venus. This Renaissance commonplace possessed both profundity and adaptability, and could be applied cosmically, politically, or socially; to friendships and loves, or to the completion of the individual human personality. By taking such a conception as the central idea of his books on love Spenser is able to include a very great deal, for relationships and cross-relationships like those suggested in the true concord of Cambel, Triamond, Canacee and Cambina, or in the imperfect concord of Venus and Diana, can be economically suggested. The idea of discords tempered was not only familiar to Spenser—it could not have failed to be that—but seems far more than an accepted commonplace. It is present elsewhere in *The Faerie Queene* and elsewhere in the poems. In cosmic terms, *An Hymne of Love* tells how love at the creation of the world set the elements in order,

> tempering goodly well
> Their contrary dislikes with loved meanes,

while in the human terms of the *Amoretti* the warring lovers are bound at last in a league that no discord can spill. It is through divine or human love that concord was most readily presented.

So in the two central books of *The Faerie Queene* the discords, discords incompletely or falsely resolved, and discords properly tempered in concord, are displayed through the behavior of different characters in similar situations, the characters being elucidated by their common reference to figures of classical myth; and these figures are themselves capable of considerable manipulation, since their attributes or their stories had already been seen as giving them a certain ambiguity of meaning. The two on whom I propose to concentrate by way of example, Venus and Diana, make an appearance in the poem in their own persons. Together, they form one point of reference for several of the characters: the problem of relationship, of concord, which they pose is developed in a series of variations.

Venus and Diana make their very spirited joint personal appearance in the third book, and are closely connected there with their respective wards, Amoret and Belphoebe. They are introduced, indeed, by way of explaining the nature of Belphoebe and, later, of Amoret. Their encounter takes place because Venus, searching for her lost child Cupid, enlists Diana's aid in finding him, and their conversation on the subject strikes a rather curious note. It has been described as a débat through which the two unfriendly goddesses reach a reconciliation, but one might more accurately term it a rather suspect alliance in which the two opposing principles are ready surreptitiously to borrow each others' functions, a false imitation of concord. Each is spiteful and jealous, but it is Venus who comes off best in the encounter with her suggestion that Diana's train of nymphs may not be quite what it seems. Here, she hints, is precisely the place for her to start looking for Cupid. The nymphs may well be hiding him; he may even now be present, disguised as one of them. The quarrel is smoothed over, but the suggestion that a hidden relationship exists between Diana's followers and Cupid is firmly established. It emerges into the next stage of the story, where the goddesses, searching for Cupid, instead find and adopt the twin children born without inherited sin,

> Pure and unspotted from all loathly crime,
> That is ingenerate in fleshly slime.          (III.vi.3)

Why these two, who never know each other during the course of the existing poem, are presented as twin sisters, has often been considered. One modern scholar dismisses the relationship as a caprice on Spenser's part, but more usually it is suggested that their virtues are of equal value, or are complementary. It is also possible that the sisters, offspring of a single birth, are complementary in the sense that they should not have been parted, and that their relationship underlines, or is underlined by, that of Venus and Diana, who stand opposed to each other and yet have a devious and hidden kind of kinship.

The kinship had been hinted at often enough, in art and in literature, and it could have various meanings, serious or frivolous, sound or suspect, according as emphasis was placed. It survived vigorously until the early eighteenth century, when that understanding Spenserian Matthew Prior used it in his *Cloe Hunting,* and it occurs in a stanza, translated from Marot, which was printed following the *Amoretti:*

> As Diane hunted on a day,
> She chaunst to come where Cupid lay,
>   his quiver by his head:
> One of his shafts she stole away,
> And one of hers did close convay,
>   into the others stead:
>     With that love wounded my loves hart,
>     but Diane beasts with Cupids dart.

Cupid shoots with the arrows of Diana, Diana with the arrows of Cupid; a kind of complicated interchange is set up in which chastity becomes a weapon of love, or uses love as a weapon. That arrows were used by both Cupid and Diana made an appropriate hinge on which such relationships could turn. And Diana's ward Belphoebe the huntress grows up to wound Timias

> Through an unwary dart, which did rebound
> From her faire eyes and gracious countenance          (III.v.42)

even as she tries to cure the wound he has already received from the cruel shaft of the foster. Indeed there is in the remote and radiant figure of Belphoebe something of the strangeness of the Venus/Diana exchanges. In the course of her pursuit of a wounded beast she is led straight to the wounded Timias, one quarry replacing another. So in Book II, where she first and briefly appears, the same pursuit leads her to Trompart and the hidden Braggadocchio, whom she almost shoots in mistake for her rightful quarry, the wounded hind.

In that earlier appearance Belphoebe is, of course, modelled on the appearance of Venus, in the guise of a huntress nymph, to Aeneas in Vergil's first book. Spenser's is an intricately beautiful passage in which both the Venus aspect and the Diana aspect suggested by the Vergilian parallel are emphasized and enriched. The long description is full of the sensuous imagery of the Canticles, while Belphoebe's clothes are an elaborately decorative and gorgeous version of the simple robe and buskin of the huntress. The analogy with Venus/Diana here is usually seen as relating to the allegorical meanings which were attributed to Vergil's Venus by Neoplatonic commentators, Venus Urania manifesting herself in active life, "the beauty of moral ideals." Some such meaning is certainly applicable to the Belphoebe of Book II, and indeed remains applicable to her appearance in Book III, for throughout there is attached to her a splendor, a suggestion of the rarefied and ideal. But in the third book, where she takes a much greater part in the action, this does not quite account for her. She is here not only the embodiment of an ideal, momentarily revealed; she is rather a person seen as, and behaving as, an ideal. Her remote and not quite human aspiration is seen in relation to another theme; her innocence is considered in its effects upon ordinary fallen humanity. When Timias wakes from his faint to see her, we are referred back to Book II by his speech,

> Angell, or Goddesse do I call thee right?
> What service may I do unto thee meete,

> (III.v.35)

which echoes the speech of Trompart and, with differences, that of Aeneas before him. We are still to remember Belphoebe as Venus/ Diana, and still to appreciate her fineness. But the reminder is straightway followed, here, by the débat of the two goddesses, suggesting that in this book a further aspect of the Venus/Diana connection is to be explored, though without negating the first. Belphoebe acts out her story with Timias, and in doing so she shows herself from another point of view, that of human relationships. She accepts the love of Timias as the adoration due to her, and as requiring no return. As Diana's huntress, she can be loved, but the love must be manifested as worship; yet it is not clearly distinguished from Timias's tenderness to the wounded Amoret, her unknown complement and twin, which is regarded as a breach of faith. "Is this the faith, she said, and said no more." And Timias is returned to her grace through the agency of a dove, bird of Venus as well as of peace, with her present to him tied around its neck, a jewel like a bleeding heart. But in or out of favor the situation is at no point presented as a true good for Timias, for by it he is not inspired to greatness but is kept from his proper task, the quest, as Arthur's squire, for glory. Refusing to make himself known

to Arthur, who is wasting time in looking for him, he lives uselessly
and ignobly, "all mindlesse of his owne deare Lord." His devotion, it
seems, should be to something else.

Spenser is here showing us, I think, not the result of worship of an
ideal, but the result of worship of the lady *as* an ideal, and he regards
it with sympathy and with scepticism. What Belphoebe demands, and
Timias attempts, is shown in action as a very uneasy thing. Her excellence remains, but it is too simple and one-sided an excellence for a
complicated world. Genuine in itself, it yet produces a confusion of
effects it never intends, when Belphoebe emerges from her own isolated
"earthly paradise" in the midst of the forest of the passions. In the
real world, the arrows of Diana can have an effect hard to be distinguished from that of the arrows of Cupid; the chase of honor can turn,
however unintentionally, into the chase of love. Belphoebe, set apart
by her innocent birth and by Diana's training, and at home in her own
paradise, seems never fully to comprehend the people she meets; her
behavior is not quite adapted to a fallen and a complex state. The
nonhuman nobleness which is a tribute to a queen operates a little
differently in the moral world of the poem as a whole.

Like Belphoebe, Amoret is brought up in a highly specialized environment, and again like her sister she demonstrates the problems
raised, in the real world, by the simplifications which are in place in
an earthly paradise. But where Belphoebe is martial and fiercely
aspiring, Amoret is wholly submissive, for she is reared by Venus in
"true feminitee," "In all the lore of love, and goodly womanhead."
As a child she is brought up in the Garden of Adonis, for which in a
sense her innocent birth fits her. The Garden, one knows, is a complicated place, but so far as it concerns Amoret it is simple enough,
Venus's joyous earthly paradise,

> the first seminarie
> Of all things, that are borne to live and die,
> According to their kindes.                                    (III.vi.30)

There

> of their owne accord
> All things, as they created were, doe grow,
> And yet remember well the mightie word,
> Which first was spoken by th'Almightie lord,
> That bad them to increase and multiply.                       (vi.34)

As a place of natural generation, it is like the Golden Age—"There
is continuall spring, and harvest there / Continuall"—or more pre-

cisely the paradisal images suggest that it is a kind of Eden, where sensuality is spontaneous, frank, and blameless as in the prelapsarian garden. An etymological connection was of course made. The Garden is walled, protected, but threatened: Time the destroyer is already within the wall, Adonis's boar is imprisoned but alive. Here as in Eden is potential disaster, and the innocent joy of the Garden is as precarious as Amoret's is soon seen to be. It exists only by the rigorous exclusion of whatever may bring harshness and pain. The Cupid who is allowed to enter is not the annoying child or the hostile tyrant, but the benevolent husband of Psyche and father of Pleasure. He must lay his sad darts aside and leave the "spoiles and cruelty" with which he has ransacked the "world," the real and painful and fallen world, and here Psyche, her troubles over, brings up Amoret with the child pleasure. In this aspect, the Garden is essentially the same as Love's heaven or paradise in *An Hymne of Love,* the dream of the miserable lover in the real world, a place free from "the gnawing envie, the hart-fretting feare." This paradise, like the Garden, is the home of Pleasure, and she dwells there without pain and without blame. A similar distance from painful reality is suggested in the reference to the Garden of Adonis in Book II, where it occurs as the equivalent of Eden in the Elfin History, the place where the first Elfe, newly created by Prometheus, finds the first Fay. Again the parallel is with innocence, with love and indeed with life itself as natural, simple, and protected, lacking all fierceness or self-assertion. To attain concord, here, is made unnecessary, for the discord which it should surmount is not allowed to intrude. Instead of Mars, Adonis, an Adonis who hunts no longer; and even Cupid's weapons must be left outside the walls.

From this protected happiness Amoret has to go into the "world" of "spoiles and cruelty," of strife and inherited sin, where even love is also war; into Venus' other domain, denoted by her Temple, guarded as it is by Hate and Love, their hands forcibly linked by Concord. In the "world," the meaning of Amoret's mythological background as Venus's ward is developed and defined by its relation to the tradition of courtly love. This is itself used metaphorically to express a certain attitude to human relationships which has its classical and its modern, as well as its medieval, forms, and which owes its enduring power to its expression (though its distorted expression) of a truth: that in personal relationships, and in love as the most intense and so most representative of such relationships, there is always an element of hostility. The truth as realistically and maturely interpreted can be found in the *Amoretti,* which are built up partly through variations on this theme. The lady is warrior, tyrant, even traitor, the lover is huntsman, and both fear the prison of love, the loss of liberty to the other. Yet at the close of the sequence the hostility is resolved, the prisoned birds sing, the spider and the bee live in eternal peace. But there are other handlings of the theme in which love stops eternally short of concord, in which the warfare and the chase are perpetual and mutual, in which each feels and inflicts pain, and endless revenge is disguised as affection. And of course the distortion is itself equally true to human life, and is portrayed by Spenser with equal insight.

It is this which the submissive and feminine Amoret, reared in a place from which all hostility is barred, and wholly lacking in the aggressive self-reliance which characterizes her huntress sister, has now to face. All assertion of self she sees as menacing and terrible, and what to Scudamour is a mere convention of behavior becomes to her an obsessive reality. Scudamour fights twenty knights, enters the Temple of Venus, and terrifies Amoret's guardians with his shield, on which, since he is "Cupid's man," the sincere but conventional courtly lover, is emblazoned the cruel Cupid excluded from the Garden of Adonis, "Cupid with his killing bow / And cruell shafts." He then leads out the protesting Amoret as the prize of his prowess, while the statue of Venus, with the doubtful quality she possesses in the human world, laughs her approval of the desecration of her Temple. Cupid may be shut out of the Temple, replaced by his small and harmless brothers; yet Scudamour his representative is, as he himself suggests, drawn in to that same Temple by its appurtenances, the danger, the parade of modesty, the white-robed virgin priestesses, the exclusive femininity. Venus, the great natural creative power of the universe, is ready to depend for the fulfillment of her purpose in the human world upon hostility, the weapons of Diana and the spoils of Cupid, upon exclusiveness set as a snare for violence. Human happiness, after all, is no part of her concern.

This, at least, is how Amoret comes to see her situation, when she has been taken from the Temple as Eurydice was taken from the underworld. The comparison is Scudamour's, proud of an enterprise as dangerous as that of Orpheus; the irony is Spenser's, for as Eurydice was lost again from the threshold of the living world, so is Amoret, on the day of her wedding, lost to the deathlike enchantments of Busyrane, and imprisoned in her own obsession. The shadowy Maske of Cupid which conveys her away contains some of the conventional denizens of the Temple of Venus and of the courtly tradition, Danger, and Doubt; but now their traditional function is changed, and from the lady's devices against the lover they have become the torturers of the lady herself. Of them there are as many

> as there be phantasies
> In wavering wemens wit, that none can tell,
> Of paines in love, or punishments in hell.

> (III.xii.26)

Busyrane, who sacrifices Amoret to the destructive Cupid, is presumably named from Busiris, who made human sacrifices to his own god in Egypt. He appears in the mythological commentators and in Diodorus and Apollodorus, but most relevantly in the *Ars Amatoria,*[1] where he is directly related to the Ovidian (and in part courtly) conception of love as hostility and deceit, a perpetual strife in which *concordia* is seen as no more than the momentary defeat of one cruelty by another. Ovid's Busiris is an illustration of the theme that love is the result of deceit, which should be avenged by deceit. "Let them fall into the snares they have set." The victim is equally the hunter and should, as victim, suffer, so Amoret's Doubt and Danger are turned in more terrible form against her. Busyrane's house is decorated everywhere with the predatory and treacherous loves of the gods: gods as bulls or serpents, love which kills as Semele and Daphne were killed.

> Yet was thy love her death, and her death was thy smart.

> (III.xi.36)

Everywhere is portrayed the mutual horror of a situation in which each punishes and is punished, "all Cupids warres they did repeate." Amoret is freed by Britomart, through whom she unthinks her obsession as Busyrane is made to unread his spells, but she is still not free from the cause of the obsession, the fear of assertion as necessarily destructive. Still "His will she feard." Her lack is explained or typified in her past history, and she will not be free until her own soft submissiveness is joined with its opposing principle, gentleness with self-assertive "will" or, in one of Spenser's figures in Book IV, the dove with the falcon. The incompleteness and consequent distortion suggested by the separation of the sisters must be overcome, as it is, in the first version of the poem, in the union of Amoret and

[1] Similar conclusions as to the probable connection of Busyrane with the *Ars Amatoria* have been reached by Mr. Thomas P. Roche, in a paper, "The Challenge to Chastity: Britomart at the House of Busyrane," delivered at the conference of the Modern Language Association in December, 1959. [Published in *PMLA*, LXXVI, 4 (September, 1961), 340–4. Included in revised form in *The Kindly Flame* (Princeton, 1964), pp. 72–88.—ED.]

Scudamour. The hermaphrodite image there used is a symbol of marriage, but of marriage as itself a symbol of the necessary concord of opposites on which the world depends, and individual human welfare also.

In the second version of the poem, this union is displayed not in Amoret's story but in Britomart's. Britomart stands between the separated sisters as an example of completed and integrated human nature, "amiable grace and manly terror" both, the great champion who can help knights and ladies alike because in her are united the masculine and the feminine, the self-sufficient and the dependent, passion and chastity. In her Venus and Diana, Venus and Mars, are in true and unsurreptitious relation. She is accepted on her own terms as knight and as lady, neither potential destroyer nor potential victim; and, herself an example of concord, she achieves a further concord in her connection with Artegall.

How Britomart has become the invincible knight, strong because loving, loving because strong, we are shown after her first appearance in the poem, in the account of her love for Artegall. She has seen him first, and uncomprehendingly, in the magic mirror, and her immediate response has something of Amoret's confused horror. She hints of it to her old nurse Glauce as if it were a brutal and destructive visitation, love for a shadow, unnatural and leading to death. The passage is based on the Vergilian *Ciris,* but it echoes also the talk of Ovid's Myrrha and her nurse in the *Metamorphoses,* and it is related to Scylla, Biblis, Pasiphae, and the whole Ovidian context of perversity and pain. But through the commonsense wisdom represented by Glauce, and through the sense of personal responsibility represented by Merlin, Britomart learns that human affections are guided by divine purpose, that her eyes were led to the mirror by a higher power than Venus, and that her vision of Artegall will lead to the fulfilling of heavenly destiny for centuries to come. The looking glass has shown her not a shadow, an illusion, but a fuller truth than she could otherwise see, for it is a little image of the world, a glass globe

> Like to the world it selfe, and seem'd a world of glas.

> (III.ii.19)

Its virtue is to "shew in perfect sight, / What ever thing was in the world contaynd," "What ever foe had wrought, or frend had faynd." For Britomart love is a mirror of truth, a means to fulfillment through the concord of necessary opposites in herself, in her union with Artegall, and in the history of her race. For Merlin's account of the

future history of Britain, where she and Artegall and their descendants
are to rule, is more than a compliment worked in for the benefit of
Elizabeth Tudor. It serves to convince Britomart that no personal
situation is merely personal, but may have results that go far beyond
ourselves. For her love becomes an instrument of divine providence,
and she accepts completely the responsibility of the fully human being
for its fellows. Her part, Merlin tells her, is to fit herself to cooperate
actively with a creative and purposeful destiny:

> Therefore submit thy wayes unto his will,
> And do by all dew meanes thy destiny fulfill.

> (III.iii.24)

Merlin's prophecy is throughout in terms of the divine, and just,
will, which deals with the Britons as did Jehovah with the Hebrews,
supporting, checking, punishing; and in this process the union of
Artegall with Britomart, of impulsive force with restraining wisdom,
of justice with equity, is to play an essential part, culminating in
the reconciliation of Briton and Saxon under the house of Tudor,
mingling the blood and the attributes of each. In Britomart's story,
the theme of concord is taken beyond the realm of the personal; what
the others cannot attain is for her only a first step. Throughout, her
sense of destiny and responsibility keeps her on her quest where the
others, even Arthur, can be distracted, and always what is stressed is
her constancy, courage, and perfect balance of qualities. She is, in the
phrase of the moralizers of the myths, the true Venus/Diana, or Venus
*armata*, as even her name may suggest: Britomartis, the nymph whose
apotheosis as the moon goddess Diana Dictynna is told in the *Ciris*.
Later, in the prophetic dream of Book V, Britomart becomes Isis the
Queen, the power in whom, as Plutarch and Apuleius would show, all
the goddesses are made one, Cybele, Minerva, Venus, Diana Dictynna.
In the union of Isis with Osiris is the true justice which sustains the
universe.

Complementary to the theme developed through Amoret and Venus,
Belphoebe and Diana, is the related one more briefly hinted at in the
figures of Artegall and Marinell, again in relation to Britomart, who
both represents success and helps them, in their degree, to achieve it.
Here it is Achilles who is the point of classical reference, himself a
sorry failure in the achieving of personal balance and presenting, in
his single figure, an uneasy seesawing of opposites, extremes of ag-
gression and passive submission. Artegall owns Achilles' armor and
emulates his wrathfulness, and he re-enacts also some of the labors of

Hercules. Whether or not Spenser was acquainted with accounts of the ancient rites and statues which accentuate this ambiguity in both heroes, the common classical and medieval treatment would have provided ample material. For Hercules, the subjection to Omphale, re-enacted by Artegall, and death through Deianeira; for Achilles, the disguise among women to escape the danger feared by his mother Thetis, devotion to the Amazon Penthesilea, who thus conquers him even as he kills her (this too lies behind Artegall's defeat by Radigund), and a shameful death at the hands of the effeminate Paris through subjection to Polyxena. These episodes had become, in Comes, Statius, Ovid's *Metamorphoses* and *Ars Amatoria,* and the non-Homeric versions of the siege of Troy, as important as the wrath of Achilles, and their shadowy presence in the adventures of Artegall and Marinell suggests how a nature which cultivates one aspect of itself to the exclusion of its opposite may be overthrown and enthralled by that opposite. Both are exaggeratedly masculine characters; Artegall is first known not as the champion of justice but as the wrathful, wilful knight of *salvagesse sans finesse,* the "tyrant" of the woods where he was reared and the "tyrant" of the tournament of Book IV. He is conquered by the beauty of Britomart, his sword falling from his hand, but in the same way he is conquered by Radigund, submitting as totally to the wrong female warrior as to the right. Scudamour's taunt to him at the earlier defeat, that he is

> now become to live a Ladies thrall,
> That whylome in your minde wont to despise them all
>
> (IV.vi.28)

turns to literal truth in his degrading subjection to Radigund. Artegall lives as the warrior who must either subjugate or be subjugated, who is either all pride or all "humblesse meek." The vision in Isis Church shows what the final harmony is to be. The fierce and at first inimical beast Osiris/Artegall, now tyrannically wrathful and now fawning, is to become with Britomart complete justice, the union of opposed principles operating as the instrument of destiny.

The investigation of true and false concord which I have suggested as one function of the main characters is further emphasized in the story of Marinell and Florimell. As creatures of sea and of meadows, wave and flower, these two provide a version of the theme which underlines its cosmic scope; here one is aware of concord as a universal law. But the story, interlinked with and carefully related to those of Amoret, Britomart, and the rest, suggests also what I must now emphasize, that the mythological connections with which this paper has been concerned form only a part of the complex organization of these books. Adonis, the dead yet living god, and the hunt of death and of love with which he is connected, form another organizing center of meaning, and from it stem the events of the forest, into which character after character plunges, among the "Beares, Lions, and Buls, which romed them around," and the events, also, just outside the forest, in the house of Malecasta. But the subject of the Renaissance Adonis and his hunt is too vast, and its role in *The Faerie Queene* too complex, to be more than touched on here, and it is enough perhaps to suggest that it is linked with that of Venus and Diana as another, yet related, point of reference. Through it, love as destruction or as creation, and death as an end or as a beginning, are shown as part of that structure which is the concord of the world. The flight and pursuit of Florimell, who is imprisoned under the sea for the traditional seven months of darkness, contribute to this theme, but she contributes also to the meaning to which this paper is limited, concord within human nature and between human beings. In this aspect she too is a type of human incompleteness, relating to Amoret, Britomart and Belphoebe in terms of concord and of course of chastity, for each of them portrays one kind of chastity and one kind of love.

Florimell's search for the knight Marinell proves to be very different from Britomart's steady search for Artegall. From the beginning it is in effect a mindless flight, dispersing and distracting the knights from their quests. Only Britomart, apparently rightly, refuses to follow "beauty's chase." A chase, a hunt, is indeed what it soon proves to be, and one of peculiarly futile nature; a flight which, like that of the eternally fleeing nymph, initiates and intensifies pursuit and so helps to bring about the very chase which it is intended to escape. Florimell fears good and bad without distinction, "fears every leaf," and is compared time and again to a dove, a hind, fleeing without discrimination from whatever approaches it. When she first flies past with the streaming hair which is in these books the mark of feminine power she is compared also to a comet, the blazing star "with flaming lockes dispred" which bodes misfortune. Like it, she has no ill intentions of her own, yet she is a source of confusion, turning even Arthur aside into the forest because she seems, in her momentary appearance, something like Gloriana herself. On the other hand she can also be parodied, to the conviction of most of the characters concerned, by the false spirit which is summoned to imitate and impersonate her and which "all the wyles of wemens wits knew passing well." Only when flight is no longer possible for Florimell, and she has been compelled to resist by her own will and resourcefulness the power of Proteus, can she reach Marinell, who has himself been changed by the action of Britomart. Originally a minor Achilles, fiercely acquisitive yet weakly self-protective, Marinell grows after his wounding by Britomart into a being capable of pity. And at last these two, negative and even destructive in isolation for all their beauty, are tempered and absorbed into the creativeness of the sea, now no longer the cruel source of Marinell's riches, cast up from "the wreckes of many wretches" upon the Precious Shore, but a place of fecundity and life.

Spenser's theme of reconciliation requires more intricacy in the shaping than do the subjects of some other books of *The Faerie Queene*, for this is a quest in which one cannot expect to meet one's temptations neatly in turn, as in the achieving of temperance. The way to true *concordia* is shown by presenting also several mistaken ways which yet resemble the true. But Spenser's knowledge of the human mind is as accurate here as elsewhere, and his methods though more intricate are no less planned. Through his interlinked stories he develops his truth that concord is in every sphere a state of equilibrium, not of subjugation and submission, flight and pursuit, that the war of opposites is one which both contenders are, in a sense, to win, for each is necessary to the completion of the other.

# The Legend of Justice:
# The Idol and the Crocodile

*by William Nelson*

The appeal to golden antiquity as a standard by which to measure the life of this world is a recurrent theme in *The Faerie Queene*. It is nowhere given greater emphasis than in the Legend of Justice, the Proem taking its departure from the age of Saturn:

> For during Saturnes ancient raigne it's sayd,
>> That all the world with goodnesse did abound:
>> All loved vertue, no man was affrayd
>> Of force, ne fraud in wight was to be found:
>> No warre was knowne, no dreadfull trompets sound,
>> Peace universall rayn'd mongst men and beasts,
>> And all things freely grew out of the ground:
>> Justice sate high ador'd with solemne feasts,
> And to all people did divide her dred beheasts.          (Proem.9)

The action of Artegall's story is set in the generation following this happy age, a time when virtue still flourished but "then likewise the wicked seede of vice/ Began to spring." When Artegall was a child, Astraea, goddess of justice, lived on earth and it was she who trained him in her ways. But as men waxed wicked she returned to her heavenly home leaving to the hero her iron groom Talus and the golden sword Chrysaor as legacy. He is her heir, and his moral qualities as administrator of justice are the subject of his legend. His task is to imitate—not to restore—the natural justice of the age of Saturn.

Appropriately, therefore, Artegall appears in the guise of a hero of ancient myth, a founder of civilization like the euhemerized gods of the *Library of History* of Diodorus Siculus. He is introduced as the peer of Bacchus and Hercules whom the poet describes as the civilizers and lawgivers of the East and the West, and he is compared to Osiris,

From William Nelson, *The Poetry of Edmund Spenser* (New York: Columbia University Press, 1963), pp. 256–75. Copyright © 1963 by Columbia University Press. Reprinted by permission of the publisher.

father of Hercules according to the genealogies of Spenser's time.[1] His conquest of the Souldan is likened to Hercules' slaying of the tyrant Diomedes; he is enslaved and dressed in woman's clothing by Radigund as Hercules by Omphale. Arthur shares this Herculean character by virtue of his victory over Geryoneo, son of the three-bodied giant that Hercules slew. And as Hercules conquers the shape-shifter Achelous so Talus masters the shape-shifter Malengin.

Artegall's name, like that of his beloved Britomart, is full of meanings. He is the equal of Arthur, in a sense his alter ego since he fathers the line of British kings culminating in Arthur reborn as the Tudor dynasty. "Art-egall" suggests his role as the knight of equity. But the primary allusion is to an ancient king of Britain whose history is recorded by Geoffrey of Monmouth. Geoffrey's Arthgallo began his rule as a very bad king indeed:

> He made it his business everywhere to smite down the noble and upraise the base; to take away from the rich that which was their own, and to heap up untold treasure for himself.

The barons found this intolerable and deposed him, setting his brother Elidur in his place. The loyal Elidur managed at length to restore the crown to Arthgallo, who by this time had learned to distinguish right from wrong:

> Arthgallo, accordingly, reigned ten years, and did so amend him of his former misdeeds, as that now he did begin to abase the baser sort and to exalt the gentler, to allow every man to hold his own, and to do right justice.[2]

This kind of justice, however it may disturb modern conceptions, is fundamental to the teaching of the Legend of Artegall.

The egalitarian giant whom Artegall encounters in the second canto is an advocate of the program of Arthgallo's first reign. He rests his case upon the admitted fact of the progressive worsening of the state of the world:

[1] See Isabel Rathborne, *The Meaning of Spenser's Fairyland* (New York, 1937), pp. 88–9.

[2] *Histories of the Kings of Britain* (Everyman's Library), III. xvii. Geoffrey (IX.xii) mentions another Arthgal, earl of Warwick, among the noblemen who paid allegiance to Arthur. Richard Grafton (*Chronicle at Large* [London, 1809], I, 83) expands this bare reference: "In this tyme also I finde mencion made of a noble and valiant man called Arthgall, and he was the first Erle of Warwike, and he was one of the knightes of the round Table of King Arthure. . . . This Arthgal tooke a Beare for his beast because the first sillable of his name which is Arth, in the Britishe speche, and is in English a Beare." Spenser may have had this Arthgal in mind as an allusion to the Dudley family.

> Seest not, how badly all things present bee,
> And each estate quite out of order goth?
> The sea it selfe doest thou not plainely see
> Encroch upon the land there under thee;
> And th' earth it selfe how daily its increast,
> By all that dying to it turned be?
> Were it not good that wrong were then surceast,
> And from the most, that some were given to the least?     (ii.37)

He then announces his program of reform: he will pull down the mountains and make them level with the plains; he will destroy the distinctions of power and wealth that obtain among men. Evidently he is a follower of those Hebrew and Christian scholars who held that the earth was created smooth and round, like a ball or an egg, and that its rugged deformation was the result either of God's curse after the Fall or of the action of the Flood.[3] He presumes to fulfill Isaiah's prophecy that in the last days God will make low the high mountains (2:12–14). His program derives from the assumption that the balance of the golden age—golden precisely because it was close to the perfection of the created universe—was a balance of equalities. This state of things he undertakes to restore "In sort as they were framed aunciently."

The giant is wrong on two counts, in his understanding of the nature of the golden age and in his effort to return to it. It is true, of course, that the world is degenerate. In the Proem, the poet complains,

> Me seemes the world is runne quite out of square,
> From the first point of his appointed sourse,
> And being once amisse growes daily wourse and wourse.

The stars and the planets move "at randon"; men are now "transformed into hardest stone." But the harmony of the golden age was not one which gave equal weight to heaven and hell, fire and air, king and peasant. Rather it depended upon the fulfillment of its proper task by each part of the universe:

> For at the first they all created were
> In goodly measure, by their Makers might,
> And weighed out in ballaunces so nere,
> That not a dram was missing of their right.
> The earth was in the middle centre pight,

---

[3] For a study of this tradition, see Marjorie Hope Nicolson, *Mountain Gloom and Mountain Glory* (Ithaca, N.Y., 1959), Chapter II. See also D. C. Allen, "A Note on Spenser's Orology," *Modern Language Notes*, LXI (1946), 555–6.

> In which it doth immoveable abide,
> Hemd in with waters like a wall in sight;
> And they with aire, that not a drop can slide:
> Al which the heavens containe, and in their courses guide.   (ii.35)

The balance is one of order and function, no part lacking its "right." It is associated with the idea that everything in creation by its essential quality has a "natural place" which it seeks. By means of this doctrine Aristotle accounted for the free fall of heavy objects, the rising of fire, and all other motions which are apparently not enforced by the violence of an external power. Beatrice explains to Dante at the end of the first canto of *Paradiso* that all the natures of the world tend to move toward the stations assigned to them by the divine plan and that it is for this reason that he rises effortlessly toward the empyrean. And since the natures of this world are infinitely diverse the giant's desire to set all at the same level is contrary to the way of justice.

Nature has made a difference between man and woman and given to each different powers. Therefore the roles they justly play in this world are different. Spenser makes the point by contrasting two encounters between knight and lady similar in every respect except their conclusions. After a fierce battle, Artegall succeeds in overthrowing the Amazon queen Radigund. He is at the point of delivering the final blow when he is overcome by the beauty of her face, bathed though it is in sweat,

> At sight thereof his cruell minded hart
> Empierced was with pittifull regard,
> That his sharpe sword he threw from him apart,
> Cursing his hand that had that visage mard:
> No hand so cruell, nor no hart so hard,
> But ruth of beautie will it mollifie.                          (v.13)

As he is now disarmed, Radigund is able to impose her will upon the hero and to enslave him, dressing him in woman's clothing and setting him to the female tasks of spinning and carding. His "wilfull defeat" by the Amazon almost precisely parallels his fight with Britomart in the sixth canto of Book iv. This too is a terrible battle in which Artegall at last gains mastery. He lifts up his hand, ready "to worke on her his utmost wracke," but the sight of her angel's face (marred with sweat like Radigund's) numbs his arm and the sword falls to the ground from his slack fingers. Scudamour comments:

> Certes Sir Artegall,
> I joy to see you lout so low on ground,
> And now become to live a Ladies thrall,
> That whylome in your minde wont to despise them all. (IV.vi.28)

The beauty of Britomart, like that of Radigund, tames the "salvage knight" and makes him "thrall." Yet the result of this encounter we must deem a good and that of the other an evil.

It is just both that man should excel woman in strength and that feminine beauty should vanquish the heart of a gentle man. But when she has won her battle, Britomart's "wrathfull courage gan appall,/ And haughtie spirits meekely to adaw."[a] At last, after his long suit,

> she yeelded her consent
> To be his love, and take him for her Lord,
> Till they with marriage meet might finish that accord. (IV.vi.41)

But the Amazon is of another metal, and she does not take Artegall for her lord. Having made the mistake of accepting her condition that the loser in battle must forever obey the victor, Artegall is forced to subject himself to her lordship:

> Tho with her sword on him she flatling strooke,
> In signe of true subjection to her powre,
> And as her vassall him to thraldome tooke. (v.18)

The relationship is torment for both, for Artegall because he must fill "A sordid office for a mind so brave," for Radigund, now enamored of him, because she cannot bring herself

> To serve the lowly vassall of her might
> And of her servant make her soverayne Lord (v.27)

Such a state is unjust because it is against nature:

> Such is the crueltie of womenkynd,
> When they have shaken off the shamefast band,
> With which wise Nature did them strongly bynd,
> T'obay the heasts of mans well ruling hand,
> That then all rule and reason they withstand,
> To purchase a licentious libertie.
> But vertuous women wisely understand,
> That they were born to base humilitie,
> Unlesse the heavens them lift to lawfull soveraintie. (v.25)

---

[a] adaw: daunt.

The last line, of course, is intended to justify the reign of Elizabeth as a legitimate exception to the general rule. It need not be taken as mere timeserving, for Sir Thomas Elyot in the *Defence of Good Women,* written in the reign of Henry VIII, and Calvin in a letter dated 1554 make the same exception.[4] Apart from that line, however, the two stories taken together constitute Spenser's comment on the theme of marital sovereignty in its relation to the justice of nature.

The giant is wrong also in his desire to restore the golden age. For if the world is mutable, it is so in accordance with God's behest. In the Cantos of Mutabilitie, Spenser undertakes to resolve the paradox of the changeful creation of an unchanging creator. Here, as in the episode of the Garden of Adonis, he is content to say that change is servant, not master:

> the earth is not augmented more,
> By all that dying into it doe fade.
> For of the earth they formed were of yore,
> How ever gay their blossome or their blade
> Doe flourish now, they into dust shall vade.[b]
> What wrong then is it, if that when they die,
> They turne to that, whereof they first were made?
> All in the powre of their great Maker lie:
> All creatures must obey the voice of the most hie.          (ii.40)

Without venturing to question the inscrutable ways of that Maker, the knight of Justice must imitate the law of nature as best he can. By so doing he obeys the laws of reason. Such as keep those laws, Richard Hooker declares, "resemble most lively in their voluntary actions that very manner of working which Nature herself doth necessarily observe in the course of the whole world. The works of Nature are all behoveful, beautiful, without superfluity or defect; even so theirs, if they be framed according to that which the Law of Reason

[4] See James E. Phillips, Jr., "The Background of Spenser's Attitude toward Women Rulers," *Huntington Library Quarterly,* V (1941–2), 5–32, and "The Woman Ruler in Spenser's *Faerie Queene,*" *ibid.,* pp. 211–34, and Kerby Neill, "Spenser on the Regiment of Women," *Studies in Philology,* XXXIV (1937), 134–7. Phillips quotes the letter from Calvin to Bullinger: "Concerning female government, I expressed myself to this effect, that seeing it was contrary to the legitimate course of nature, such governments ought to be reckoned among the visitations of God's anger. But even so, the grace of God sometimes displayed itself in an extraordinary way, since, as a reproach to the sloth of men, he raises up women, endowed not after the nature of men, but with a certain heroic spirit, as is seen in the illustrious example of Deborah."

[b] vade: pass away.

teacheth." [5] The giant denounces as unjust the advantage gained by a hungry ocean on the kingdom of the shore. But Artegall finds nothing inequitable in the ocean's transfer of land from the island belonging to Bracidas to that of his brother Amidas, for though it is change it is change adjudged by nature. It is equally right, therefore, that Bracidas should possess the treasure which the sea took from Amidas to give to him.

Although the giant's scales cannot erase the difference among kinds or annul the decisions of nature, they do have a proper function. Artegall urges him to use them to weigh against each other two "wrongs" or "falses" in order to discover which of the pair is the greater. Spenser has here in mind the Aristotelian argument concerning the just distribution of goods. A transaction is unjust when one party has too much and the other too little. Justice is the mean between these two wrongs or defects since it gives to each party not what is absolutely equal but "equal in accordance with proportion." Wrong may be balanced against wrong, while right sits "in the middest of the beame alone."

When the giant tries to counterpoise wrong and right, however, he finds that his scales will not work. False slides off the weighing pan; all the wrongs that he can lay together will not weigh down a little right. The principle is given dramatic demonstration when the false Florimell is set in the balance with the true in the presence of the knights invited to Marinell's wedding. To men's eyes they are equally beautiful, but

> Streight way so soone as both together met,
> Th'enchaunted Damzell vanisht into nought:
> Her snowy substance melted as with heat,
> Ne of that goodly hew remayned ought,
> But th'emptie girdle, which about her wast was wrought.     (iii.24)

The astonished assembly must conclude, with the giant, that "by no meanes the false will with the truth be wayd." In the light of truth, falsehood is negative, unreal. This is no longer Aristotle.

In the age of gold, while Astraea dwelt on earth, "all loved vertue," force and fraud were unknown, and justice resided in men's hearts. When she departed at the coming of brazen times, according to Spenser's favorite mythographer Natalis Comes, she left as her legacy the

---

[5] *Of the Laws of Ecclesiastical Polity, Books* I to IV (Everyman's Library, 1925), I.viii.9 (p. 182).

written law, written because in the decaying world men no longer obeyed the unwritten precepts of natural justice.[6] A written law requires power to enforce it:

> For vaine it is to deeme of things aright,
> And makes wrong doers justice to deride,
> Unlesse it be perform'd with dreadlesse might,
> For powre is the right hand of Justice truely hight.      (iv.1)

This power Spenser identifies with the goddess's gift to Artegall of the iron man Talus whom classical story described as regularly making the rounds of Crete armed with the laws inscribed upon tablets of brass:

> His name was Talus, made of yron mould,
> Immoveable, resistlesse, without end.
> Who in his hand an yron flale did hould,
> With which he thresht out falshood, and did truth unfould.      (i.12)

The hunt for truth is one of Talus' functions; he is also responsible for the punishment and exposure of those judged guilty. He pursues relentlessly the guileful villain Malengin who tries to escape first by running and then by turning himself successively into fox, bush, bird, hedgehog, and snake. When Munera hides from justice,

> Talus, that could like a limehound winde her,
> And all things secrete wisely could bewray,
> At length found out, whereas she hidden lay
> Under an heape of gold.      (ii.25)

In his role as executioner he chops off her hands and feet (not as brutal as it sounds for they are made of gold and silver) and nails them on high for the edification of all. The punishments which he and Artegall administer are regularly made public for their deterrent effect: Sanglier must carry about the head of the lady whom he has killed, Pollente's severed head is pitched upon a pole, Braggadocchio is hung by the heels, Trompart's face is "deform'd with infamie."

Although he is invulnerable and irresistible, Talus has his limitations. When Radigund subdues Artegall he makes no move to rescue his master, for he must obey the judging intelligence and not act on his own. Nor is his flail suitable for use in war (ix.44). When Arthur engages in his perilous fight with the Souldan Talus awaits the outcome:

---

[6] *Natalis Comes Mythologiae* (Frankfurt, 1581), pp. 117ff.

> by his stirrup Talus did attend,
> Playing his pages part, as he had beene
> Before directed by his Lord; to th'end
> He should his flaile to final execution bend.　　(viii.29)

This quarrel between the Prince and the Pagan lies outside his province. Only the flashing brilliance of Arthur's shield, the revelation of truth by the grace of God, can decide it. When that decision has been made human justice can play its part.

There are other attributes besides power necessary to make the administrator of justice feared and obeyed. It seems at first inappropriate to endow the just man with cunning, but if criminals are guileful, the keepers of order must be clever enough to catch them. "Craft against vice I must apply," says the Duke in *Measure for Measure*. Solomon cunningly decided the parentage of a child, and Artegall follows his example in proving a lady to belong to one and not to another claimant. The wily Malengin falls into a snare set by Arthur and Artegall. As so often in *The Faerie Queene*, the point is that the morality of an action lies in the nature which performs it and in its purpose, not in itself. For a knight to let go of his shield and to waver in battle appears to be shameful, and it is indeed so in the case of Sir Burbon, despite his excuse:

> when time doth serve,
> My former shield I may resume againe:
> To temporize is not from truth to swerve,
> Ne for advantage terme to entertaine,
> When as necessitie doth it constraine.
> Fie on such forgerie (said Artegall)
> Under one hood to shadow faces twaine.
> Knights ought be true, and truth is one in all:
> Of all things to dissemble fouly may befall.　　(xi.56)

Yet in his own fight with Grantorto, Artegall also lets go of his shield and stoops his head before his enemy's blows. But he is no timeserver. He looses his shield in order to encumber his opponent whose axe is caught in it; he shuns his strokes, but

> No shame to stoupe, ones head more high to reare,
> And much to gaine, a litle for to yield　　(xii.19)

Since Artegall's end is good, only Detraction can accuse him of treachery and unmanly guile.

But Justice does not consist merely of a hunt for the truth, punishment of the guilty, and insistence upon reverence for authority and

the code of law. These attributes of terror, mortality, and force represent only half of the charge which Duke Vincentio gives over to his
deputy Angelo at the beginning of *Measure for Measure:*

> we have with special soul
> Elected him our absence to supply,
> Lent him our terror, dress'd him with our love
>
> Hold therefore, Angelo:
> In our remove be thou at full ourself.
> Mortality and mercy in Vienna
> Live in thy tongue and heart.
>
> Your scope is as mine own,
> So to enforce or qualify the laws
> As to your soul seems good.[7]

Love, mercy, the qualification of the law are part of Justice too. At
the feet of Queen Mercilla, as she sits in sovereign majesty, there lies
a sword

> Whose long rest rusted the bright steely brand;
> Yet when as foes enforst, or friends sought ayde,
> She could it sternely draw, that all the world dismayde.          (ix.30)

That rusted weapon, like the rusted armor which Piers calls on Cuddie
to celebrate in the October eclogue, is the sign of power so great that
it is rarely used. So too is the huge lion beneath her feet

> With a strong yron chaine and coller bound,
> That once he could not move, nor quich[c] at all;
> Yet did he murmure with rebellious[8] sound,
> And softly royne,[d] when salvage choler gan redound.          (ix.33)

The potentiality of the sword and the lion create the majesty and
dread of temporal authority. But the sword is not drawn, and the lion
is chained.

The queen who restrains this power is called Mercilla, and she holds
a scepter in her hand, "The sacred pledge of peace and clemencie."
Her maids of honor are the Litae, a bevy of white-clad virgins, daughters of Jove,

> those they say
> Upon Joves judgement seat wayt day and night,

---

[7] I.i.18–20, 43–6, 65–7.

[8] The editors of *Works* elect the 1596 reading "rebellions" in preference to
"rebellious" which appears in later editions.

[c] quich: stir.                                    [d] royne: growl.

> And when in wrath he threats the worlds decay,
> They doe his anger calme, and cruell vengeance stay.
>
> They also doe by his divine permission
> Upon the thrones of mortall Princes tend,
> And often treat for pardon and remission
> To suppliants, through frayltie which offend.          (ix.31–32)

Jove's threat to destroy the world recalls the wrath of Jehovah, and the calming of that wrath the mercy of Christ.

In the opening stanzas of the tenth canto, immediately following the episode of the trial at the court of Mercilla, the poet raises and avoids the question as to whether mercy is a part of justice or derived from it. He is content to say that mercy, like justice, was bred in the Almighty's seat and "From thence pour'd down on men, by influence of grace." He then weighs their roles:

> For if that Vertue be of so great might,
> Which from just verdict will for nothing start,
> But to preserve inviolated right,
> Oft spilles the principall, to save the part;
> So much more then is that of powre and art,
> That seekes to save the subject of her skill,
> Yet never doth from doome of right depart:
> As it is greater prayse to save, then spill,
> And better to reforme, then to cut off the ill.          (x.2)

The one "virtue" is concerned with keeping inviolable the statutes of law. It forbids Portia to do what Bassanio asks:

> Wrest once the law to your authority:
> To do a great right, do a little wrong

The written "part" must be saved, even if the human "principal" spills, for otherwise

> many an error by the same example
> Will rush into the state[9]

The other "virtue," however, begins with the individual whom the generality of statute ignores. Spenser associates it with "equity." The French political philosopher, Jean Bodin, describes the relationship of law and equity in terms very like those used by the poet of justice and mercy:

> For that to say truely, the law without equitie, is as a bodie without a soule, for that it concerning but things in generall, leaveth the particular

[9] *Merchant of Venice*, IV.i.211–12, 217–8.

circumstances, which are infinit, to be by equalitie sought out according to the exigence of the places, times, and persons: whereunto it behoveth the magistrat or judge so to apply the laws, whether it be in tearmes of justice, or in matter of estate, as that thereof ensue neither any inconvenience nor absurditie whatsoever. Howbeit yet that the magistrat must not so farre bend the law, as to breake the same, although that it seeme to be right hard: whereas it is of it selfe cleere enough.[10]

Since it deals with individuals rather than with codified abstractions equity may be understood as the legal equivalent of the quality of mercy, and so an English judgment of the year 1589 describes its function: "to soften and modify the extremity of the law." [11] The innocent and upright judge therefore stands, as Bodin puts it, "in the middle betwixt the law and the equitie thereof: but yet to bee himselfe in the power of the law, so as is equitie in the power of the magistrat: yet so as nothing be by him deceitfully done, or in prejudice of the law." In the course of the development of the English legal system equity itself became institutionalized and the problem of reconciling it with the code became a constant plague. But for Spenser as for Bodin justice and mercy, law and equity, are opposed only in the sense that life and death are opposed in the Legend of Holinesse, and they are at one in that sense also. Although "it is greater prayse to save, then spill," the merciful judge "never doth from doome of right depart."

The strange vision which Britomart sees in the Temple of Isis, goddess of equity, sets sword and scepter, rigor and clemency, against each other and resolves their opposition. Like Mercilla with the lion at her feet is the silver statue of Isis, her foot upon a sleeping crocodile. The dream begins with the transformation of Britomart into a monarch, her moonlike miter changed into a crown of gold, her linen stole into a red robe. Her state of beauty and felicity is broken by a hideous tempest which blows the holy fire about and is at the point of destroying the temple and all within it. In this crisis the crocodile wakes and devours both flames and tempest. Grown great and proud in his power he threatens to consume the goddess herself. But he is beaten back by Isis' rod, his pride turning to humility, and he sues for grace at the idol's feet,

[10] *The Six Bookes of a Commonweale*, trans. Richard Knolles, 1606, ed. K. D. McRae (Harvard University Press, 1962), p. 764. See also Aristotle, *Nicomachean Ethics*, v.10.

[11] Cited by J. Wilson McCutchan, "Justice and Equity in the English Morality Play," *Journal of the History of Ideas*, XIX (1958), 405–10. The case involved the Earl of Oxford.

> Which she accepting, he so neare her drew,
> That of his game she soone enwombed grew,
> And forth did bring a Lion of great might;
> That shortly did all other beasts subdew. (vii.16)

When Britomart wakes, understandably dismayed by her experience, the priests of the temple explain to her that the crocodile represents "The righteous Knight that is thy faithfull lover," and is really Osiris,

> That under Isis feete doth sleepe for ever:
> To shew that clemence oft in things amis,
> Restraines those sterne behests, and cruell doomes of his. (vii.22)

Her vision, then, is a universalized form of such a story as Shakespeare tells in *Measure for Measure*. Sleeping law—Shakespeare compares it with a sleeping lion and again with "an o'ergrown lion in a cave" [12] —invites chaotic disorder and the destruction of the realm. Stern force is required to suppress the turmoil but unchecked becomes itself destructive. Only when law is restrained by clemency, when a union of the two occurs, does majesty show itself stable, victorious, and fruitful.

This ideal union is illustrated by the trial of Duessa before the court of Mercilla. The episode is colored throughout by obvious reference to the trial of Mary Queen of Scots, but the topical meaning only slightly affects its function as an integral part of the exposition of the theme of the book. The guilt of Duessa is hidden behind her "great countenance and place" and the rare beauty of her appearance. The appeal for mercy depends upon these qualities and also—here the historical occasion dictates—upon

> Daunger threatning hidden dread,
> And high alliance unto forren powre (ix.45)

Prince Arthur, sitting on one side of Mercilla, is deeply affected by the lady's unhappy state, while Osiris-Artegall, on the queen's other side, is constant against her. When Zeal, attorney for the prosecution, proves her guilty of murder, sedition, incontinence, adultery, and impiety, even Arthur repents of his "former fancies ruth" and joins in the unanimous verdict of the court. Now the court, which is the law, calls upon "Mercilla myld" to punish the prisoner,

> But she, whose Princely breast was touched nere
> With piteous ruth of her so wretched plight,
> Though plaine she saw by all, that she did heare,
> That she of death was guiltie found by right,

---

[12] *Measure for Measure*, II.ii.90; I.iii.22.

> Yet would not let just vengeance on her light;
> But rather let in stead thereof to fall
> Few perling drops from her faire lampes of light;
> The which she covering with her purple pall
> Would have the passion hid, and up arose withall.          (ix.50)

The death of Duessa is relegated to a sidelong mention in the following canto, the emphasis falling on the "strong constraint" which required Mercilla "With more then needful naturall remorse" to allow
the sentence to be carried out. Insofar as the episode refers to the
historical trial of Mary the poet is justified in the way he tells the
story since Queen Elizabeth was indeed strongly urged by Parliament
and her Council to remove the Marian threat, and although she signed
the death warrant she at least pretended to be angered by its execu-
tion. But for the central purpose of the Legend of Justice the conclusion to be drawn is that "it is greater prayse to save, then spill."

If Mercilla presiding over the trial of Duessa is prefigured by Isis
with the crocodile under her foot, Grantorto at the trial of Irena has
as his symbol the idol Geryon[13] and the fiend under the altar. The
contrast between Isis and Geryon is emphatic and detailed. For the
beautiful silver goddess there is the monstrous golden god. For the
openly terrifying male crocodile there is a fiend with the face of a
maid,

> To hide the horrour, which did lurke behinde,
> The better to beguile, whom she so fond did finde.          (xi.23)

Isis restrains her terror; Geryon calls his forth. Her priests are devoted
ascetics who drink no wine not only because it addles the brains but
also because it is, or represents, blood. The guardians of the chapel of
Geryon are a strong garrison led by a seneschal "That by his powre
oppressed every one," and to the idol is sacrificed

> The flesh of men, to Gods owne likenesse framed,
> And powring forth their bloud in brutishe wize,
> That any yron eyes, to see it would agrize.          (x.28)

The chapel of Geryon stands for the reverse of justice, or tyranny.
One such tyrant is Geryoneo, son of Geryon and builder of the
chapel. He guilefully takes advantage of the widow Belge and once
he has won her confidence shows his true nature by "tyrannizing,

---

[13] The association of Geryon with Spain is traditional. Spenser has transferred
his three bodies to his own fiction, the son Geryoneo. Wonderful to relate, classical
myth gives to Geryon's father, sprung from the blood of Medusa, the name of
Chrysaor, Artegall's sword of Justice! (Hesiod, *Theogony*, ll. 280ff.)

and oppressing all," and sacrificing her children, one by one, to the
fiend in the chapel. It is given to Arthur to rescue her and the last
two of her offspring and to destroy both the idol and the fiend. As in
the trial of Duessa, the political intention is transparent, the lady
Belge and her children representing the Low Countries and the prov-
inces into which that realm was divided, Geryoneo the Empire, and
Arthur the righteous power of England.

Artegall's final task is the saving of Irena. He is himself in part
responsible for her plight, because the delay occasioned by his "thral-
dome" to Radigund has brought the captive lady whom Gloriana
assigned him to rescue into the direst jeopardy. The effeminacy of
that imprisonment so takes on a new meaning. It illustrates not only
the unnaturalness of the subjection of man by woman but also the
enfeeblement of justice held in fetters by pity, and more generally
the diversion of the gentle man from his proper work in the world
by the power of feminine beauty. The poet cites Antony, Samson, and
Hercules as other examples of great warriors who failed in the performance of their duty because they allowed themselves to be tied by
women. In order to fulfill Gloriana's behest Artegall must harden himself against the attraction of Britomart and go sternly on his way, accompanied only by Talus. If Osiris must never be unbridled, neither
must he be emasculated.

"Irena" in Greek means "peace," and a "myld Eirene" has already
been numbered among the Litae, or Hours, attending Queen Mercilla.
Peaceful femininity imprisoned by Grantorto makes a double contrast
with righteous Artegall enchained by the warlike Amazon. Righteousness must be governed by clemency, not pride, so that Britomart must
overcome Radigund to set matters right. And mild peace is in dire
jeopardy when injustice rules, so that Artegall must conquer Grantorto. But even this comparison does not exhaust the complexity of
Spenser's web of parallels and contrasts. Irena's predicament is the
foil of Duessa's. Duessa is of "great countenance"; Irena a "tender
rose." Duessa comes to Mercilla's realm with the treasonable intention
of killing the queen; Irena, relying on Artegall's promise to fight for
her,

> Did thither come, where she afrayd of nought,
> By guilefull treason and by subtill slight
> Surprized was, and to Grantorto brought,
> Who her imprisond hath, and her life often sought. (xi.39)

Duessa is tried by legal process, Irena by a parody of the law, in effect
by brute force. It is striking evidence of the primacy of Spenser's moral

intention, I think, that a partisan of Mary Queen of Scots might find reason to identify her with pitiful, oppressed Irena rather than with proud, treacherous Duessa.

When Artegall defeats Grantorto, we know by their names and by their histories that right has conquered wrong. But an ignorant world looking only upon the superficialities of the action cannot know. When Talus inflicts grievous punishment is he just or cruel? When a knight lets go of his shield is he a coward or a skillful warrior? How can one distinguish between clemency and weakness? As Artegall comes away from the scene of his last victory he is assailed by Envy, Detraction, and the Blatant Beast who rail at him

> Saying, that he had with unmanly guile,
> And foule abusion both his honour blent,
> And that bright sword, the sword of Justice lent,
> Had stayned with reprochfull crueltie,
> In guiltlesse blood of many an innocent:
> As for Grandtorto, him with treacherie
> And traynes having surpriz'd, he fouly did to die.                (xii.40)

Slander is a crime, and the slanderous poet who abused Queen Mercilla is properly punished by having his tongue nailed to a post. But defamation is part of the necessary burden of the righteous hero. So Shakespeare:

> No might nor greatness in mortality
> Can censure scape; back-wounding calumny
> The whitest virtue strikes. What king so strong
> Can tie the gall up in the slanderous tongue? [14]

Artegall forbids Talus to chastise Detraction:

> So much the more at him still did she scold,
> And stones did cast, yet he for nought would swerve
> From his right course                                            (xii.43)

For the law cannot justify a just man; his justification must lie within himself, in his certainty of his own righteousness. Artegall knows himself "from perill free."

In the circumstances of the summoning of Artegall to Faerie court before he has completed his task of reforming Irena's "ragged commonweal" there is a clear reference to the recall of Lord Grey from Ireland in 1582. Detraction's charge of "reprochefull crueltie" had in fact been made against Grey and appears to have been the principal

---

[14] *Measure for Measure*, III.ii.196–9.

reason for the Queen's dissatisfaction with his government. This matter of Ireland, taken together with the account of Arthur's rescue of Belge, his aiding of the wavering Sir Burbon (the Bourbon, Henry of Navarre), his Armada-like battle with the Souldan, and the trial of Duessa-Mary, constitutes a kind of history of the chief political events in England of Spenser's own times. It fills that place in the Legend of Justice which is taken by the marriage of the Thames and the Medway in the fourth book, by Merlin's prophecy and the volume of *Briton moniments* in the third and second, and by the account of England's return to true religion in the first.

Although allusion to the affairs of the nation plays a larger part in the Legend of Justice than in the other books of the poem, the principal concern remains "ethice" rather than "politice." The discourse deals with the nature of those who act justly rather than with the nature of just action. The latter theme is not absent: it appears, for example, in Artegall's debate with the giant who would level the mountains and in his restoration of male sovereignty to the land of the Amazons. Even in these instances, however, the moral problem is central. The vulgar who flock about the giant support him "In hope by him great benefite to gaine," not because they find his arguments convincing. And the Amazon women reject rule, reason, and the authority of man "To purchase a licentious libertie." The dominant interest of the book is in the moral qualities and moral dilemmas of a righteous man, and this is true even when the poetic figure is drawn from the realm of politics. The point of the episode of Sir Burbon is not that he did a wrong thing but that he did it for "love of lordship and of lands," that he served the time. Mercilla pronouncing sentence at the end of the trial of Duessa would have been Queen Politic. Since she sheds a tear instead she is Queen Natural.

# The Virtuous and Gentle Discipline
# of Gentlemen and Poets

## *by William V. Nestrick*

As flies, "in whottest summers day, / Do seize vpon some beast, whose flesh is bare," literary historians have swarmed over the human creations of Spenser's imagination in Book VI of *The Faerie Queene*. What they have pretended to find matters less than what prompted them to look in this particular book. The superabundance of historical and biographical criticism, in this case, can be traced to a general failure to find enough in the poem itself to permit a coherent and convincing interpretation of the poem's total meaning.

Ample reason exists for the literary historian's interest in the book. First, the book follows the *Legend of Artegall* in which Artegall's battles for fair Irene and Arthur's for Belge clearly refer to contemporary events. Secondly, Spenser reintroduces Timias, who definitely represents Raleigh in Book IV. Although Spenser works Timias into the allegorical frame by portraying him as a victim of scorn, disdain, deceit, malice, and infamy, he does have to go out of his way in the narrative scheme to reconcile Arthur and Timias. Then, too, Calidore, the paragon of courtesy, begins to look like a portrait of one of Spenser's contemporaries. The Elizabethan who saw the ideal courtier wander through pastoral scenes and rescue a maiden from a tiger could hardly fail to recognize the Elizabethan courtier *par excellence* and the author of *Arcadia*. But the choicest tidbit for this kind of criticism can be found in Canto X. Spenser suddenly interrupts his narrative to describe Colin Clout piping for rings of naked ladies. Colin Clout would attract little enough attention if Spenser had not so obviously made Colin a mouthpiece for the poet both in *The Shepheardes Calender* and in *Colin Clouts Come Home Againe*. With Colin appears a damsel who is decked out in all the graces of courtesy even though she is only of low degree. Like Eliza in the April

From *English Literary History*, XXIX, No. 4 (1962), 357–71. Copyright © 1962 by The Johns Hopkins Press. Reprinted by permission of The Johns Hopkins Press.

eclogue of *The Shepheardes Calender,* she is elevated to the position
of a fourth Grace. But at this point, Spenser forces us to remember
that *The Faerie Queene* is not some kind of identification game. The
fourth Grace utterly lacks any identifiable aspects; she has a completely poetical existence.[1] Spenser cared less about the identity of
Colin's shepherdess than about the figure his poetry could create. If
Spenser thought of Sidney when he created his ideal courtier, he depicted the ideal qualities he saw in Sidney. A recognition of Sidney
does not fulfill the purposes behind this poetry. If Spenser drew
Calidore with Sidney in mind, he made no attempt to copy specific
and realistic details of his subject. He *perfected* the nature of Sidney's
courtier. He never troubled with the outward shows; the validity of
his imitation rested upon the resemblances of inward thoughts. An
interpretation of Book VI, then, must focus on what the poetry is
*doing.* Those flickering correspondences between Gloriana's Land of
Faery and Elizabeth's England can, at most, illuminate some of the
processes of the poet's imagination.

As an alternative to this historical view of the sixth book, another
order may be found in following parallel developments in three levels
of the poem, levels not imposed *ab extra* but indicated by Spenser
himself in his organization and design: (1) the comments of the poet's
*persona* on the specific book he is engaged in writing; (2) the projection of these comments onto a dramatic level in which conflicting
attitudes about the function of poetry are played off against each other
in the figures of Colin Clout and Calidore before a final resolution,
and (3) the allegorical level with its palpable design of defining and
inculcating the virtue of courtesy.

In the Proem, Spenser begins to express an emotional involvement
which reaches its climax (but not its dénouement) in Canto X:

> The waies, through which my weary steps I guyde,
> In this delightful land of Faery . . .          (VI. Proem. 1)

He feels delight in the sweet variety "Of all that pleasant is to eare
or eye," but he also recognizes his "tedious trauell." Although the

---

[1] M. Pauline Parker, in *The Allegory of the Faerie Queene* (Oxford, 1960), while
acknowledging the inadequcy of interpreting the Arcadian idyll as Philip Sidney's
marriage with Frances Walsingham, cannot resist the temptation to hint that the
fourth Grace may be Elizabeth Boyle, and once the identity of Colin Clout and
Spenser has been recognized, he [*sic*] feels it necessary to explain the whole vision
of Acidale in historical or biographical terms: "Perhaps at that moment Calidore
represented not Sidney, but Raleigh, who had come to him in Ireland, his Arcadia,
if also a scene of battlegrounds, and had awakened in him again the ambition of
the court, dispelling who knows what other poetic projects" (p. 255).

poet overcomes any decay of might, this feeling of weariness still intrudes. The presence of these two feelings implies a question: How is it that the Land of Faery, the creation of the poet's mind, can evoke the disparate feelings of delight and weariness? If he needs variety to divert him from his tedious work, why doesn't he stop writing? The word "guide" defines the nature of these feelings in terms of modes of poetic statement. Spenser guides himself according to a plan. In the *Letter to Raleigh,* he calls that plan "a continued Allegory," and allegory demands discipline; it imposes a framework within which the poet must work. Moreover, it must be complete. It requires a clear intellectual conception of the embryonic abstraction before its birth into concreteness. A consistent emotional response to experience will not suffice. In the first stanza of Book VI, Spenser is admitting his difficulty in following the allegorical path. He prefers those little outgrowths in which he can bring his full poetic imagination to bear: the Garden of Adonis, the Temple of Busyrane, the Thames-Medway wedding, and the Pastorella episode. Through these little departures from the straight and narrow way, where the techniques of amplifying the setting and characters are symbolical or occasionally simply descriptive rather than allegorical, Spenser escapes the rigor of allegory.

The feeling of escape to some pleasant place recurs throughout the book. Tristram, for example, seeks asylum from Cornwall where his usurping uncle remains a potential danger. Indeed, the whole pastoral episode may be considered as an interlude in the allegorical chase of the Blatant Beast. The hot chase dissolves into the scene of piping and caroling shepherds. The sweating Calidore intrudes anomalously in this atmosphere of relaxation. The same idyllic and removed quality appears more consciously in the etymology of "Acidale" as "free from care," [2] thus making Canto X an explicit recognition of this pattern in the book.

Spenser continues to develop the theme of the escape from weariness and tedium by a recurrent image pattern. The conventional Elizabethan ship conceit occurs more frequently than in the other books. Generally, the figure includes the idea of getting to a restful port. Stylistically, Canto X is at the center of this figure. In Acidale, Venus used "to repose / And rest her selfe, as in a gladsome port" (VI.x.9).

---

[2] W. Renwick, *Spenser Selections* (Oxford, 1923), p. 202, quoted in the notes to VI.x.viii.9 of the *Variorum Edition,* by Edwin Greenlaw and others (Baltimore, 1948).

With this figure, Calidore phrases his request to stay in the pastoral world. He envies Melibœ's life which is so free "From all the tempests of these worldly seas, / Which tosse the rest in daungerous disease" (VI.ix.19). As if to exemplify the contentment which the mind itself can create, he asks Melibœ's permission to live in the simplicity of the rustic world:

> Giue leaue awhyle, good father, in this shore
> To rest my barcke, which hath bene beaten late
> With stormes of fortune and tempestuous fate,
> In seas of troubles and of toylesome paine.                    (VI.ix.31)

A recurrent figure of the poet's voice appears in the speech of the principal character. The distance lessens between the formal poet and Calidore.

Finally, the poet himself refers to the guidance he has given his own poetry and compares his work to a ship "Whose course is often stayd, yet neuer is astray" (VI.xii.1). The poet continually elaborates upon a single image that embodies the development of thematic, philosophical, and artistic concerns within the work. In the Acidale description, the ship figure emphasizes the cessation of tensions: after a voyage, the ship comes to port. Calidore's voice grows closer to the poet's within the same simile. The final use of the ship image, however, comes as a surprise. From the very beginning, Spenser characterizes the restful delights of poetry as escapes; he calls out a warning that he needs a rest from his tedious works. The ship may stray from its course for diversion and then return. Suddenly, in the last canto, he claims his course "is often stayd, yet neuer is astray." When he appears to digress, as in Canto X, he is merely lingering over a scene which lies directly in his course. The final use of the ship simile suggests that the "digressions" form part of the book's total meaning. The poet continually presents himself as a controlling as well as a creative force in the poem.

Again and again, the voice of the poet can be heard through the narrative. The last stanza, like the first in the book, reflects upon the poem as a whole:

> Ne may this homely verse, of many meanest,
> Hope to escape his venemous despite,
> More then my former writs, all were they clearest
> From blamefull blot . . .                    (VI.xii.41)

Nowhere else in *The Faerie Queene* does Spenser involve himself so intimately with his work. This personal tone pervades the last book, as in the attack of the Blatant Beast: "Ne spareth he the gentle Poet's rime" (VI.xii.40). Through the strong intrusion of the personal poetic voice, Spenser creates an awareness of the poet shaping the work. He urges the fundamental identity of the poet standing outside the work and the poet piping for the Graces on Acidale.

The first level of Spenser's *persona* and his attitude toward the book necessarily leads to the second level, on which he dramatizes these conflicting attitudes in the figures of Colin Clout and Calidore. Poetry on this level is just as much a "subject" as courtesy on the allegorical level. As the focal point of the book, Canto X makes the poet central:

> That iolly shepheard, which there piped, was
> Poore *Colin Clout* (who knowes not *Colin Clout?*)
> He pypt apace, whilest they him daunst about.          (VI.x.16)

The offhand comment, "who knowes not *Colin Clout*," directs the reader to those works in which Colin has appeared before—and in which the identification of Spenser and Colin takes place. Spenser *controls* the amount of material extraneous to the poem which may be admitted.

Two attitudes balance each other in this scene. The first is the fundamental identity of the poet who creates the vision and the poet within the vision. Simultaneously, an attitude of separation opposes the identity to create an objectivity that saves Canto X from any charge of watery emotionalism. Structurally, the canto separates the poet and Colin Clout. Every effort gives distance. The dance of the Graces to Colin's music occurs in a highly artificial pastoral world. To the demands of a literary convention the poet must subordinate personal emotion. The vision itself breaks into the whole narrative flow and suspends the story. Gradually Spenser directs the eye from the foot of the hill, where a gentle flood tumbles down, to the top, where a spacious plain spreads itself. Even the birds order themselves in a hierarchy of song. Through this descriptive sequence, Spenser physically elevates the dancing maidens and their poet above the normal pastoral world. He *frames* the vision by suggesting the way it appears to Calidore.[3] Rarely is the vision brought into direct ex-

---

[3] A. C. Hamilton senses the closeness of the poet to Calidore, although he overlooks Spenser's clear separation of himself from Calidore as well as from Colin Clout by having Calidore as the mediator between the poet and the vision: ". . . it is not Calidore's vision, but the poet's. It is as difficult not to see the poet intruding himself into the poem, as it is not to see Shakespeare in the role of Prospero with the breaking of the pipe, the dissolving of the vision, and our

perience. At each point, Calidore's stationing is emphasized:

> Vnto this place when as the Elfin Knight
> Approcht . . .
> . . . . . . .
> He nigher drew, to weete what mote it be;
> . . . . . . .
> And in the midst a Shepheard piping he did see.    (VI.x.10)
> He durst not enter . . .    (VI.x.11)
> Much wondred *Calidore* at this strange sight. . . .    (VI.x.17)

When he rose out of the wood, "They vanisht all away out of his sight" (VI.x.18). He has marred all. The delicate texture of this poetry, the sheer lyricism of the celebration of the shepherd lass's beauty cannot support the intrusion of Sir Calidore. He is as out of place as was the sweating knight among the dancing shepherds. Visions of pure beauty and love constantly dissolve before our eyes. The Brigants lay waste to the pastoral world. Such parallels occur throughout the book, almost as if the poet were thinking ahead to the last two stanzas in the *Two Cantos of Mutabilitie*. In the most boorish manner, Calidore bursts in upon the quiet delight of Serena and Calepine. The romantic state of Serena and Calepine parallels almost exactly that of Priscilla and Aladine (VI.ii.16,43):

> a iolly Knight,
> In couert shade him selfe did safely rest,
> To solace with his Lady in delight:
> His warlike armes he had from him undight
> For that him selfe he thought from daunger free.    (VI.iii.20)

Again and again, Spenser or one of his characters undrapes an intimate scene of restful delight. Such scenes exemplify the sweet variety that Spenser *and Calidore* find along their tedious way. Calidore does the same things that Spenser claims he himself is doing in this book. The early cantos and the last canto present a simple allegory of Calidore's pursuit and defeat of the Blatant Beast. Between these sections are all those scenes of beautiful variety, the escape into (almost) pure poetry, interrupted only by the arrival of Sir Calidore. The changing modes of poetic statement reflect the central conflict of poetic impulses. Canto X brings the exemplars of these conflicting modes together. Spenser has translated the poetical conflict which on the level of the poet-*persona* was between "sweet variety" and "tedious trauell" into

---

awareness (but surely the poet's too) that his work is being rounded out." *The Structure of Allegory in The Faerie Queene* (Oxford, 1961), p. 202.

the contrast between Calidore and Colin Clout, the one the hero of the
allegory, the other the main figure in the lyric outburst of the episode
on Acidale. The lyrical romanticism of the vision vanishes as soon as
the hero of the epic and allegorical sections intrudes. Calidore can
only wonder, "But why when I them saw, fled they away from me?"
(VI.x.19). The poetic impulses of discipline and freedom appear to
conflict.

At almost every opportunity, Spenser exults in a freedom from
discipline. Lacking all arms, Calepine chases after a bear, but this very
lack of arms, this release from restraint, proves to be an advantage.
The metaphorical description of the case fully communicates this
sense of freedom:

> like an Hauke, which feeling herselfe freed
> From bels and iesses, which did let her flight,
> Him seem'd his feet did fly, and in their speed delight. (VI.iv.19)

There is an almost childlike joy in these lines. At the opposite extreme,
the Hermit advises Serena and Timias to abstain from pleasure, restrain the will, subdue desire and bridle loose delight.

In Meliboe and his family Spenser finds this restrained and disci-
plined ideal of life to be the means of realizing the ideal of freedom.
The family and Calidore fall to their supper

> With small adoe, and nature satisfyde,
> The which doth little craue contended to abyde.          (VI.ix.17)

Although Spenser might have described the magnificence of nature in
providing for the natural needs of the body, he gives a distinctly ascetic
tinge to the meal. The supper of moderation leans in the direction of
the less frequently encountered evil in order to keep well away from
the superfluities of the courts with "the worlds gay showes" (VI.ix.22)
which Meliboe has left. For Meliboe, the shepherd's life is one of discipline insofar as he has chosen it with full knowledge of all the
pleasures (now perceived as vanities) which the court had to offer.
Yet Calidore sees that this life, in fact, provides a sense of internal
freedom, and he admires his host for

> Leading a life so free and fortunate,
> From all the tempests of these worldly seas.              (VI.ix.19)

This ideal of freedom does not afford the riotous excesses of libertine
naturalism, but instead unfetters the spirit from the "idle hopes," the
pride and ambition which Meliboe experienced during his ten years
at court.

This conflict between poetic discipline and freedom parallels a conflict in the conception of the virtue courtesy on the allegorical level, for the nature-nurture dichotomy as the basis of courtesy only translates to another stage the alternatives of freedom and spontaneity versus discipline. Since Spenser brings the principle of decorum to courtesy, the Salvage Man shows a form of courtesy appropriate to his degree. He is misshapen and *undisciplined*. He is courteous by gentle blood (nature). Tristram, on the other hand, has adorned his courtesy with the "goodly thewes" (VI.iv.38) of discipline (nurture). The child Calepine gives to Matilde exemplifies the predominant conception of the potential of nurture. Calepine presents the babe in whose spirit

> ye may enchace
> What euer formes ye list thereto apply,
> Being now soft and fit them to embrace;
> Whether ye list him traine in cheualry,
> Or noursle vp in lore of learn'd Philosophy. (VI.iv.35)

Nurture alone will not suffice for courtesy. Nature without training will produce the comic, but true, courtesy of the Salvage Man. The ideal figure of courtesy combines both nature and nurture, each complementing the other. (And in a parallel way, Spenser can only achieve the total unity he claims for the poem through a fusion of discipline and freedom in the poetry.) This whole concern with nature and nurture is crystallized in the metaphorical description of virtue. Calepine uses the image in his description of children like the one he gives to Matilde:

> those braue imps were sowen
> Here by the Gods, and fed with heauenly sap,
> That made them grow so high t'all honorable hap. (VI.iv.36)

The virtue of courtesy begins as a seed; but the seed's cultivation will play a large part in the form the virtue takes. Spenser develops this dominant image more carefully in the Proem. He invokes the Muses:

> Reuele to me the sacred noursery
> Of vertue . . .
> . . . .
> Since it at first was by the Gods with paine
> Planted in earth, being deriu'd at furst
> From heauenly seedes of bounty soueraine,
> And by them long with carefull labour nurst,
> Till it to ripenesse grew, and forth to honour burst.
> (VI.Proem.3)

As the focal point of the book, Canto X reveals this metaphor in the description of Pastorella "With heauenly gifts from heuen First *enraced*" (VI.x.25).

The resolution of the *apparent* conflict between freedom and discipline on the level of courtesy takes place quite easily in a harmonious combination of nature and nurture. But it is important to see how Spenser resolves the much more difficult conflicts on the two other levels in terms of poetry. On the levels of the poet and his work and the pastoral episode with Calidore and Colin, the conflict between the poetic impulses of discipline and freedom naturally enough centers around the use of conventions; since the Elizabethan poet like Spenser works in conventions, he is immediately faced with the literary necessity of infusing some vital substance as a personally and freely creative force into an otherwise dead form of discipline. The tenth canto is the testing ground for attempts to reconcile freedom and discipline in poetry. Again, this interpretation does not merely hypothesize about Spenser's intentions but tries to offer some explanation for the ordering of the materials already present in the poem. The importance of recognizing the manipulation of a convention *per se* can be deduced from the fact that in the vision of Acidale Spenser remolds specific conventions used in earlier cantos and endows them with a meaning beyond the conventional. At every point, then, the *total effect* is achieved by the *combination* of free inspiration working through the discipline of a convention.

For a new conception of poetic description, one need only compare the description of Serena (VI.viii.42) with that of the fourth Grace (VI.x.13–14). Serena, every bit as white as the fourth Grace, is hardened by the physical quality of the imagery (*e.g.*, the alabaster breast). The Song of Songs style is in itself a convention found in some of the best Elizabethan sensual poetry. The body's sexual appeal lies close to the surface. Serena's belly becomes an altar; her thighs, a triumphal arch, "and thereupon The spoiles of Princes hang'd, which were in battel won." Only the most fantastic extension of wit could conceive of the altar and the arch; the hyperbolic comparisons, because they are exaggerated, prevent the formation of any healthy attitude towards the body. In contrast, the description of the fourth Grace lavishes no attention upon the individual parts of her body. She and the Graces are simply naked. All the mythological ornamentation goes into her crown. Her beauty appears to the senses through the rose garland and the fragrant odors of the flowers. Otherwise she is all light. Nowhere does sexual experience suggest itself.

A more obvious convention occurs in the story of Mirabella. She receives her punishment, "when *Cupid* kept his court,/ As he is wont at each Saint Valentide" (VI.vii.32). The Court of Love makes use of accepted (pre-established) characters: Cupid, the jury, and the defendant. The story of the Graces also involves established mythological figures. But because Spenser is going to relate the Graces to his theme of courtesy, he must recreate the Graces as myth:

> These three on men all gracious gifts bestow,
> Which decke the body or adorne the mynde.     (VI.x.23)

They achieve mythic stature as they fulfill and realize the dominant image of heavenly forces planting the seeds of virtue. The Graces adorn, but, as sign and symbol, they reveal, in their own naked simplicity, the ultimate spiritual nature of the gifts. They freeze into their final mythic identity as the figures of a tradition in the visual arts:

> two of them still froward seem'd to bee,
> But one still towards shew'd her selfe afore;
> That good should from vs goe, then come in greater store.
>
> (VI.x.24)

By using the word *good*, Spenser avoids the suggestion of material benefits present in the Stoical interpretation of this sculptural arrangement as signifying giving, accepting and returning; he thus expands the allegory to fit into a larger moral and religious framework. The Graces adorn the shepherdess as the subject of the poet. With the opening invocation to the Muses, Spenser ties both Graces and Muses together. In the Proem, the Muses well into the minds of mortal men, "And goodly fury into them infuse." In the language of poetic signs, the Graces dramatize the act of the poet's divine inspiration.

In the episode of the Graces, Spenser transforms the convention in which he is working. The vision projects the first description of Pastorella:

> Vpon a litle hillocke she was placed
> Higher then all the rest, and round about
> Enuiron'd with a girland, goodly graced,
> Of louely lasses, and them all without
> The lustie shepheard swaynes sate in a rout,
> The which did pype and sing her prayses dew,
> And oft reioyce, and oft for wonder shout,
> As if some miracle of heauenly hew
> Were downe to them descended in that earthly vew.     (VI.ix.8)

The elements of pastoralism all appear, but little beyond the convention exists in these lines. The impulse of discipline keeps the poetry faithful to the tradition of an *Arcadia*. In the vision of the Graces, the discipline remains, but Spenser combines the convention with the natural poetry of *Epithalamion*. With care, he imitates the beautiful nature of a gentle flood:

> His siluer waues did softly tumble downe,
> Vnmard with ragged mosse or filthy mud.          (VI.x.7)

Spenser gives an impression of reality in the words "ragged" and "mud." Yet he avoids anything like naturalistic detail by defining the silver waves in opposition to the "ragged mosse or filthy mud." Spenser does not create a poetry wholly and artificially abstracted from real experience, for the moss and mud require some reference to the real world.

To recreate the pastoral convention, Spenser introduces the richness of classical allusion in Ariadne's crown. The felicitous correspondence in the heavenly hue of Pastorella between nature, the gods and man becomes more vividly dramatized in the picture of the Graces.

The poetic mode of Pastorella and her world is transformed into the vision of the four Graces. Canto X foreshadows the changes which Pastorella and her convention undergo in the remainder of the book. In this final change of poetic mode, Spenser again reworks, for purposes of contrast, a previously used poetic form. The brigands' capture of Pastorella bears too close a resemblance to the savage nation's capture of Serena to escape notice. Somewhere in the imaginative lacuna between Serena and Pastorella, Spenser transforms the Greek romance of Underdown's *An Ethiopian History* and Sidney's *Arcadia*. The Serena episode has all the trappings of the convention. Unlike the piping Shepherd poets, the savages are "Whooping, and hallowing on euery part" (VI.viii.40). The pagan sacrifice leads to the conceit in the description of Serena:

> her bellie white and clere,
> Which like an Altar did it selfe vprere,
> To offer sacrifice diuine thereon.          (VI.viii.42)

In their lurid actions, the villains almost rape their sacrifice, but "religion held euen theeues in measure" (VI.viii.43). This perverted and ironic suggestion of religion is precisely the point Spenser elaborates in Pastorella's capture. Through the brigands, Spenser symbolically lays waste the pastoral convention. All but the very spirit of the convention dies. The pure light of Pastorella's "starry beames" remains. And even she is contaminated by the carcasses that surround her, those encumbering shepherds of conventional discipline without inspiration, Spenser rises above the sheer plot of the romance. His poetry becomes elemental as it deals with the ultimate forces of life and death:

> But making way for death at large to walk:
> Who in the horror of the griesly night,
> In thousand dreadful shapes doth mongst them stalke,
> And makes huge hauocke, while the candlelight
> Out quenched, leaues no skill nor difference of wight.    (VI.xi.16)

Hell itself replaces the earlier pagan sacrifice. And in these "hellish dens," dwells the King of Hell, the Captain whose heart is "inly burnt with flames most raging whot." Metaphorically, Spenser continues to oppose the heavenly and hellish: Pastorella, as the pure spirit of the pastoral world, is "Like a sweet Angell twixt two clouds vphild: / Her louely light was dimmed and decayed" (VI.xi.21). Then, a more successful Orpheus saving his Eurydice from the underworld, Calidore battles his way "into th'open light." Pastorella undergoes the cycle of life, death and rebirth: "So her vneath at last he did reuiue, / That long had lyen dead, and made againe aliue" (VI.xi.50). Spenser's thought centers around the rebirth of Pastorella, and rebirth plays a part in the most effective moment in the elaborate machinery of Pastorella's reunion with her parents, when Claribell softly weeping says, "And liuest thou my daughter now againe?/And art thou yet aliue, whom dead I long did faine?" (VI.xii.19). As in *The Winter's Tale,* the feeling of rebirth and regeneration prevails. Both works fuse the Greek romance with Christian myth. Although courtesy is primarily a secular virtue, its religious tones should not be missed. At the climax of the book, the Blatant Beast attacks religion—not simply the accouterments Spenser fought in *The Shepheardes Calender,* but the spiritual core of religion. The Blatant Beast demolishes the Monastery, "Regarding nought religion, nor their holy heast" (VI.xii.24).

What holds true for courtesy holds true for the book's second subject, the definition of poetry: the very element added to revitalize the Greek romance, the spiritual and Platonic aspect of Christianity, is essential to courtesy. Similarly, the principle that virtue consists in inward thoughts and not in outward shows finds its parallel in poetry as it is defined in Canto X: unlike the savages' sacrifice of human flesh to their false gods, the poet (Colin Clout) offers a tribute to the heavenly principles by celebrating the virtue of his lass. He pictures in her all the grace of divine resemblance, chastity, and beauty. Poetry, like courtesy, is not self-contained. Courtesy reveals itself in civil deeds, all decorously ordered to the degree and demands of a given situation. In the vision of the Graces, Colin receives his poetic inspiration from his subject. Similarly, the shepherd lass receives her apotheosis only through the medium of poetry. Mirabella was at fault for scorning her knightly loves: "For beautie is more glorious bright and clere,/The more it is admir'd of many a wight" (VI.vii.29). Poetry and courtesy both demand a kind of selflessness. Coridon lacks true courtesy because he fears to approach the tiger that threatens Pastorella: "His life he steemed dearer then his frend" (VI.x.35). Calidore is always self-sacrificing and generous. His virtue of courtesy increases by *reflection.* Just so with Colin Clout; his honor as poet depends upon his conveying, in the language of signs, the essence of the Graces. The Grace episode clarifies an essential unity in the book. One's own virtue increases as others reflect it. Spenser fulfills the promise he made to the "most dreaded Soueraine," "That from your selfe I doe this vertue bring,/ And to your selfe doe it returne againe" (VI.Proem.7). Colin's shepherdess is the handmaid of Gloriana. Her light reflects that of Gloriana:

> Sunne of the world, great glory of the sky,
> That all the earth doest lighten with thy rayes,
> Great *Gloriana,* greatest Maiesty.                                        (VI.x.28)

Spenser separates himself from Colin Clout because his relationship with *The Faerie Queene* (the poet-*persona* of the first level) can become clear only to the extent that he objectively defines the relationship between Colin Clout and the unknown shepherdess (the second, "dramatic" level). The poetic conventions discipline personal identification and inspiration.

If Spenser is to make good his claim that although his course has been stayed, he has never strayed, then the pastoral interlude which seems to serve primarily to introduce poetry as a thematic concern must also be functionally related to the allegorical level. And, indeed, the interlude has its allegorical justification: it brings love into the realm of courtesy. Venus resorts to Acidale (VI.x.9), and the Graces are "handmaids of Venus." Mythologically, love brings "all the complements of curtesie" (VI.x.23). In the Platonic purity of the Graces, Spenser affirms Bembo's discourse on the ennobling effects of love in the training of the young courtier in Castiglione's *The Courtier.* Thus Spenser places the Legend of Courtesy squarely in the tradition of the conduct book and encompasses the entire work—including the pastoral episode—in a single convention. Love not only helps in the definition of courtesy but also has a reciprocal function in giving the book a formal unity. While the poetry gains its graces from the lyricism of love, Spenser has his eye on the total design of the book; "The generall end therefore of all the booke is to fashion a gentleman or noble person in vertuous and gentle discipline." The freedom of personal emotion and inspiration works hand-in-hand with a discipline of form, just as the gentle mind needs gentle deeds and the outward shows need inner thoughts to fulfill the ideal of courtesy.

# The *Mutabilitie Cantos*:
# Archaism and Evolution in Retrospect

## *by Harry Berger, Jr.*

The view of experience expressed in and as Spenser's poetry is shaped by a radically historical consciousness. It is historical in two reciprocal aspects: the objective character of Spenser's vision is *evolutionary;* its subjective mode is *retrospective.* The present essay will explore these terms in the specific context of the *Mutabilitie Cantos,* but I shall preface my interpretation with some remarks of a more general nature in order to clarify my use of these terms. By evolutionary I mean that we may find in Spenser's poetry an overall developmental pattern in which three vectors coalesce: from lower to higher, from simpler to more complex and, of course, from earlier to later. These vectors run parallel courses in the history of the individual psyche and in that of culture or civilization. The relation between these two courses is reciprocal. Haeckel's discredited biogenetic formula, "ontogeny recapitulates phylogeny," covers one side of it: the individual organism (the microcosm, the human or psychic *discordia concors*) manifests in compressed form the development of culture from its earler childhood phases to its later more sophisticated phases. The normal and normative growth of human consciousness and conscience is from a relatively narrow, simplistic or elementally "pure" perspective to a broader, more complex and comprehensive perspective. In early or in regressive stages, for example, distinguishable areas tend to blur or overlap, as when the mind fails to perceive or respect the boundaries between itself and the world, man and God, self and other, love and hate, heaven and earth, the divine and the chaotic or natural sources of energy. The other side of the reciprocity between psyche

Pp. 146–49 of this essay constitute a modified version of the opening pages of "Archaism, Immortality, and the Muse in Spenser's Poetry," to be published in *Yale Review,* LVIII (1968–1969). Some paragraphs of the earlier version were in turn revised from "Spenser's View of Experience," *Studies in English Literature,* VIII (Winter, 1968), 1–18.

and culture is the effect of the microcosm on any phase of the larger order: here Spenser agrees with Plato, Virgil, and others in depicting the institutions and products of "early" culture as dominated by, expressive of, those tendencies of the psyche which are usually described as childlike, autistic, superstitious, sensuous.

The subjective mode of Spenser's historical vision is retrospective: he looks back into the past from his own *here and now*. In his early or archaic world, action is caused for the most part by the large-scale play of forces which, though psychic as well as cosmic, operate outside of any individual will or consciousness. Book III of *The Faerie Queene* is especially ordered to suggest how entirely independent actions and episodes, occurring in widely separated places and moments of the Spenserian world, are triggered in such a way as to produce a meaningful coalescence whose import could not possibly be grasped by any of the figures involved, except perhaps for gods and prophets (and even their perspectives are limited in ways to be discussed below). The driving purpose of this organic system of forces is beyond its conscious members because both system and purpose are retrospectively fashioned by the poet, and only tentatively, temporarily, fulfilled in his own time. The possibility of prophecy is founded on deterministic presuppositions, and a leading characteristic of Spenser's "primitive" age is the manifest domination of behavior by extra-human forces whose influence tends toward the conservation or restoration of an archaic state of affairs. As psyche and culture develop, this collective and determined mode of behavior gradually yields to the more active and original assertions of individual souls. When the center of will, decision, and activity is located in the individual consciousness, archaic determinism gives way to retrospective determinism as the dominant organizing mode.

When cosmic and primitive influences dominate, the forms of existence tend to be at once unstable and universal (i.e., recurrent, generic or archetypal). When psychic and rational influences dominate, the forms tend to be personal, unique and potentially more stable; at the same time, the forms of discord, evil, danger and temptation are subtler, therefore less easily located and contained. Fundamental to this model is Spenser's conviction that no moment of union or reconciliation, of relief or triumph, is to be construed as absolute—absolute either in the sense of being final, or in the sense of being totally one-sided. Every triumph or resolution at a lower level of existence or an earlier phase of experience releases new and different problems at a higher level or a later phase. This will be oddly demonstrated in the *Muta-*

*bilitie Cantos,* where the vision of cosmic harmony which triumphantly concludes canto vii in the medieval mode triggers a new brief lyric moment of anxiety in the closing stanzas.

The full vision of the pattern I have been describing is seldom attained by characters within the Spenserian world, while its complex and articulated unity is a condition attained by soul, state, or culture only in relatively advanced phases of its career. And only in such phases does the imagination double back to activate the tacit or latent elements—the primitive and palingenetic factors—of experience in order to set the present moment within its developmental context. As I suggested before, Spenser presents the latest form of experience both *in* his work and *as* his work. The historical sense which is the defining mark of that work asserts itself in his effort to locate the various elements of his poetic *discordia concors* at their proper temporal distances from the present. His poetry thus represents in its complex form all the phases which preceded it and which it, in effect, supersedes. This representation is achieved by means of the technique of *conspicuous allusion:* the depiction of stock literary motifs, characters, and genres in a manner which emphasizes their conventionality, displaying at once their debt to and their existence in a conventional climate—classical, medieval, romance, etc.—which is archaic when seen from Spenser's retrospective viewpoint.

The *Mutabilitie Cantos* provide the most concise and complete embodiment of Spenser's historical consciousness. Explicitly lyric or self-referential in mode, the poem not only directs our attention toward the "modern" narrator, it also reveals the effect of his retrospective narrative on his own feelings. Spenser uses conspicuous allusion to organize the poem along evolutionary lines: its three sections—canto vi, canto vii, and the final two stanzas[1]—develop what is in effect an ontogenetic recapitulation of the phases of experience from pagan through medieval modes of imagination to the lyric (and renaissance) present. Canto vii, the medieval phase, includes, infolds, and transcends the two simple pagan modes (epic and pastoral) of the comic sixth canto. The later moment is a more complex, more finely articulated revision of the earlier moment, which it redirects and transforms; but it is itself distanced and superseded in the poem's concluding stanzas.

---

[1] Cf. the different triadic scheme in Donald Cheney, *Spenser's Image of Nature: Wild Man and Shepherd in "The Faerie Queene"* (New Haven, 1966), p. 246; he divides canto vi into epic and pastoral sections, resolved in the "didactic synthesis" of canto vii.

If we look carefully at the six-stanza proem we shall see that all the themes, attitudes and problems to be displayed throughout the work are present here in a special and temporary form, i.e., dominated by a limited viewpoint which will change as Spenser moves through the poem:

> What man that sees the ever-whirling wheele
>     Of Change, the which all mortall things doth sway,
>     But that therby doth find, and plainly feele,
>     How MUTABILITY in them doth play
>     Her cruell sports, to many mens decay?
>     Which that to all may better yet appeare,
>     I will rehearse that whylome I heard say,
>     How she at first her selfe began to reare,
> Gainst all the Gods, and th'empire sought from them to beare.
>
> But first, here falleth, fittest to unfold
>     Her antique race and linage ancient,
>     As I have found it registred of old,
>     In Faery Land mongst records permanent:
>     She was, to weet, a daughter by descent
>     Of those old Titans, that did whylome strive
>     With Saturnes sonne for heavens regiment.
>     Whom, though high Jove of kingdome did deprive,
> Yet many of their steeme long after did survive.
>
> And many of them, afterwards obtain'd
>     Great power of Jove, and high authority;
>     As Hecate, in whose almighty hand,
>     He plac't all rule and principality,
>     To be by her disposed diversly,
>     To Gods, and men, as she them list divide:
>     And drad Bellona, that doth sound on hie
>     Warres and allarums unto Nations wide,
> That makes both heaven and earth to tremble at her pride.
>
> So likewise did this Titanesse aspire,
>     Rule and dominion to her selfe to gaine;
>     That as a Goddesse, men might her admire,
>     And heavenly honours yield, as to them twaine.
>     At first, on earth she sought it to obtaine;
>     Where she such proofe and sad examples shewed
>     Of her great power, to many ones great paine,
>     That not men onely (whom she soone subdewed)
> But eke all other creatures, her bad doings rewed.

For, she the face of earthly things so changed,
  That all which Nature had establisht first
  In good estate, and in meet order ranged,
  She did pervert, and all their statutes burst:
  And all the worlds faire frame (which none yet durst
  Of Gods or men to alter or misguide)
  She alter'd quite, and made them all accurst
  That God had blest; and did at first provide
In that still happy state for ever to abide.

Ne shee the lawes of Nature onely brake,
  But eke of Justice, and of Policie;
  And wrong of right, and bad of good did make,
  And death for life exchanged foolishlie:
  Since which, all living wights have learn'd to die,
  And all this world is woxen daily worse.
  O pittious worke of MUTABILITIE!
  By which, we all are subject to that curse,
And death in stead of life have sucked from our Nurse.

By the end of the poem Spenser will stand before us as *a man* in
meditation, responding personally to what he has made and seen. But
here he introduces himself in a more detached stance as *a poet* who
will use an old story to exemplify and embellish the power of mutability. At first he separates himself from the audience ("What man . . .")
whose concern he will delineate in fiction. His attention moves back
to the pagan genealogy and its sources, mentioning not only Mutabilitie's ancient lineage, but also the antique account of the lineage.
"Faery Land" seems to have two references: to his own literary world
or imagination, the myths and fictions devised by the poet of *The
Faerie Queene;* and to the "antique rolles" in the "everlasting scryne"
(I.Pr.2) of the Muses, the fictions, myths, and legends recorded throughout history. The association of the everlasting *scryne* (from *scrinium,* a
chest or casket for manuscripts) with antique rolls and of "records
permanent" with "registred of old" suggests something fixed early
in culture, therefore permanent but not necessarily adequate. This
kind of permanence sets itself over against that of "the ever-whirling
wheele," and it therefore embodies the wish to resist inevitable change,
to memorialize for all time a particular vision or solution that arose
in response to a particular situation. As the ever-whirling wheel is an
early and defective view of the dynamic recurrence that yields the
constancy of Nature, so this archaic permanence is a defective prevision
or imitation of that on which Nature and the poet meditate at poem's
end. In the second and third sections, these simple opposites—whirl

and permanence—will converge and interpenetrate, will move forward and inward from the reconciling cosmic symbolism of the medieval mind to the lyric present in which the poet stands, altered yet still unreconciled—even more deeply divided, in fact, by what he has envisaged.

Something like this larger pattern of movement is condensed in the proem, though it takes a different direction. Stanzas 2–4 comprise a relatively matter-of-fact rehearsal in the antique pagan mode of canto vi. Stanza 5 anticipates canto vii by introducing Nature and allowing Judaeo-Christian echoes to filter in. As the poet lists Mutabilitie's evil effects in stanzas 5 and 6, the rhythm and feeling of his rhetoric build toward the exclamation—"O pittious worke of MUTABILITY!"— and toward the final couplet that at once generalizes the curse and draws it close by the use of the first person plural. Like the blatant beast at the end of Book VI, Mutabilitie seems to rush from the remote past into the poet's present as her influence spreads throughout the universe and into the human domain where Justice and Policy have been abused. The proem thus ends at a nadir. Having moved from the position of detached narrator, the poet now joins his mortal audience, plainly feels the effect of what he has found or invented, and actualizes the grimmest possibilities of the opening lines.

These lines imply a limitation of vision and response most explicitly glossed by the proem to Book V, which the sentiments expressed in stanza 6 echo in more condensed form. The man that sees the ever-whirling wheel may not see beyond it, and as a result he *plainly* feels mutability as entirely evil. In addition to *clearly* or *vividly*, the word *plainly* carries the sense of *directly, flatly, simply.* Spenser here depicts an objective attitude, a general frame of mind, and then adopts it as his own. It is nevertheless adopted with a degree of detachment as the *wrong* attitude, one that affects his view of life, that will affect his poem, and that is modified in the course of narration. In Book V and the *Mutabilitie Cantos,* he locates this attitude in the poetic first person in order to dramatize it, give it play, and put it to the test. The attitude is the basic problem—the enemy, as it were—with which both poems deal. It is an attitude that in one form Spenser stated directly at the beginning of *A View of the Present State of Ireland.* Irenius reports the received opinion that it is Ireland's "fatall destinie" that no purposes "mente for her good" can succeed in reforming that miserable nation, perhaps because of "the *very Genius* of the soile, or influence of the starres, or that Allmighty god hath not yeat Appointed the tyme of her reformacion or that he reserveth her in this unquiet state still, for some secrete skourge, which shall by her Come into Englande." Eudoxus pooh-poohs this opinion as the "vaine Conceipt of simple men" and attributes the trouble rather to "the unsoundnes of . . . Counsells and Plottes." He then offers the commonplace criticism, perhaps most familiar to us in Edmund's famous soliloquy on Gloucester's self-deception, that "it is the manner of men that when they are fallen into anye Absurditye or theire accions succede not as they woulde they are ready allwaies to impute the blame theareof unto the heavens, soe to excuse their owne follies and imperfeccions. . . . it is the manner . . . of desperate men farre driven to wishe the utter ruine of that which they Cannot redresse. . . ." [2]—the manner not only of the egalitarian giant of *The Faerie Queene* (V.ii), for example, but also of the justice of Talus and Artegal and, to some extent, of Spenser's own vision of actuality in that book.

When Spenser dramatizes this "vaine Conceipt" at the beginning of the *Mutabilitie Cantos,* he immediately connects it with the "records permanent" of antiquity. It is the response "of simple men," the pessimistic fatalism of the vulgar mind "farre driven." At the same time it is characterized as regressive by being "historically" located in an archaic framework of pagan conceptions and images. The essence of this framework lies in the polarity between Mutabilitie and Nature as Spenser initially presents it—*initially*, that is, because the idea of nature in vi.5–6 will be radically altered in the figure of Natura who dominates canto vii.[3] Nature in vi.5–6 has already succumbed to mutability, who *brake* her laws, *changed, did pervert,* and *alter'd quite* her original estate and the world's fair frame. Stanza 5 tends to push Nature back into Eden and identify the reign of her enemy with the whole history of fallen man,[4] though the general pagan context diffuses the Edenic reference so that it is suggestive of any conception of the first golden age. This idea of nature has already been outmoded because it projects unrealistic expectations; it is based on a longing for too perfect and fixed a state of nature. Under the pressure of actual life, so unguardedly sanguine a hope dialectically produces its opposite, that is, the despairing acceptance of negative mutability as life's ruling

[2] *Variorum* 9.43–4. The connection has been made by John Danby, *Shakespeare's Doctrine of Nature* (London, 1949), pp. 35–8, and related to Spenser's description of Nature at vii. 5–6.

[3] Noted by Sherman Hawkins, "Mutabilitie and the Cycle of the Months," in *Form and Convention in the Poetry of Edmund Spenser,* ed. William Nelson (New York and London, 1961), p. 86f.

[4] In *Paradise Lost,* Milton ascribes a similar attitude to the God of Book III. Cf. my "Archaism, Vision, and Revision: Studies in Virgil, Plato, and Milton," *Centennial Review,* XI, 1 (Winter, 1967), 46ff.

principle, which in turn generates the wish to escape back into the paradisaic state of nature. Wish-fulfillment and nightmare are simple contraries, twinned and mutually intensifying impulses, neither of which is more realistic than the other. We may thus translate the fabled triumph of mutability over sublunary nature into its psychological equivalent: it is the triumph of a view of earthly life that "sees the ever-whirling wheele" of entropic change as the nature of things, having succeeded an inadequate and fragile view of nature as a pleasure garden where all things endure forever just as they were when "establisht first / In good estate, and in meet order ranged." In terms of the mythology of Book V, this radical counterswing from the golden to the iron age, from Saturn to Jove, is signified by the departure from earth of Astraea, whose virginity symbolizes classical disdain and self-withholding exclusiveness. Her desire to resist change, to retain in its purity her ruthlessly idealistic and aprioristic justice, is related to the feeling that the present decay of justice, politics, and ethics may have been determined from creation by the mechanics of physical change:

> Me seemes the world is runne quite out of square,
> From the first point of his appointed sourse,
> And being once amisse growes daily wourse and wourse.　(V.Pr. 1)

This is archaic determinism, whose premise of irreversible decline dissipates the possibility of second thoughts and second chances, of rebirth, redemption, and revision.[5] It encourages the violent repressiveness of iron-age justice in Jove, Hercules, Artegal, Talus, and the stoic censors.

The opposed visions of the ever-whirling wheel and the ever-abiding happy state are permanent possibilities for the mind, but they represent an archaic mode of seeing and feeling. Therefore they "may better yet appeare" in the *whylome* form recorded early in man's psycho-cultural history. In signalling his return to this mode, the poet dramatically enacts the urge to escape time, change, and history. During the remainder of the sixth canto this assumption of the archaic perspective is comically sustained by a number of parodistic devices that I shall now discuss:

1) To attribute all evil to mutability, "to impute . . . unto the heavens" the blame for human follies and sins and failures, is the first stage of a time-honored mode of evasion.[6] The next stage is to devise

---

[5] Cf. "Archaism, Vision, and Revision," pp. 26–8 and 33–8.
[6] Cf. Cheney, *Wild Man*, pp. 240–1; Hawkins, "Cycle," p. 84; Kathleen Williams, *Spenser's World of Glass: A Reading of The Faerie Queene* (Berkeley and Los Angeles, 1966), pp. 225–6.

a way of producing an Ultimate Solution in a single encounter, and this is accomplished by condensing all evils into an allegorical or mythological scapegoat who may then be defeated by a more powerful divine embodiment of order. Helpless man may thus surrender both his responsibility and his power, may relieve himself of moral efficacy and effort, consigning the good fight to the cosmic forces of Darkness and Light. This is a return not only to primitive, but also to childlike, sensibility—thus the appropriateness of Spenser's recourse to an old fairytale. From the total evil plaintively delineated in the first six stanzas he withdraws into a purely recreative world of ancient fable and into a comic portrait of the way in which antique genres—the high and low styles of heroic bombast and pastoral homeliness—render and cope with the problem of mutability.[7]

2) The opposition between simple change and simple permanence, black mutability and golden nature, plaintive and recreative attitudes, high and low styles, points toward an attempt stylistically to imitate an archaic pattern mentioned in the beginning of this essay—the separation of elements into pure and mutually exclusive contraries. Such divisiveness is already the essence of the fable action in this canto, from the first mention of Mutabilitie's antique lineage through the facing-off with Cynthia and Jove to the new arrangement of these contraries in the pastoral digression. The action of the canto is so disposed as to emphasize the catabolic process of fragmentation, the breaking down of primeval and unstable compounds: chaos/earth/heaven; Uranus/Titan/Saturn and Saturn/Jove; Jove/Hecate/Bellona (the latter two being opposed principles of order and disorder); male and female, old and young, separating off from the primal family matrix; the members of the ruling Olympian pantheon set at odds among themselves by Mutabilitie's assault (vi.23); the hints of a composite goddess splitting into Hecate, Cynthia, and Diana; Mutabilitie by implication dividing into Faunus and Diana, the lustful voyeur and the Astraean destroyer of Ireland's "first . . . good estate"; the uneasy pastoral alliance between Ovidian mythic and Irish actual landscapes.

This pattern penetrates the division of the canto into high and low styles. The inherent contrariety between epic and pastoral perspectives is intensified by Spenser's comic exaggerations of the devices which characterize each mode: in the former, bombastic rhetoric, heroic vaunting and "flyting," Homeric formulas, cosmic muscularity, panoramic vistas, and in general the fusty, expansive, and broad-planed

---

[7] Cheney (*Wild Man*, pp. 241–2) remarks on the tone of "detached, ironic wit" informing the first third of the canto (i.e., the heroic episode).

way of at once magnifying and simplifying problems;[8] in the latter, the problems reduced, lightened, dissipated in homely analogies, rustic minutiae, buffoonery, sylvan diversions, minor woodland metamorphoses, and echoes of Spenser's own early literary play.[9]

The pastoral episode is not comic relief, for the simple reason that it is no less serious than the heroic episode, in which the inflated presentation is continually punctured. The conflict between Mutabilitie and Cynthia, for example, is little more than a scuffle between oversized schoolgirls (vi.13), and Jove ends five thundering stanzas in a wheedle: "ceasse thy idle claime thou foolish gerle" (vi.34). Both episodes are equally comic and recreative, equally acts of withdrawal into ancient fairyland from the grimmer vision of the opening stanzas. The more intricate and pressing human issues, the problems of justice and polity, are introduced at the beginning and conspicuously ignored. Early epic and pastoral are portrayed from the standpoint of the present as pure contraries that fall on either side of real life; the poet climbs upward and backward to Jove's heaven until Jove is about to be passed by (vi.35–36), at which point he runs downward to make a new beginning in Cynthia's unfallen wood.

3) In canto vi, Mutabilitie, Cynthia, Mercury, Arlo Hill, and to some extent the other gods, including Jove, all suffer the same ignominious fate at the hands of their author; they are *desymbolized,* for they are more cosmic, portentous, and epic at the beginning of the canto than at the end. Spenser first flashes the full range of symbolic references while converting the referents to mythic or allegorical personifications, then conspicuously ignores or abandons these references for the literal play of his story. Withdrawal into the recreative now of storytelling is heightened by the fact that most of the symbolic references that are present-as-excluded are plaintive. Mutabilitie begins as the ever-whirling wheel of entropic change, is personified before being blamed for the sum total of human vicissitudes, and, immediately after the proem, drops off these first two stages to become merely a very large, aggressive, and upward-mobile woman with some of the qualities of Britomart and Radegund. Spenser's obvious relish in heroic parody, the enjoyment with which he gratuitously elaborates details of dialogue and description, produce something like a cartoon-strip world whose heroine is a version of Superwoman; but it is a world seen through the eyes of *Mad* magazine.

---

[8] Examples in Stanzas 3, 7, 10–12, 21; 20–21, 26–33; 3, 14, 18, 22, 30; 7, 10, 22; 8, 10, 14, 19, 23.

[9] Examples in stanzas 47–8; 39, 48, 50; 46, 49; 41–2; 40–1, 51, 53.

This recreative desymbolizing is historical in its implications, because Spenser directs us to the more recent identities of the gods as
planetary forces before he moves back to animate their older mythological images as Ovidian dramatis personae. Cynthia and Mercury
are introduced in astronomical guise (vi.8,14), but are immediately
converted to emblematic or mythological figures. Mutabilitie climbs
to the "Circle of the Moone" and Cynthia's "bright shining palace,"

> All fairely deckt with heavens goodly *story;*
>   Whose silver gates (by which there sate an *hory*
>   Old aged Sire, with hower-glasse in hand,
>   Hight Tyme) she entred, were he liefe or sory:
>   Ne staide till she the highest *stage* had scand,
> Where Cynthia did sit, that never still did stand.

> Her sitting on an Ivory throne shee found,
>   Drawne of two steeds, th'one black, the other white,
>   Environd with tenne thousand starres around,
>   That duly her attended day and night;
>   And by her side there ran her Page, that hight
>   Vesper, whom we the Evening-starre intend:
>   That with his Torche, still twinkling like twylight,
>   Her lightened all the way where she should wend,
> And joy to weary wandring travailers did lend. . . .

(vi.8–9, italics mine)

The italicized puns pivot the scene from astronomical space and function to theatrical or emblematic fiction, and this process is completed
in the symbolic reversal whereby Vesper's torch becomes the subject,
and his twilight only the comparison, of the simile. By the time Mutabilitie has laid hold of Cynthia—"raught forth her hand / To pluck
her downe perforce from off her chaire" and threatened to club her
with "her golden wand" (vi.13)—the hieratic emblems have themselves
given way to physical action that on the one hand is heightened by
epic scale and rhetoric and on the other hand is comic, even pastoral,
in its inconsequence. A multi-level stage set replaces the spheres, em-
bellishing an action invented and controlled by the myth-making
mind. This frames the foreground artifice—the reduction to purely
visual and spatial terms of a subject whose essential meaning is temporal.

Desymbolizing is a contrastive technique that, while dividing the
surface narrative from its significant background, keeps both before
us. We are encouraged to feel that the narrative obscures the themes
that generate and organize the plot of the fable. We learn at the be-

ginning of the canto that the superlunary world is about to be threatened by mutability. The heroine's ascent through the spheres therefore acts out some contemporary commonplaces in a pessimistic or apocalyptic vein. Perhaps it also alludes to current changes in astronomical and cosmological theory. Toward the end of the epic section, we are given glimpses of the hidden order that will emerge in canto vii. Jove begins to use legal jargon (vi.33). Mutabilitie, whose ultimate ambition was presented earlier as a martial attempt to displace "highest Jove" from his palace in the "highest sky," aims beyond Jove (vi. 34–36) and wants to plead her case before "the highest him," the "God of Nature." Jove is grudgingly forced to accede, and bids "Dan Phoebus Scribe her Appellation seale." By this time Mutabilitie has become more beautiful, or at least her physical stature and beauty are noted by Spenser, the gods, and Jove (vi.28, 31–34) for the first time only after she has ascended to Jove's palace. This alteration will be clarified in the next canto, when the beauty of change is emphasized, but here it seems a purely gratuitous and *ad hoc* touch.

4) All this points toward a purposeful disjunction between the underlying order apparent to the medieval Christian imagination of canto vii, and the misguided, obscure anticipations of the pagan mythopoesis that dominates canto vi. This disjunction, the fourth and final aspect of canto vi to be discussed, reinforces the conspicuously digressive quality of the narrative. It sets off the instability of the characters and, occasionally, of the narrative. It heightens the comic effect of inflatedness and irrelevance that attends the posturing of the gods. For, looking back from stanzas 33–36, we see the episode in an entirely new light. Mutabilitie's real problem is procedural and falls within the legal domain of Right, not the martial domain of Might: she wants a hearing and apparently has to go through channels and attract the attention of the proper authorities to get one. This lends her previous wranglings the air of legalistic maneuvers. Her transactions with Cynthia, Mercury, and Jove retrospectively assume this character, whereas Jove's feeble effort at seduction (vi.34) seems motivated not solely by lust, but also, as she points out, by his desire to keep her from putting her case before the court. As the plot action moves closer to the higher and later system of forces disclosed in the next canto, it reveals the influence of that system with increasing clarity.

From this standpoint, the heroic pagan gestures are at once more meaningless in themselves and more significant as expressions of limited responses. There is very little real action or conflict in the

episode, and even this is continually interrupted or deflected: the
tussle with Cynthia, the interchange with Mercury, the military council of the gods, the assault on heaven, and the interview with Jove are
all broken off (vi.17, 19, 24ff., 35–36) for apparently arbitrary reasons
before they produce any serious consequences. Plot and narrative
therefore seem ruled by contingency and whim, by unforeseen oc-
currences and unexpected reactions. Against this pattern, such resound-
ing passages as the following are faintly ridiculous, especially the final
example, in which the advent of mutability reduces the ancient psycho-
pomp to his Lord's legman:

> Eftsoones she cast by force and tortious might,
> Her [Cynthia] to displace. . . .                                    (vi.10)

> Fearing least Chaos broken had his chaine,
> And brought againe on them eternall night. . . .                    (vi.14)

> Doubting least Typhon were againe uprear'd,
> Or other his old foes, that once him sorely fear'd                   (vi.15)

> And there-with-all, he on her shoulder laid
> His snaky-wreathed Mace, whose awfull power
> Doth make both Gods and hellish fiends affraid:
> Where-at the Titanesse did sternely lower,
> And stoutly answer'd, that in evill hower
> He from his Jove such message to her brought,
> To bid her leave faire Cynthias silver bower;
> Sith shee his Jove and him esteemed nought,
> No more then Cynthia's self; but all their kingdoms sought.

> The Heavens Herald staid not to reply,
> But past away, his doings to relate
> Unto his Lord. . . .                                               (vi.18–19)

The antique thunder, the fear of the recurrence of old catastrophes,
the portentous gesture with the caduceus—these items, all futile or
beside the point, contribute to Spenser's image of the archaic mind.
Together with the emergent influence of the medieval *concordia discors*—the process of gradual, ordered change silently moving and
modifying these *antickes*—they suggest that mind's inflated self-image,
its tendency toward violent and headlong yet easily deflected impulses,
its backward-looking reliance upon ancient precedents, and its consequent ignorance of or resistance to Nature's message that all things
"by their change their being doe dilate." [10]

[10] So Orgoglio's "auncient" porter and foster father Ignaro, "An old old man, with
beard as white as snow," who held "the keyes of every inner dore," but could not

Thomas M. Greene has described the "perpetual *becoming*" of Spenser's characters while their "status and meaning and concreteness . . . shift and fade and recombine," [11] and this is exemplified in a pointedly contrapuntal manner by the *Two Cantos of Mutabilitie*. What unfolds in the seventh canto as cyclical and developmental change, appears at the surface of canto vi as random motion and instability. The gods not only shift from planets to characters, they suffer sudden changes of quality and whim, as when the stern titaness becomes beautiful and Jove is moved from anger to desire. Both Mutabilitie and Mercury experience, then *boldly* overcome, unexpected impulses of fear (vi.17–18; 25–26). When Mutabilitie and Cynthia face off, the latter is momentarily infected with her enemy's nature ("sterne countenaunce and disdainfull cheare," vi.12). Cynthia's demotion to her earthly domain, in the pastoral digression, seems to intensify this influence. She destroys her *locus amoenus* just as the titaness had destroyed golden nature. As if in reaction to her closer involvement with mutable earth and lustful males, she waxes Astraean in her self-withholding disdain (vi.42) and her anger at folly and weakness (vi.51, 54–55).[12]

The pastoral digression is the most interesting example of instability, because it is the speaker himself who is affected: Spenser introduces Arlo Hill as a place of revelation "Where all, both heavenly Powers, and earthly wights, / Before great Natures presence should appeare," but presents himself as distracted immediately after by the thought of his own earlier pastoral portrait of that region of Munster ("my old father Mole, whom Shepheards quill / Renowmed hath with hymnes fit for a rurall skill," vi.36). He spends the next stanza vacillating:

> And, were it not ill fitting for this file,
> > To sing of hilles and woods, mongst warres and Knights,
> > I would abate the sternenesse of my stile,
> > Mongst these sterne stounds to mingle soft delights;
> > And tell how Arlo through Dianaes spights
> > (Beeing of old the best and fairest Hill
> > That was in all this holy-Islands hights)
> > Was made the most unpleasant, and most ill.
> > Meane while, O Clio, lend Calliope thy quill.      (vi.37)

---

use them, since "as he forward moov'd his footing old, / So backward still was turnd his wrincled face" (I.viii.30–1).

[11] *The Descent From Heaven* (New Haven and London, 1963), pp. 330–1.

[12] Cf. Cheney, *Wild Man*, pp. 245–7. Faunus has often been recognized as an allegorization of bestial man, but the gist of such an identification, if it is to be allowed, is that this is a pointedly biased and contemptuous estimate of man from the god's, and goddess', angle of vision.

The fact that the conditional is negative in force, and that Calliope is more appropriate for great Nature's trial than for Faunus' minor tribulations, suggests that Spenser has controlled the impulse to digress. But this only accentuates the about-face of the next lines, in which he appears to yield to his caprice in spite of himself.

As an alternative to the prospective trial, the pastoral episode may strike us even more sharply as reversion and diversion—reversion to an obviously fanciful mixture of outmoded Spenserian, Irish, and classical myths of the permanence-mutability conflict, and diversion from the glimpse of cosmic order to a playful explanation of the entropic change that still prevails on earth. The problems raised in the opening stanzas of canto vi re-enter in much diminished and localized form. Well-known metamorphic catastrophes are alluded to but averted.[13] The canto concludes with a kind of black joke upon Ireland—Diana's "heavy haplesse curse" that specifies that wolves should

> all those Woods deface,
> And Thieves should rob and spoile that Coast around.
> Since which, those Woods, and all that goodly Chase,
> Doth to this day with Wolves and Thieves abound:
> Which too-too true that lands in-dwellers since have found.
>
> (vi.55)

Having looked through the archaic or youthful mind's anthropomorphic window on the world, Spenser ends on a Eudoxian note that makes light of that whole realm of explanation: "men fallen into any Absurditye . . . are ready allwaies to impute blame theareof unto the heavens, soe to excuse their owne follies and imperfeccions." It is the explanation, not the problem, that is parodied, for the canto, like the six-stanza proem, ends with a sudden return to the present and to the nearness, the actuality, of the dark "state of present time" in Ireland. It ends, furthermore, upon a more intensely pessimistic note: "desperate men farre driven . . . wishe the utter ruine of that which they Cannot redresse." The destructive wish flashing forth in the final stanza makes the Ovidian *pourquoi* story and "the image of the antique world" seem frivolous by contrast—a flight into the recreative mode of imagination, with its focus upon the pleasures of fancy and the ornaments of verse.[14] It is the mode most appropriate to the poet

---

[13] Noted by Cheney, *Wild Man*, p. 246; see also Richard N. Ringler, "The Faunus Episode," *Modern Philology*, LXII, 1 (August, 1965), 12–19, for a detailed study of these averted catastrophes.

[14] Unless one reads this topically and introduces Elizabeth in Diana's clothing. Even so, this could hardly cancel the atmosphere of play that bathes the earlier

in his youthful phase, but when revived in its pure form in a later
stage, it is a function of the escape impulse.

This conclusion frames the next canto within the motivational
context that will lead ultimately to the concluding two stanzas. For
if things are still bad on earth, maybe they will work out more happily
in heaven. If a grasshopper flight over Ireland touches down on bumpy
terrain, maybe a higher flight, a more panoramic view, an increase in
distance, an Astraean remoteness, will resolve the discords and ugli-
ness into a satisfying pattern. I think it is important to keep this context in mind when reading canto vii. Otherwise the more obviously
positive and triumphant aspects of the vision of order may appear to
solve all problems in a real and unqualified manner, which certainly
is not the case so far as Spenser is concerned. The opening stanzas of
canto vii register with some delicacy the degree and kind of resolution
we may expect, and they also stand dramatically as a reaction to the
pastoral interlude.

> Ah! whither doost thou now thou greater Muse
>   Me from these woods and pleasing forrests bring?
>   And my fraile spirit (that dooth oft refuse
>   This too high flight, unfit for her weake wing)
>   Lift up aloft, to tell of heavens King
>   (Thy soveraine Sire) his fortunate successe,
>   And victory, in bigger noates to sing,
>   Which he obtain'd against that Titanesse,
> That him of heavens Empire sought to dispossesse.
>
> Yet sith I needs must follow thy behest,
>   Doe thou my weaker wit with skill inspire,
>   Fit for this turne; and in my feeble brest
>   Kindle fresh sparks of that immortall fire,
>   Which learned minds inflameth with desire
>   Of heavenly things: for, who but thou alone,
>   That art yborne of heaven and heavenly Sire,
>   Can tell things doen in heaven so long ygone;
> So farre past memory of man that may be knowne.

Except to classify the digression under a new and more general category
(the mortal poet's insufficiency), he speaks as if it had not occurred and
the woods had not been defaced. Looking forward, he describes Jove's
prospective victory as much more complete than it in fact will be. The
language of the second stanza promotes a momentary blurring of pagan

---

stanzas. The topical reference would enter only toward the end, abruptly, and this
would intensify the contrast discussed here.

and Christian muses and divinities, but insofar as we feel the presence of the pagan muse, we are allowed to suspect that she is capable of nepotism. The final couplet fills out the chronological relations in the poem. The happening on Arlo Hill occurred too long ago to be remembered by man; the contemporary poet must woo a muse whose usefulness arises not only from her transcendence but also from her antiquity. "So farre past memory of man" refers to both and leaves temporarily unresolved the location of the event; as a vision of pagan-Christian concord, it is culturally "later" than the vision of canto vi, yet Nature's trial and judgment are pushed very far back into the past and/or very high up in heaven. We may feel that it is the image of a wished-for stabilization of order that occurred at the beginning of time, and this may lead us to see in canto vi an inadequate pagan version, in canto vii a more adequate medieval version, of the same mythical event.

The medieval account reflects more accurately than its predecessor the essential feature of that mythical event, namely, its promise of a cyclical natural order whose processes recur throughout the course of time. This superiority is made evident in a number of ways, though space does not permit more than a brief itemization.

First, canto vii reconciles the antique contraries of epic and pastoral, contracting the expansive and relatively vacant regions of canto vi into the narrow, densely packed confines of its middle ground (vii. 3–4).[15] In canto vi, the poet's eye ranged through the ancient heaven and earth, going where the action was. In canto vii, the action and characters come to Arlo Hill.

Second, the desymbolized figures are, so to speak, *re*symbolized. The gods resume their planetary functions, and their influence is felt not only on earth but also in the zodiac. The literal reaches of the two-level pagan cosmos are infolded in Arlo Hill, which, desymbolized by the poet and Diana in canto vi, now regains its symbolic value as an apocalyptic height. Mutabilitie cannot be contained within her own personification; she stands for processes that are beyond her not only because they are diffused throughout the natural universe, but also because they have values diametrically opposed to those the titaness affirms. Although she is conveniently defeated and *whist* in the single action of the trial, this is the classic Spenserian feint: the defeat of an externalized and localized enemy diverts attention from the continuing and deepening effectiveness of the enemy within; Mutabilitie is limited mainly by the rigid qualities and archaic personification to which

[15] Cheney, *Wild Man*, p. 246; see note 1 above.

"she" lays claim, and the disappearance of the titaness corresponds to the infiltration of all nature by mutability.

In this connection, it is significant that Mutabilitie talks so much. She is a real windbag, and Spenser's judgment upon Faunus is surely meant to rub off on her:

> He could him not containe in silent rest;
> But breaking forth in laughter, loud profest
> His foolish thought. A foolish Faune indeed,
> That couldst not hold thy selfe so hidden blest,
> But wouldest needs thine owne conceit areed.
> Babblers unworthy been of so divine a meed.                    (vi.46)

Had Faunus followed the example of the goddess Natura—stayed hidden and kept as still as possible—he would have seen what he wanted to see. The more Mutabilitie speaks, the more she imposes and expresses herself as a personality, the clearer her limitations become; if she only gets what she, as a titaness, claims, it will be much less than what mutability, as a process, covers. Her prosopopoia is thus itself a primitive form of self-seeking and self-deceiving arrogance, as Nature points out: "thy decay thou seekst by thy desire" (vii.59). The ultimate stage of resymbolization would be *depersonification,* in which the referent breaks free from its containing symbolic form. Thus released, it is open to new forms and to new life in later times. This process is already under way as we move from the aggressive pagan individuals of canto vi to the impersonal concord of forces and functions shining more clearly through the figures and emblems of canto vii. More retrograde and stubborn than the others, Mutabilitie is almost the last to get the word.

Third, the organization of Nature's concord in canto vii is dominated by the form of the cycle, or round. This form appears not only in the obvious pageant of seasons and months, but also in the stanzas on Nature (vii.5–13), discussed below, and in the larger unit of the canto as a whole, which moves from benign Christian Nature through Mutabilitie's older vision of negative elemental change (vii.17–26) and back to a benign nature that has dilated to assimilate mutability's influence. Both cantos together may also be viewed on this cyclical model in terms of the semantic pattern, symbolizing——desymbolizing ——resymbolizing, which binds the movement of the whole poem into a single action.

Fourth, the cyclical pattern is not one of simple recurrence, but rather one in which recurrence is part of a larger evolutionary movement. In this movement, the older and simpler elements are at once negated and upheld (*aufgehoben,* Hegel's term for the one process divided into these two contrary moments). Mutabilitie and the gods persist in the same attitudes they held before, even while debating planetary influence. In his one stanza of rebuttal, Jove cites that influence as evidence for his previous claim: it is true, he admits, that all things under heaven are changed by Time,

> who doth them all disseise
> Of being: but, who is it (to me tell)
> That Time himselfe doth move and still compell
> To keepe his course? Is that not namely wee
> Which poure that vertue from our heavenly cell,
> That moves them all, and makes them changed be?
> So them we gods doe rule, and in them also thee.                    (vii.48)

His language is purged of the old heroic thunder, but the archaic resistance to change lurks in the legalism, *disseise,* which usually connotes *wrongful* or forcible dispossession. Mutabilitie's discourse on the elements is similarly located between the old and the new: it is related to the mock-heroic business of canto vi very much as the "philosophical" discourse in *Metamorphoses* XV is related to the metamorphoses of Ovid's first fourteen books; and as a piece of Lucretian materialism, it aims at demythologizing the elemental processes, for example,

> So, in them all raignes Mutabilitie;
>   How-ever these, *that Gods themselves do call,*
> Of them doe claime the rule and soveraity. . . .
>                                    (vii.26, italics mine)

At the same time, the argument reveals its proponent's antique and limited viewpoint in reducing the principle of life to "unsteady ayre" (vii.22) and in selectively dwelling upon changes that reveal only instability, unpredictability, hostility, or decline. Her summation concisely recapitulates that early vision and early state of world order that the medieval concord passes by and upholds *as* early, as fulfilling necessary yet partial functions in an evolving universe of whose real nature those functionaries are scarcely aware:

> Thus, all these fower (the which the ground-work bee
> Of all the world, and of all living wights)
> To thousand sorts of Change we subject see:
> Yet are they chang'd (by other wondrous slights)
> Into themselves, and lose their native mights;
> The Fire to Aire, and th'Ayre to Water sheere,

> And Water into Earth: yet Water fights
> With Fire, and Aire with Earth approaching neere:
> Yet all are in one body, and as one appeare.                    (vii.25)

Echoing this stanza at the end, Nature corrects and reinterprets the process, thus emphasizing Spenser's evolutionary view that things sustain and enrich themselves through self-surrender to the fated influences of time—fated because communicated from whole to part. Nature finds

> that all things stedfastnes doe hate
> And changed be: yet being rightly wayd
> They are not changed from their first estate;
> But by their change their being doe dilate:
> And turning to themselves at length againe,
> Doe worke their owne perfection so by fate. . . .
>
> (vii.58)

At once dynamic and organic, cyclical and developmental, this explanation is in direct contrast to Mutabilitie's image (emphasized by her jaggedly disjunctive "Yet . . . yet . . . yet" construction) of the elements fighting each other, becoming each other, and finally falling into the undifferentiated "one body."

In a rough way, the process of reinterpretation affects all the large-scale relations between the two cantos. The discourse on elemental flux may be linked to the earlier myth of the revolt of the titans by reference to Natalis Conti's reading of that myth as a symbol of *elementorum mutationes*.[16] Mutabilitie's ascent to the house of Jove is translated from image to argument (vii.49–55) when she describes, in Ptolemaic order, changes in the planetary gods. Her beauty appears as the beauty of change in Nature's pageant. Jove's attempt to make her his mistress finds a parallel in his statement (vii.48) that although time and change rule in the lower world, they are controlled by the *vertue* poured "from our heavenly cell." The references to Astraea and Diana in the cycle of months (vii.37,39) allude glancingly to the rigor and questionable justice of the golden-age sensibility that dominated canto vi. All these parallels dramatically exhibit Nature's message that things—in this case, conceptions or interpretations—"by their change their being doe dilate." The continuity of cultural ideas is guaranteed by demythologizing the older pagan version and resymbolizing it in the newer medieval context.

---

[16] Suggested by Robert Kellogg and Oliver Steele in their edition of *Books I and II of The Faerie Queene* (New York, 1965), p. 405. See Natalis Conti, *Mythologiae*, VI.20 (Padua, 1637), p. 342.

The various characteristics of canto vii are vividly present in the set
of stanzas devoted to Nature—not only those, noted above, that make
its vision "later" and more positive than that of canto vi, but also those
that arise from its deliberately imposed limits and exclusions. The
latter are suggested by the sorting-out process that occupies the following stanzas:

> Now, at the time that was before agreed,
>     The Gods assembled all on Arlo Hill;
>     As well those that are sprung of heavenly seed,
>     As those that all the other world doe fill,
>     And rule both sea and land unto their will:
>     Onely th'infernall Powers might not appear;
>     Aswell for horror of their count'naunce ill,
>     As for th'unruly fiends which they did feare;
> Yet Pluto and Proserpina were present there.

> And thither also came all other creatures,
>     What-ever life or motion doe retaine,
>     According to their sundry kinds of features;
>     That Arlo scarsly could them all containe;
>     So full they filled every hill and Plaine:
>     And had not Natures Sergeant (that is Order)
>     Them well disposed by his busie paine,
>     And raunged farre abroad in every border,
> They would have caused much confusion and disorder.

> Then forth issewed (great goddesse) great dame Nature,
>     With goodly port and gracious Majesty;
>     Being far greater and more tall of stature
>     Then any of the gods or Powers on hie:
>     Yet certes by her face and physnomy,
>     Whether she man or woman inly were,
>     That could not any creature well descry:
>     For, with a veile that wimpled every where,
> Her head and face was hid, that mote to none appeare.

> That some doe say was so by skill devised,
>     To hide the terror of her uncouth hew,
>     From mortall eyes that should be sore agrized;
>     For that her face did like a Lion shew,
>     That eye of wight could not indure to view:
>     But others tell that it so beautious was,
>     And round about such beames of splendor threw,
>     That it the Sunne a thousand times did pass,
> Ne could be seene, but like an image in a glass.

> That well may seemen true: for, well I weene
> That this same day, when she on Arlo sat,
> Her garment was so bright and wondrous sheene,
> That my fraile wit cannot devize to what
> It to compare, nor finde like stuffe to that,
> As those three sacred Saints, though else most wise,
> Yet on mount Thabor quite their wits forgat,
> When they their glorious Lord in strange disguise
> Transfigur'd sawe; his garments so did daze their eyes.
>
> (vii.3–7)

As Spenser's earlier tongue-in-cheek reference (vi.36) to Arlo—"Who knowes not Arlo-Hill?"—may have suggested, it is hardly a mythic or literary landmark, and the contraction of the natural universe to a somewhat eccentric locale works like a signature. Whatever vision we are about to see will fit the modest scope of this poet's purposes and may be expected to answer the previous episode. The visionary place must not again be allowed to decline into a figure of contemporary actuality at its worst. The polarity between recreative and plaintive modes, like that between epic and pastoral genres, must be reconciled in the synthesis of the later moral mode, as in the vision on Mount Acidale.[17] Thus Spenser begins by reversing the pattern of decline and instability that marked the previous canto and by opposing to the sad-brow complaint of vi.1–6 a creative sequence that depicts something like an accelerated cosmogony and theogony: first, the sharing out of the universe among heavenly, earthly, and infernal gods and powers, described in descending order and logically followed by Pluto and Proserpina—logically, because they carry us back from the depths to vernal earth and are admitted not only as seasonal gods, but perhaps also as pagan divinities sustained and revised by subsequent allegorization; next, the multitude of natural kinds and creatures on whom order must be imposed just as, in other Spenserian contexts, *eros* aligns the elements emergent from chaos (*HL* 71–91); third, the appearance not of the fecund source itself, but of its personification. Nature is described first as a goddess and then as greater than the gods, first as possibly mortal (male or female) and then as a transcendent mystery, first as the primitive form of Venus (the Magna Mater, goddess of lions and the law of the claw)[18] then as a later conception, the

---

[17] Cf. my "A Secret Discipline: *The Faerie Queene*, Book VI," in *Form and Convention*, ed. Nelson, pp. 70–1.

[18] Cf. the reference to Cybele, *Faerie Queene* IV.xi.28.

symbol of heavenly beauty (Sapience).[19] The image takes on added
richness if seen to include and develop Spenser's own earlier images,
especially the veiled Venus of IV.x–xi:

> So fertile be the flouds in generation,
> So huge their numbers, and so numberlesse their nation.

> Therefore the antique wisards well invented,
> That Venus of the fomy sea was bred. . . .

In rejecting the lion-headed figure, preferring the sun-headed figure,
and comparing himself to the biblical observers of the Transfiguration,
Spenser at once moves Nature more definitely toward a Christian context and affirms his own selective and retrospective presence. His reference to Chaucer and Alanus two stanzas later specifies the Christian
context as medieval, but also as secular and literary: Chaucer, the
"pure well head of Poesie" did not dare describe such radiance,

> But it transferd to Alane, who he thought
> Had in his Plaint of kindes describ'd it well:
> Which who will read set forth so as it ought,
> Go seek he out that Alane where he may be sought.           (vii.9)

In following his *auctor's* example, he fixes the image at a certain historical distance from the present. At the same time, in stanzas 8 and
10, he establishes Nature in a *locus amoenus* reminiscent of the *Foules
parley* as well as of his own ideal gardens: the earth "her self of her
owne motion" produced a pavilion of trees that seemed to do homage
to Nature and "like a throne did shew"—"Not such as Craftes-men by
their idle skill / Are wont for Princes states to fashion"; flowers "voluntary grew / Out of the ground," and seemed richer "then any tapestry, / That Princes bowres adorne with painted imagery." Human art
and government are together excluded from this idyllic order whose
ease and security are guaranteed by a transcendent power of nature.
It is typical of this familiar pastoral logic that it blends subhuman
and superhuman nature together to produce a model of sure spontaneous behavior in which the subjects (*natura naturata*) both automatically and voluntarily express the will of the ruler (*natura naturans*)—a model free of the pride and weakness of fallen human nature.

The infernal powers, the "confusion and disorder" that call forth
the "busie paine" of Nature's Sergeant, the lion-headed goddess, the

---

[19] These two figures are, in a way, simple opposites: the primitive and terrible
earth mother under or within nature, and the Neoplatonic Heavenly Beauty, the
hermetic Wisdom, above nature; their extremes are mediated by the descending
and rising god of incarnation and resurrection.

prideful luxury of princes—these are mentioned in order to be excluded. After a glance at his own earlier pastoral (the vernal renewal of Mole in vii.11), Spenser circles back to the epic marriage of Peleus and Thetis "On Haemus hill" (vii.12), a pagan prevision of "the *paradis terrestre* in which man lived before the apple thrown by Discord, that *diable d'enfer,* began our woe." [20] From the unfallen nature on Haemus to the resurrected nature on Thabor and Arlo, and from the archaic god's-eye view of Phoebus ("that god of Poets hight" who, they say, "did sing the spousall hymn" of Peleus and Thetis) to the saintly vision and its analogues in the redactions of later poets, Spenser overleaps the valleys of fallen nature, synoptically compressing into Arlo's middle height a history of apocalyptic moments, summits of redeemed time and purged vision. Present-as-excluded are those sociopolitical problems that lead to the breaking of the laws "of Justice and of Policie." The prohibition of the infernal powers who administer the irreversible doom of Hell is a logical consequence of this exclusion.

The creatures on Arlo are specified in terms of "life or motion"; man, if he is included, is present only as a member of this organic domain. Later, when the pageant of seasons and months reaches out to embrace human activities—love, recreation, procreation, and labor— it absorbs them into the securely determined cycles of "the lawes of Nature," cycles whose upward thrust from winter to spring and death to life is carefully emphasized. This benign pattern of continuity, positive change, and birth and rebirth is condensed into the familiar paradoxes of the brief concluding description of Nature:

> This great Grandmother of all creatures bred
> Great Nature, ever young yet full of eld,
> Still mooving, yet unmoved from her sted;
> Unseene of any, yet of all beheld. . . .                    (vii.13)

The antithesis "unseene/beheld" is blunted by the fact that the latter term may mean "possessed." Nature is possessed by, held in the forms of, all its creatures, and is therefore visible to its creatures, perhaps also is viewed mentally as in a vision. This is a more dynamic, powerful, and beneficent figure than the goddess described at vii.5–6, and Spenser's circling back to the second passage from the first gives the effect of an advance, for he has shifted attention from her garments and visual presence to her operations and inner nature. The paradoxes are interpreted by the preceding stanzas in such a way as to infold both the cyclical and developmental patterns, since the renewal is cultural

[20] Hawkins, "Cycle," p. 87.

and linear as well as seasonal and recurrent. The underlying matrix, "full of eld," gives rise not only to various living kinds but also to various human conceptions of nature. Thus great Nature may be the effect as well as the cause of all creatures—"of all creatures bred."

The ideal and idyllic qualities of this medieval vision derive from its dialectical relation to canto vi; it is *an* improvement over the pagan viewpoint, but not *the* final improvement. As a reaction to the golden-age pessimism underlying canto vi, it swings a little too far in the opposite direction, providing not a tentative *discordia concors,* but a carefully purified *concordia discors* whose climax is the cycle of seasons and months. In its elliptically emblematic reference to—and coordination of—human, seasonal, and zodiacal phenomena, this pageant attains to a cosmic synthesis sufficiently panoramic in scale to minimize the subtle yet fundamental problems of social life and human relations.[21] The vast network of psycho-social and psycho-cultural problems considered throughout *The Faerie Queene,* and especially in its last three complete books, is admitted in allusions, echoes, and oblique references. But it is present-as-excluded; it is either resolved into the limited context of nature's round, or muffled, pushed into the background, by the hieratic quality of the pageant. What the poet stresses, especially in the more vivid genre-life details, are natural problems— hunger, age, heat, and cold—and these are so closely observed that they tend to divert our attention from the symbols of the other, less simple, evils.[22] By these devices, the poet reminds us of the fact that his vision of nature has been selectively refined and idealized.

This is why we must not confuse Spenser's picture of the medieval mind with what are often thought of as Spenser's medieval habits of mind. Commentators frequently have noted the medieval texture of the canto in terms of the sources and traditions behind it, for example,

for such images as the signs of the zodiac, the personification of the seasons and the months, the council of the gods, and the allegorical debate,

---

[21] So Hawkins, "Cycle," p. 92 and *passim;* my reading, however, differs from his in assuming that Spenser means the very power and perfection of his pageant to be felt as *too* perfect.

[22] Examples: the crab compared to hypocrites (35); the Nemaean lion and the implied death of Hercules (36); Astraea's abandonment of "th'unrighteous world" (37)—stanzas 36 and 37, together evoking the world of Book V, remind us that the earlier attitude of golden-age pessimism is still alive; Diana's "doom unjust" (39); echoes of various metamorphic deeds of rape and violence, here presented for the most part in benign form (32-4); perhaps also a papist reference in the "Romane floud" (42).

dozens of analogues in medieval plastic and literary art make source hunting unnecessary.[23]

For centuries the months and their labors appeared over and over again in calendars and books of hours, above the portals of cathedrals, in handbooks and encyclopedias, signifying that the divisions of time . . . are part of the divine plan, and that by labor man works out his own place in it. The medieval man who paused to contemplate the great stone calendar over a church door found various meanings there, . . . and all of them apply to Spenser's Calendar.[24]

If this vision is particularly attractive to Spenser, it is not because he is uncritically traditional or unconsciously medieval. The medieval mind may have believed in this vision as a divine and providential work, a panoramic picture of God's real order of nature. But Spenser employs the technique of conspicuous allusion in this canto not only to distance that vision in terms of cultural time, but also to emphasize its artistic and artificial quality. The essence of the order is so clearly dependent upon and communicated by its artistic organization, the whole harmony of the natural universe is so dramatically foreshortened and its rhythms condensed by Spenser's symbolic shorthand, that we are impressed primarily by the synoptic power of the human poet's imagination. This impression is heightened by the forms that comprise the network of allusion: literature, pageantry, emblematic imagery, ancient cosmological speculation, the arts of relief and illumination, judicial process, and debate.

The two cantos I have just discussed develop a cosmic rather than a microcosmic vision; their subject is the harmonious order of the physical and organic universe; the domain of the human psyche and society as such is not included as an object in that field; human attitudes have been externalized into pagan and medieval world views. The concluding stanzas move beyond the vision into the mind that has unfolded it and into the lyric moment evoked by that unfolding:

> When I bethinke me on that speech whyleare,
>> Of Mutability, and well it way:
>> Me seemes, that though she all unworthy were
>> Of the Heav'ns Rule; yet very sooth to say,
>> In all things else she beares the greatest sway,
>> Which makes me loath this state of life so tickle,

---

[23] Kellogg and Steele, *Books I and II*, p. 404.
[24] Hawkins, "Cycle," p. 88.

> And love of things so vaine to cast away;
> Whose flowring pride, so fading and so fickle,
> Short Time shall soon cut down with his consuming sickle.
>
> Then gin I thinke on that which Nature sayd,
>     Of that same time when no more Change shall be,
>     But stedfast rest of all things firmely stayd
>     Upon the pillours of Eternity,
>     That is contrayr to Mutabilitie:
>     For, all that moveth, doth in change delight:
>     But thence-forth all shall rest eternally
>     With Him that is the God of Sabbaoth hight:
> O that great Sabbaoth God, graunt me that Sabaoths sight.

There is an uncertainty of tone reflected especially in the ambiguous syntax of the first stanza, lines six and seven: (1) "This thought makes me loathe this unstable life, and makes me (to) cast away the love of things"; (2) "I am loth to cast away this state of life and this love of things." As an adjective, *vaine* could modify either *love* or *things:* the love may be vain not because things are vanity, but because all such attachments are doomed; things are loved because they flower into brief beauty, perhaps in vain. In the adverbial position, *vaine* enforces the second alternative: the state of life and love of things may be vainly put off if no experience or vision can attain to what lies beyond the mutable whirl. Similarly, the often noted doubt about *Sabbaoth* (meaning either rest or host) carries the unresolved feeling through to the end: (1) "Grant me the vision of that final rest"—or, more forcefully, "Grant me its prospect, put it within reach"; (2) "Grant me a vision of that Host"—the armies of the saved, the children of the spirit, the Host assembled at the end of time. He wants to get beyond the clutches of change, and the first emphasis is simply upon escape. But he also wants to carry the variety up with him—"all things firmely stayd." The doubts of the first stanza suggest the added possibility that he may be asking to see this vision *now,* while alive, since he cannot be certain of what is to come. And though these stanzas have been described as moments of prayer, they express, as Watkins has put it, "desire rather than affirmation." [25] The final line is not a great leap through faith; it is a slow and guarded turning *toward* prayer and faith, moving from mere indication ("Him that is . . .") through half-apostrophe ("O *that* great Sabbaoth God") to the final direct exhorta-

[25] W. B. C. Watkins, *Shakespeare and Spenser* (Princeton, 1953), p. 72; John Arthos, *On the Poetry of Spenser and the Form of Romances* (London, 1956), p. 198.

tion. It is as if, should he turn too quickly, too hopefully, too unguard-edly, nothing would be there.

Though the conclusion may be called plaintive, this does not mean that—in Greene's words—if Spenser's faith "is indeed a refuge here, it is a lonely and bitter one." [26] For we have moved, through the two cantos, from one sort of complaint to another, and from a plaintive attitude dramatically, impersonally, given play by the man-as-poet, to a plaintive attitude affecting the poet-as-man as he considers what he has made. The first complaint is based upon rejection, upon fear of life, upon disillusionment with the world, upon the desire to escape from the world as it is and return to some pristine mythical state that the mind locates before time and change. The final complaint arises from so strong an involvement in and attachment to, such utter de-light in the changing world, that the poet bemoans its fragility. "Spenser . . . has made the inevitable confession, that he loves all changing, mortal things too much, and they are betraying him. . . . the commitments to mortality have gone too deep to allow [the renun-ciation of earthly love]." [27] Having oscillated between the elemental divisions of pagan pessimism and the organic harmony of medieval optimism, he attains to a more complicated and dynamic equilibrium at the end, still looking backward, still thrusting forward, still revolv-ing doubts.

Cheney has described as follows the "mixture of opposing attitudes with which Mutabilitie is being viewed":

> One pole of this opposition is the Christian *contemptus mundi,* the feel-ing of exhaustion and disdain for this world and intense longing for the combination of absolute delight and absolute rest to be found through death in the "Sabaoths sight" hinted by nature. At the other pole is the artist's delight in the inexhaustible variety of his creation. . . .[28]

The first sentence needs some modification; the attitudes described here resemble those that reciprocally reinforce each other in canto vi (see pp. 152ff. above) and that are overcome by the shift in canto vii to the variety of natural and artistic creation. What is required after canto vi is a redistribution of values and a redirection of longing; earthly life must be enhanced, the absolute must be distanced or veiled, and the distinction between the mundane and the transcendent more

---

[26] *Descent From Heaven,* p. 323.
[27] Arthos, *On the Poetry of Spenser,* pp. 94–5.
[28] *Wild Man,* pp. 246–247.

rigorously honored. This theme is touched upon in two passages: At vi.32 Jove criticizes Mutabilitie for wanting "Through some vaine errour or inducement light, / To see that mortall eyes have never seene"; and at vi.46 Spenser chides Faunus for breaking out into laughter because he cannot contain his "great joy of some-what he did spy"—"Babblers unworthy been of so divine a meed." These are comic images of the "intense longing for . . . absolute delight" and vision, for the unveiled nearness of divinity, and for possession of the god's-eye view—a longing entailed by "disdain for this world."

The poem as a whole enacts a turning away from these conjoined opposites. Thus in canto vi the "highest heaven" is identified with Jove, whereas in canto vii we find a higher celestial region (the zodiacal sphere of the fixed stars) and clues to the very different spiritual heaven clearly disclosed only in the final stanza of the poem. The contrast of genres in canto vi intensifies the pastoral insignificance of the earthly episode; the perspective on both episodes, visually or qualitatively, is that of the gods (Mutabilitie, Jove, Diana), whereas their burden centers on the departure of a goddess from an unworthy and ruined earth, an earth seen by the uncomfortable ruling pantheon as the chief source of danger. The poet's initial gesture in canto vii is to move higher up for a more panoramic and harmonious view, then to settle into the middle region of Christian pastoral on Arlo. By the time he has described Arlo and Nature, this view has been further defined and "lowered"—located in terms of a particular cultural moment, a literary tradition, and his own limited, selective vision (his reliance on sources, his effort to make adequate comparisons, the weakness of mortal sight). This "descent" of viewpoint and desire is traced in the sequence of summits and seers: first, the easy mixture of mortal and immortal elements in the marriage on Haemus, whose singer was the god of poets himself; second, the more miraculous moment of transfiguration, seen by saintly mortals, symbolizing both the absolute transcendence of Christ, and his promise to resurrect earthly nature; third, the literary vision on Arlo, a fable invented by the humanistic poet who gives it historical distance by looking through medieval eyes and through a variety of traditional modes of expression.

This psychological movement of the point of view and of desire down into earth and history appears in other details. The second description of Nature is "lower" than the first, and though Mutabilitie calls her "Goddess" after this, the poet himself does not. The two specific references to Christian belief are both to Christ—his transfiguration and incarnation (vii.41). The pageant itself is centered on earthly activities as the focus of cosmic motions. In all these ways, then, the seventh canto reverses the upward- and outward-bound thrust of the pagan sensibility with its unguardedly childlike anthropomorphism. Canto vii places in high relief the archaic impulse to unify heaven and earth on earthly terms that presume to raise men closer to gods while actually lowering heaven to put it within the finite reach of man. The Christian answer to this centers on the paradigm of the Incarnation. Whereas the pagans envisaged their deities as human in form and behavior but remote from man in attitude, the three-personed God is mysterious and remote from man in terms of behavior, much closer to man in the manifestations of his love. The unbridgeable gap between man and a God who is Wholly Other requires God to descend. The descent, in enhancing fallen nature by expressing God's love for it, urges man to cherish not disdain it.

But from the standpoint of the sixteenth-century poet, this good news, along with its medieval edition, was delivered long ago; man's problems and attitudes were changed, but not automatically resolved thereby. Although Spenser opens himself to the consoling harmony of the medieval world view, his stylized presentation is itself a way of lowering and limiting that view, since it declares its origins in the mind and art and culture of man. The Nature of canto vii is less easily identifiable with those aspects of divine providence to which it ostensibly refers than with the creative process of poetic imagination. This is suggested by Cheney's phrase, "the artist's delight in the unexhaustible variety of *his* creation" (italics mine). The organization, emblems, images, *topoi,* and personifications (including Nature herself) are generated by the intercourse between nature as underlying matrix and the poet's mind. Toward the end of the canto, after the processes of nature have been unfolded in the discourse on elements, the pageant, and the passage on planetary gods, Natura is even more closely linked to the poet. Firmly personified at vii.57, she speaks for the first time, then vanishes "whither no man wist," concurrently with the canto's last words. "Her doome" sets forth in a plain statement what the entire canto has already enacted: The poet's moral or argument is simply placed in her mouth, and immediately after, he gives the phrase "turning to themselves at length againe" a new direction by turning to consider his own state of mind as affected by the argument.

Such an identification of nature with art places a heavy burden and a high value upon the work of the human mind and the function of man's art and vision. For where else if not here is the summit and fulfillment of created nature to be found? If, as many Renaissance and Reformation thinkers suspected, the forces of reality both transcend and differ in character from their equivalent forms in the mind, how else can they be even obscurely adumbrated? If God makes the world, it is His collaborator, man, who makes world views. However insubstantial the pageant of human forms in nature, culture, art, and play, it may yet be the only token, the only record and impress of a power that may not find expression after man has had his day: "If it be now, 'tis not to come; if it be not to come, it will be now." [29] But the

> like the baseless fabric of this vision,
> The cloud-capped towers, the gorgeous palaces,
> The solemn temples, the great globe itself,
> Yea, all which it inherit, shall dissolve,
> And, like this insubstantial pageant faded,
> Leave not a rack behind.
>
> *(Tempest,* IV.i.151–6)

poet cherishes at the end of the poem the hope that "if it be not now, yet it will come; the readiness is all. Since no man has aught of what he leaves, what is't to leave betimes? Let be."

Yet these assertions of man's shaping power can be taken seriously only if they do not claim too much, only if made tentatively and experimentally, placed in quotation marks, or in the presumptive fiction of play and poem. The magic and triumph of art reside in its ability to indicate the reality before which all art fails. When this happens, make-believe becomes "unrealistic," its tissue grows artificial, diaphanous to the point of vanishing. To be closed within the poet's secure second nature, to substitute *a world view* for *the world,* to long for solutions and resolutions not found in life, is to confuse the true *contemptus mundi* with "the feeling of exhaustion and disdain for this world." Thus Spenser shifts and opens his prospect throughout the poem, discloses new depths and distances continually emerging and continually receding. In the final moment the furthest depth is touched, but only lightly touched, for the poet's long brooding, his slow turning, his tone of reaching and beseeching, express a Sabbaoth God still moving away from man approaching.

[20] So also Prospero:

> like the baseless fabric of this vision,
> The cloud-capped towers, the gorgeous palaces,
> The solemn temples, the great globe itself,
> Yea, all which it inherit, shall dissolve,
> And, like this insubstantial pageant faded,
> Leave not a rack behind.
>
> *(Tempest,* IV.i.151–6.)

# Chronology of Important Dates

1552?     Spenser born in London.

1569     Matriculated to Pembroke Hall in Cambridge after attending the Merchant Taylors School (London) of which Richard Mulcaster was Headmaster. One of thirteen sizars, or poor students, at Pembroke. In this year John Van der Noodt's *Theatre for Worldings* was published in London, containing anonymous sonnets and epigrams which may have been Spenser's first published work.

1576     Masters of Arts from Cambridge.

1578     Secretary to John Young, Bishop of Rochester and former master of Pembroke Hall.

1579     Joined the household of the Earl of Leicester. Married Machabeus Chyld at St. Margaret's, Westminster. Publication of *Shepheardes Calender.*

1580     Went to Ireland as secretary to Arthur Lord Grey de Wilton, newly appointed Governor, and remained after Grey's recall in 1582.

1581–88     Clerk of the Chancery for Faculties, an office through which dispensations granted by the Archbishop of Dublin were channeled.

1582     Moved to New Abbey, in the vicinity of Dublin.

1585     Appointed deputy to Sir Philip Sidney's friend, Lodowick Bryskett, clerk of the council of Munster, in the south of Ireland. Spenser praised in the preface to Bryskett's *Discourse of Civil Life.*

1588–89     Took possession of Kilcoman, a large estate in Munster, and became its legal owner in 1589 or 1590.

1590     Publication of Books I–III of *The Faerie Queene.* Spenser may have brought parts of the poem to England with him the previous year when he supposedly visited London and the royal court in the company of Sir Walter Raleigh. The poem seems to have been circulated in a manuscript version during the preceding years. A stanza from Book II is quoted in Abraham Fraunce's *Arcadian Rhetorike* (1588). *Muiopotmos* published. Death of first wife (?).

1591    Awarded an annual income of £50 for life by Queen Elizabeth. *Complaints* and *Daphnaida* published.

1594    Back in Ireland by 1593 at the latest; married Elizabeth Boyle in June, 1594.

1595    Publications: *Amoretti and Epithalamion, Colin Clouts Come Home Againe.*

1596    In London again between 1595 and 1597. *Faerie Queene* Books IV–VI published; also *Prothalamion* and *Fowre Hymnes.*

1598    *Vewe of the Present State of Irelande* published. Tyrone's rebellion broke out in north of Ireland, spread to Munster, where rebels sacked Kilcoman. Spenser arrived in London late in year.

1599    Died January 13. Buried in Westminster Abbey.

1609    *Two Cantos of Mutabilitie* first appeared, published in the 1609 edition of *The Faerie Queene.*

# Notes on the Editor and Contributors

HARRY BERGER, JR., editor of this volume, is Professor of English Literature at Cowell College, University of California, Santa Cruz. He is author of *The Allegorical Temper.*

DONALD CHENEY, formerly Assistant Professor of English Literature at Yale University, now teaches at the University of Massachusetts.

MAURICE EVANS, author of several works on Renaissance poetry, was formerly at the University of Aberdeen and is presently Professor of English Language and Literature at McGill University.

ALBERT C. HAMILTON is Professor of English Literature at the University of Washington and the author of *The Structure of Allegory in The Faerie Queene.*

WILLIAM NELSON, Professor of English Literature at Columbia University, is the author of several studies on Renaissance literature, the most recent being a book on John Skelton. He has edited *Form and Convention in the Poetry of Spenser.*

WILLIAM V. NESTRICK, now a Fellow in English at Harvard University, was previously Associate Dean of Teacher Education at the City University of New York.

RICHARD NEUSE is Associate Professor of English at the University of Rhode Island. He has published studies of Chaucer and Spenser.

KATHLEEN WILLIAMS is the author of a study of Swift, several essays on Spenser, and most recently, *Spenser's World of Glass: A Reading of The Faerie Queene.* She is Professor of English Literature at the University of California at Riverside.

MARTIN L. WINE, now Associate Professor of Drama at the University of California at Irvine, was formerly Associate Professor of English at the University of Illinois.

# Selected Bibliography

## I. Editions of Spenser's Poetry:

Spenser, Edmund, *Books I and II of The Faerie Queene*, eds. Robert Kellog and Oliver Steele. New York: The Odyssey Press, Inc., 1965.

———, *Complaints*, ed. W. L. Renwick. London: Scholartis Press, 1928.

———, *Daphnaida and Other Poems*, ed. W. L. Renwick. London: Scholartis Press, 1929.

———, *The Shepheard's Calendar*, ed. W. L. Renwick. London: Scholartis Press, 1930.

———, *The Works of Edmund Spenser: A Variorum Edition*, eds. E. Greenlaw, C. G. Osgood, F. M. Padelford, and others. 10 Vols. Baltimore: Johns Hopkins Press, 1958.

## II. Book-length Studies and Essay Collections:

Alpers, Paul, *The Poetry of The Faerie Queene*. Princeton: Princeton University Press, 1967.

Arthos, John, *On the Poetry of Spenser and the Form of Romances*. London: George Allen and Unwin, 1956.

Bennett, J. W., *The Evolution of the Faerie Queene*. New York: Burt Franklin reprint, 1960.

Berger, Harry, Jr., *The Allegorical Temper*. New Haven: Yale University Press, 1957. Reprinted, Hamden: Archon Books, 1967.

Cheney, Donald, *Spenser's Image of Nature: Wild Man and Shepherd in "The Faerie Queene."* New Haven: Yale University Press, 1966.

Elliott, John R., ed., *The Prince of Poets*. New York: New York University Press, 1968.

Ellrodt, Robert, *Neoplatonism in the Poetry of Spenser*. Geneva: Droz, 1960.

Fowler, Alastair, *Spenser and the Numbers of Time*. New York: Barnes & Noble, Inc., 1964.

Greenlaw, Edwin, *Studies in Spenser's Historical Allegory*. Baltimore: Johns Hopkins Press, 1932.

Hamilton, Albert C., *The Structure of Allegory in The Faerie Queene*. Oxford: Clarendon Press, 1961.

Harper, Carrie, *The Sources of the British Chronicle History in Spenser's Faerie Queene*. Philadelphia: J. C. Winston, 1910.

Hieatt, A. Kent, *Short Time's Endless Monument*. New York: Columbia University Press, 1960.

Hough, Graham, *A Preface to The Faerie Queene*. New York: W. W. Norton & Company, Inc., 1963.

Lewis, C. S., *Spenser's Images of Life*, ed. Alastair Fowler. Cambridge: Cambridge University Press, 1967.

McLane, Paul E., *Spenser's Shepheardes Calender*. Notre Dame: Notre Dame University Press, 1961.

McNeir, W. F., and F. Provost, *Annotated Bibliography of Edmund Spenser, 1937–1960*. Pittsburgh: Duquesne University Press, 1962.

Mueller, W. R., and D. C. Allen, eds., *That Soueraine Light*. Baltimore: Johns Hopkins Press, 1952.

Nelson, William, ed., *Form and Convention in the Poetry of Edmund Spenser*. New York and London: Columbia University Press, 1961.

——, *The Poetry of Edmund Spenser*. New York: Columbia University Press, 1963.

Parker, M. Pauline, *The Allegory of The Faerie Queene*. London: Oxford University Press, 1960.

Renwick, W. L., *Edmund Spenser*. London: Edward Arnold (Publishers), Ltd., 1925.

Roche, Thomas, *The Kindly Flame*. Princeton: Princeton University Press, 1964.

Spens, Janet, *Spenser's Faerie Queene*. London: Edward Arnold (Publishers), Ltd., 1934.

Watkins, W. B. C., *Shakespeare and Spenser*. Princeton: Princeton University Press, 1953.

Williams, Arnold, *Flower on a Lowly Stalk: The Sixth Book of The Faerie Queene*. East Lansing: Michigan State University Press, 1967.

Williams, Kathleen, *Spenser's World of Glass: A Reading of The Faerie Queene*. Berkeley and Los Angeles: University of California Press, 1966.

## III. Shorter Studies and Brief Discussions:

Allen, Don Cameron, *Image and Meaning*. Baltimore: Johns Hopkins Press, 1960.

Alpers, Paul J., ed., *Elizabethen Poetry*. New York: Oxford University Press, Inc., 1967.

Colie, Rosalie, *Paradoxia Epidemica*. Princeton: Princeton University Press, 1966.

Durling, Robert, *The Figure of the Poet in Renaissance Epic*. Cambridge: Harvard University Press, 1965.

Fletcher, Angus, *Allegory: The Theory of a Symbolic Mode*. Ithaca, N.Y.: Cornell University Press, 1964.

Frye, Northrop, *Fables of Identity*. New York: Harcourt, Brace & World, Inc., 1936.

Giamatti, A. B., *The Earthly Paradise and the Renaissance Epic*. Princeton: Princeton University Press, 1966.

Greene, Thomas M., *The Descent From Heaven*. New Haven, Conn., and London: Yale University Press, 1963.

Lever, J. W., *The Elizabethan Love Sonnet*. London: Methuen & Co., Ltd., 1956.

Lewis, C. S., *Studies in Medieval and Renaissance Literature*, ed. Walter Hooper. London: Cambridge University Press, 1966.

Lewis, C. W., *The Allegory of Love*. London: Oxford University Press, 1938.

Rubel, Veré L., *Poetic Diction in the English Renaissance*. New York: MLA, 1941.

Smith, Hallett, *Elizabethan Poetry*. Cambridge: Harvard University Press, 1952.

Starnes, D. T., and E. W. Talbert, *Classical Myth and Legend in Renaissance Dictionaries*. Chapel Hill: University of North Carolina Press, 1955.

Tillyard, E. M. W., *The English Epic and Its Background*. London: Chatto and Windus, Ltd., 1954.

Tuve, Rosemond, *Allegorical Imagery*. Princeton: Princeton University Press, 1966.